Strategic Reputation Risk Management

Judy Larkin

First published 2003 by
PALGRAVE MACMILLAN
Houndmills, Basingstoke, Hampshire RG21 6XS and
175 Fifth Avenue, New York, N.Y. 10010
Companies and representatives throughout the world

PALGRAVE MACMILLAN is the global academic imprint of the Palgrave Macmillan division of St. Martin's Press, LLC and of Palgrave Macmillan Ltd. Macmillan® is a registered trademark in the United States, United Kingdom and other countries. Palgrave is a registered trademark in the European Union and other countries.

ISBN 0–333–99554–6

This book is printed on paper suitable for recycling and made from fully managed and sustained forest sources.

A catalogue record for this book is available from the British Library.

A catalog record for this book is available from the Library of Congress.

Designed and formatted by
The Ascenders Partnership, Basingstoke

10 9 8 7 6 5 4 3 2 1
12 11 10 09 08 07 06 05 04 03

Printed and bound in Great Britain by
Creative Print and Design (Wales), Ebbw Vale

Contents

Acknowledgements

I would like to thank the many people who have helped me to deliver this book. In particular, Caitlin West, and also Ellen Raphael for substantial assistance on the research and my sister, Sue Craig for considerable input on structure and editing. I would like to acknowledge expert input from Professor Ragnar Lofstedt, Director of the Centre for Risk Management at King's College, Professor Tim Traverse-Healy and Professor Frank Furedi for their kind support and also Professor Robert Worcester, Chairman of MORI for valuable input and comment. A special thank you to Malcolm Williams at Shell, Ann Sullivan at Cable & Wireless, Ann Furedi, Mike Palese of Daimler Chrysler, Mark Goyder of The Tomorrow's Company and Roger Hayes of the International Institute of Communications for their opinions and case study input. I must also acknowledge the early efforts of Tracey Brown and Dr Jane Sargent for helping me to get the show on the road. My thanks also go to Stephen Rutt and Jacky Kippenberger at Palgrave.

Finally, to the following people who provided valuable practical insights to managing reputation risk at the coal face: Deborah Allen, Edward Bickham, Michael Broadbent, Richard Bunting, Michael Caldwell, Janet Cézar Lucien Fa, Dominic Fry, Lynne Galley, Tim Halford, Kevin Hawkins, Blake Lee-Harwood, Simon Laxton, Simon Lewis, Chris Major, Steven Michell, Charles Naylor, Steven Olivant, Steven Paine, Geoff Potter, Tim Sharp, Jan Shawe, Penny Studholme, Rory Sullivan, Maxine Taylor, Paul Taylor, Mary Walsh, Ian Willmore, Ian Wright and John Wybrew.

In memory of my father,
Patrick Larkin

Introduction

There is no question in my mind that business is a formidably positive force in society today. Good business - performing and behaving with a sense of responsibility - underpins successful communities. It influences who we buy from, work for, supply to and invest in, and plays to both the rational and emotional attachments that we have with an organization. Strategic business development and revenue growth are reflections of a company's performance, but so is perceived leadership through greater visibility. Reputation is, therefore, a vital commercial asset and one which companies squander at their peril.

The influence and resources of big business today are huge and that's not necessarily a bad thing. Fifty-one out of the world's top 100 economies are corporations, representing annual revenues of $2.9 trillion (World Bank and *Fortune* magazine, 2002). The annual revenues of Royal Dutch/Shell are greater than the GDP of Morocco; those of Wal-Mart greater than the GDP of Poland and those of General Motors greater than the GDP of Denmark. Against a backdrop of economic globalization, political transition and technological transformation, business has emerged as the principal engine of growth and development in the new world order, and so it has everything to play for.

Companies can, on occasion, lose sight of the right course to navigate by focusing on short-term requirements at the expense of longer-term impacts – no surprise when share-price is king and the average life expectancy of a CEO is three years! Ignoring the wider consequences of what companies are doing can, however, create unwanted market volatility, negative scrutiny and opportunities for the growing influence of anti-business activism.Companies travelling along this route are charting a course towards a field of operational and reputational icebergs that can quickly sink the most water-tight business strategies.

Threats to reputation – whether real or perceived – can destroy, literally in hours or days, an image or brand developed and invested in over decades. These threats need to be anticipated, understood and planned for. Public perception of risk has become a constant and recurring threat to reputation. Understanding and communicating effectively around risk perception can help to reduce conflict, and gain support and trust – critical attributes in securing and maintaining customer, investor and employee loyalty. This is even more important at a time when the forces of globalization and the

Internet are pushing us from a so-called 'old world' or 'industrial economy', dependent on the value of physical assets such as property and equipment, to a 'new world' or 'knowledge economy' characterized by the intangible assets of reputation, knowledge, competencies, innovation, leadership, culture and loyalty.

These intangible assets are valued in the balance sheet as goodwill or 'intellectual capital', of which reputation and brand attributes play important parts. Some 53 per cent of the value of Fortune 500 corporations is accounted for through intangible assets – an estimated $24.27 trillion. Research conducted by Interbrand with Citibank in 1998, found that the total value of the FTSE 100 companies was £842 bn, with goodwill accounting for 71 per cent of total market capitalization. In contrast, ten years ago, goodwill accounted for less than 44 per cent of the total value, although this figure had been steadily rising over preceding decades. Another recent study by Interbrand concluded that one-quarter of the world's total financial wealth is tied up in intangible assets (Clifton and Maughan, 1999).

Why is it then, that corporations are surprised when they are faced with controversy? Exxon, Shell, British Airways, BP, Coca-Cola, Railtrack, McDonald's, Nike, Marks & Spencer, TotalFinaElf, Singapore Airlines, Renault – some of these companies are potent symbols of globalization, others are or were powerful local or regional brands, some successfully reinvented themselves from nationalized backgrounds – most have spent fortunes developing or redesigning and promoting their corporate or brand image. And yet all have failed at some point to acknowledge the commercial impact of adverse public perception on reputation in a risk setting, with chilling results.

Having worked in the field of crisis and issue management for many years, it seems extraordinary to me that business has learnt so little from its past mistakes. Coca-Cola learnt nothing from Perrier when it faced product contamination scares in Belgium and France in 1999. TotalFinaElf learnt nothing from the Exxon Valdez disaster a decade before when it had to deal with a major oil spill off the coast of Brittany at the end of 1999. By the end of 2000 Monsanto had wrecked an entire industry, as well as its own brand. Wrangling over who was to blame for a major vehicle safety failure has left the asset base of Bridgestone/Firestone in tatters and has created a serious dent in the balance sheet and reputation of Ford Motor Company, ejecting top management in the process. The British rail infrastructure company, Railtrack, self-destructed with help from incompetent policymakers in late 2001, and confidence in corporate America has slipped in the aftermath of scandals associated with Californian energy trading, Enron and Arthur Andersen, WorldCom, Xerox, Sotherby's and Tyco.

Government performance has fared no better. Surely some lessons could have been learnt and applied about 'joined-up government' in the UK from the BSE outbreak in 1996, the fuel crisis and the floods of 2000 and the foot and mouth epidemic of 2001? The US administration continues to be accused of an unhealthily close relationship with business; and European politicians are being dragged, kicking and screaming, into a new world order which calls for transparency at the expense of personal and party political corruption.

In many Western societies today, we are living in an environment of unprecedented risk aversion and perceived lack of trust. Strange, because for much of human history we have relied on gut instinct in the face of uncertainty and fared pretty well.

Reputation is built on trust and belief. Our own reputations matter to us a great deal – whether we are good at what we do or fun to be around. But in the commercial world reputation appears to have become a Cinderella asset – easily overlooked but with terrific potential! After all, it should be the biggest asset in most corporations and a high priority in the boardroom. Yet reputation isn't properly valued, is rarely fully understood and is seldom managed in a cohesive way by the people at the top.

As the examples cited above demonstrate, traditional models simply don't work any more because they ignore the essential building blocks of trust and belief. Senior managers need to think and behave differently. First, by demonstrating a clear acknowledgement of the importance of reputation in the boardroom and second, by adopting an integrated approach to reputation management and associated decision-making across the organization in exactly the same way that conventional operational risks are assessed, audited and managed. My guiding principles for avoiding relegation to the arctic and delivering successful reputation risk management, which will be explored in this book, are:

- Acknowledge that reputation is a valuable asset and needs to be actively managed at board level
- Develop a finely tuned radar and become a listening company
- Design clear and robust management systems that integrate with routine risk management processes
- Create your own code of good behaviour and assure your licence to operate
- Treat your stakeholders intelligently
- Work as if everything you say and do is public

Who should read this book?

This book makes the case for reputation as a commercially valuable asset, one that needs to be actively managed and integrated into operational risk management processes, and owned at board level, not in the PR department. It is designed to meet the needs of busy executives, who feel they are under fire from a barrage of inaccurate and misleading media reporting and activist claims about their products, services or business practices and cannot seem to cut through the 'spin' to achieve a more balanced debate.

It provides a practical and research based guide for senior managers and communications professionals, who recognize the importance of reputation and may need to make a convincing case to board level colleagues when:

- There is an urgent need to develop and resource from scratch a reputation risk management strategy
- Systems and strategies may be in place but need validation or fine-tuning through auditing or testing
- A major threat or crisis could be imminent and action needs to be swift and rigorous

In contrast to existing texts on reputation and brand management, I emphasize how enhanced reputation can contribute to commercial asset management through improved competitive performance. The flip side is that reputation loss can freeze out support and goodwill, and significantly erode the ability of businesses to successfully retain their markets, maximize shareholder value, raise finance and manage debt, and remain independent. Chapter 1 begins to address these points and gives a general overview of some of the key themes which will be addressed in more detail in subsequent chapters.

Chapter 2 examines reputation risk assessment and presents planning and management models designed to familiarize senior executives and communicators with some of the best tools available for protecting and enhancing reputation value. The models are then applied to a range of case study examples throughout the book. The chapter contains two case studies showing first, how to get reputation risk management dramatically wrong and second, how under pressure to get it surprisingly right.

Chapter 3 addresses the damage that adverse public perception of risk – whether real or perceived – can have on meeting commercial objectives, when this perception is fuelled by much greater risk aversion, intrusive and sensational media commentary and a rapid rise in direct action and campaigning by Non-Governmental Organizations (NGOs) with anti-technology and anti-business agendas. Communicating around new risks, especially when they are poorly defined or easily linked with other similar risks, is a complicated business. Risk is characterized by uncertainty and variability and there is a big difference in how experts and members of the public view hazards. Greater risk aversion in Western democracies has directly contributed to a more political and popularist regulatory framework in Europe which is demanding greater transparency and accountability on the part of business. Clearly, there are costs attached to this.

In Chapter 4, I examine the rise in activism and the incredible influence of the Internet. A key theme here is the impact of consumerism and a greater sense of individuality and rights which have fuelled enormous growth in the activities of NGOs. I'll look at some of the 'isms' that these groups focus on – environmentalism, anti-capitalism, animal activism, consumerism – as well as overlaying issues of ethics, choice, need and equity. The ability of businesses to keep up with these changes, acknowledge their importance and work with rather than against them will define success or failure in reputation management terms.

Chapter 5 examines the perceived decline of the scientific community's reputation and how this has brought about policy changes that are institutionalizing a loss in public confidence in the benefits of innovation to the material detriment of business. I will assess the commercial impact of the Precautionary Principle and outline some decision-making guidelines for anticipating and responding to these changes. This is another area of confused interpretation and application, but one which innovative companies must enter if they are to reduce the risk of a regulatory brake on new products and processes.

In Chapter 6, I'll review the emerging corporate social responsibility agenda, expanding liabilities and corporate governance and, through case study examples, consider the threats and opportunities for reputation risk management.

This book is not a critique of communication practices in business. On the contrary, as the power-house of society, business can and does play a crucial and beneficial role within communities, economies and societies. I am arguing for business to withdraw from the treacherous ice-fields of conflict management and denial, characterized by a 'decide, announce, defend' style of communication with the outside world, and move to the firmer ground of acknowledging the potential for public concern and focusing on transparency and accountability.

The principles of effective risk communication are described and applied against a range of international examples; contemporary case study analysis is used to illustrate these points with guidelines for implementation, learning points and additional reference/resource materials. The text draws on academic analysis, published and new qualitative research, and some of the easy-to-use models and metrics that I have utilized working for major corporations in helping them to anticipate and assess the impact of change on reputation and minimize the potential for crises.

While my own research demonstrates a growing awareness of the importance of reputation, delivery of robust processes for management is far from evident. So the emphasis in my book is on pragmatic and robust approaches, including some of the do's and don'ts of addressing risk perception today, as well as guidance on anticipating events and trends that will drive effective reputation risk management in the future. Some of the key questions I address are:

- Can reputation be valued?
- Where do risk issues come from and how can you decide if they matter?
- Who are your likely 'protagonists', how do they operate and what are the merits of engagement?
- What models and systems can help you to identify, prioritize, assess and successfully respond to risk issues?
- How do you know these will work?
- How can you diffuse the potential for pressure?
- If all else fails, what you should do!

The ultimate aim, of course, is not just to protect but to actually enhance the asset value of corporate and brand reputation. I hope this book will help senior executives across a range of functions to actively engage with stakeholder interests and concerns, without feeling they are plotting a course for the rocks!

CHAPTER 1

What's different about reputation today and why is there a sense of urgency?

"Minds are like parachutes, they work best when open"
LORD THOMAS DEWAR

What's in a name? – the business implications of reputation

Any name has a reputation attached to it. Reputation in a corporate context is based on perceptions of the characteristics, performance and behaviour of a company. Essentially, reputation is a reflection of how well or how badly different groups of interested people – stakeholders – view a commercial name. How do we feel about a particular organization and do we think it's good, bad or indifferent based on available information about past, present and potential performance? Corporate reputation influences the products and services we buy, the investments we make, the job offers we pursue and even the people we choose to be with. It's no different from thinking about our personal reputations, the associations attached by others to our names – are we respected? liked? sought after? emulated? ... or laughed at, loathed or avoided? Reputation implies a value judgement about the attributes of a company and is usually established over time. According to Asia's Most Admired Companies survey, "In today's turbulent economic times, a fine reputation is arguably more important than ever before. Building and maintaining reputation ... takes careful thought, meticulous planning and constant hard work over years. And it can be lost overnight." (*Asian Business Review*, 2000).

Strong reputations need to be actively managed and resourced long-term, reflecting the delivery of demonstrable performance criteria reinforced by effective communication with and between stakeholders, or resource-holders, as they are fashionably called today. Reputation needs quality information and successful relationships. Developing and nurturing each is a labour- and investment-intensive process but the results are well worth it! Reputation is, however, a delicate hybrid – which doesn't survive in adverse conditions unless it has been well protected. Equally, it needs the nutrients of transparency and accountability. Reputation is a *valuable asset* in its own right which can affect financial performance and provide a source of competitive advantage.

Reputation depends on successful relationships inside and outside the business, based on mutual trust and belief. The goodwill of those relationships can help to provide a support base in difficult times. When the going gets tough we are prepared to give a company under the spotlight the benefit of the doubt ... at any rate, maybe once! Equally, when companies achieve good reputations they can have their work cut out in continuing to strive to meet stakeholder expectations.

Benefits of effective reputation management

- Reduce tension between business, its shareholders and customers
- Reduce barriers to competition and market development
- Create a more conducive environment for investment and access to capital
- Attract the best recruits, suppliers and partners
- Secure premium pricing for products and services
- Reduce share price and market volatility
- Minimize the threat of increased regulation or litigation
- Reduce the potential for crises
- Establish trust and credibility with stakeholders

Reputation management practice

The practice of reputation management is about understanding responsibilities towards your stakeholders, including their different interests and the risks which particularly concern different groups. Risk is a constant theme in managing reputation. I regard risks to reputation as icebergs, potentially blocking the navigation channel of successful commercial and reputation strategies, a large amount of which is hidden from view, often underestimated in scale and impact. The objective is to recognize that uncertainty around current and emerging risks poses threats and also opportunities. Sound reputation management seeks to reduce the former and increase the latter.

The management of risk has become more difficult for a number of reasons. First, companies are operating and competing in a *global environment*, with risks emerging from a host of different sources and locations. It is, therefore, extremely difficult to keep up with potential risks and to know how best to respond if they occur. Second, companies are under much greater *scrutiny* than ever before. They are being watched by an array of groups, connected by a global electronic media and the Internet, allowing instant access to and transmission of information – factual and perceptual – between many millions of consumers. Third, calls for *transparency* in corporate performance and behaviour place new pressures on business to inform, share, and consult with stakeholders on a range of issues that may affect them. Finally, *stakeholder perception* is the biggest change-maker of all. The emotional dynamics of risk perception can instantly negate the facts, making redundant reams of documentary evidence confirming the safety of a new food process or life-saving medicine.

Risks to reputation are many and diverse. They no longer constitute mere physical failure – a manufacturing fault or accident – and, in any case, companies in the twenty-first century are learning how to minimize and manage these risks more effectively through formal risk and crisis management procedures. Some of the types of risks that are more prevalent today are listed below:

Example reputation risks

- Security failure
- Product/service shortfall
- Competitor targeting
- Bad behaviour
- Unfair employment practices
- Damage to health, safety or the environment
- Inconsistency in policies/practices
- Poor governance/ethics
- Regulatory intervention
- Threat of litigation
- Adverse stakeholder perception

Reputation risk can be considered in terms of corporate reputation, corporate brands, family brands and in terms of individual product brands. *Corporate brand* equity relates to the attitudes and associations that stakeholders have of a company as opposed to an individual product –

which may be very different. Usually the corporate brand is always present somewhere on a product or service package. For some firms, however, the corporate brand is virtually the only brand used, for example, Nike, General Electric, Motorola, Virgin and CNN. Other companies may have *family brands*, defined as a brand that is used in more than one product category but is not necessarily the name of the company itself. Examples of family brands include Weight Watchers and Mercedes Benz automobiles. An *individual brand* is restricted to one product category, such as a rock star, clothing range or drink and may, therefore, appeal only to a specific consumer group. Further sub-division of a brand occurs by designating a specific item or model type, for instance, Visa offers 'classic', 'gold', 'platinum', 'signature' and 'infinite' versions of its credit card. Corporate reputation, however, plays to our individual expectations, aspirations and needs as consumers, and to our beliefs as citizens. It describes the *rational* and *emotional* attachments that stakeholders form with a company, which is why perception is the driving force behind management success or failure.

Corporate reputation has undoubtedly become an increasingly important issue for CEOs and the top management team, and many now recognize this.

In a recent study by *Chief Executive Magazine*, conducted by Hill & Knowlton/Yankelovich, 96 per cent of CEOs indicated that they believe reputation is very important, and 65 per cent dedicate more time to this subject than they did five years ago. According to the 2001 MORI annual survey of Britain's Captains of Industry, when asked "What are the most important factors you take into account when making your judgement about companies?" CEO respondents viewed the salience of financial performance as less significant than in 1997 (down 16 points to 59 per cent). Factors relating to reputation, however, were regarded with increased importance (up 14 points to 60 per cent).

Risks to reputation must, therefore, be fully acknowledged at the highest level as an integral part of the overall risk management process and as a catalyst for protecting and enhancing customer, employee and shareholder value. The financial impact of reputation loss can be catastrophic, whether through a decline in revenue as a result of a product boycott, asset value depletion from a brand collapse, resource diversion from fixing problems, increased cost of capital as a result of share premium erosion, exposure to predatory takeover, costlier compliance through regulatory intervention or even bankruptcy.

Acknowledging the value of reputation and understanding the diversity of risks that can damage it is what reputation risk management is about.

Managing reputation – both the risks and opportunities inherent in such a valuable asset – affects all parts of the organization.

The development of business reputation is a reflection of the fact that we are becoming more interested in issues beyond specific product characteristics and associations. Ralph Larson, former CEO of Johnson & Johnson says, "Reputations reflect behaviour you exhibit day in and day out through a hundred small things. The way you manage your reputation is by always thinking and trying to do the right thing every day."

How can reputation be valued?

The biggest hurdle in making the case for building, maintaining and managing reputation is how to measure it effectively. There are many measures and a degree of woolliness around most of them. However, selectively, they can provide useful criteria for developing reputation risk management strategies. Reputation surveys in well regarded business publications are commonly seen to provide a good sense of which corporations are admired by opinion formers and management peer groups. *Fortune* magazine, *The Financial Times* and *Asian Business Review* are among the best examples of the so-called 'Reputation Quotient' (RQ) perceptual measure, providing some interesting comparisons, both in the criteria and interview bases that they use, and in their individual rankings over time (see Appendices).

A key trend from *Fortune* magazine's Most Admired Companies survey is that in charting performance, the companies listed are more likely to: (a) use return-based methods of measurement – assets, equity, capital and shareholder value, rather than profits; and (b) focus on customer and employee-based measurements. Almost 60 per cent of the Most Admired Companies rely on customer indicators such as satisfaction, loyalty, and market share. Forty per cent also chart retention, career development and other employee-orientated measurements – more than three times the percentage of companies that didn't make the list (*Fortune* magazine, 2000). A good reputation has an impact on the bottom line. It allows firms to hire and hold onto talented workers, attract investors, customers and partners, launch successful products and win market share – all factors that affect financial performance.

Selection criteria, however, are not particularly robust, depending on opinion rather than a formal evidence base. Recent research (Weber Shandwick and Fombrun, 2001) suggests that people make their judgements about corporate reputation according to attributes within six categories – emotional appeal, calibre of products and services, financial performance, workplace environment in terms of quality of management and employees, and commitment to being a good corporate citizen, referred to as corporate social responsibility.

It is much easier to make the case for valuing reputation by pointing to the costs associated with major mismanagement and/or communication failure. Companies that have been the subject of crisis situations, perceived to be either badly handled or the result of significant operational failure – particularly where the result has been loss of life, injury, large-scale environmental damage or asset reduction – have experienced share premium erosion, market share loss, debt-rating decline, litigation and unwanted regulatory costs. And where organizations have failed to communicate effectively in the immediate aftermath of a crisis, research indicates that the consequences of adverse public perception, media scrutiny and pressure for tougher regulation means that the degree of financial loss can be greater, longer and more difficult to recover from. Our own and other research estimates suggest that the financial impact of major crises can be considerable.

Table 1.1 *The cost of crises*

Corporation	Event	Estimated costs $m
Pan Am	Lockerbie	652
Union Carbide	Bhopal	527
Exxon	Valdez spill	16,000
Perrier	Product recall	263
Occidental	Piper Alpha	1400
P&O	Zeebrugge	70
Barings	Collapse	1200
Ford/Firestone	Product recall	5000
Coca-Cola	Product recall	103
TotalFinaElf	Oil spill	100
Monsanto	GM crops	2–3000

These losses include expectations of future clean-up costs, litigation and reparation costs, as well as the impact of more restrictive legislation which can affect whole industries. The costs also include negative perception and loss of regard in the eyes of customers, investors, employees and communities. Experience from these and other major crises of recent years indicates that:

- Insurance liability cover alone will not protect shareholder value
- Recovery largely depends on management ability
- Share price can be an effective measure of post-crisis management
- Investment in effective communication and reputation management *before* a crisis situation is critical in conserving value (Knight and Pretty, 1997)

Revenue growth, strategic business development, and resource expansion contribute to the way in which asset value and management are assessed. So does perceived leadership through greater visibility (Fombrun, 1996).

Investment in establishing a good reputation is similar to having an insurance policy which can provide protective cover for well regarded companies in times of intense pressure. A study based on *Fortune* magazine's 15th annual survey of America's Most Admired Companies, which followed the stock market crash in 1987, indicated that shares in the top ten public companies recovered faster and suffered less, while shares in the ten least admired companies fell three times as far (Brouillard Communications and Yankelovich Partners, 1998). In addition, the value of future returns on investment is derived, in part at least, from the positive attitude – and therefore endorsement – of stakeholders towards a business. Approval of a company's strategic growth plans facilitates more attractive financial valuations.

Over the past 20 years, the gap between a company's balance sheet and the value placed on it by investors has been widening significantly. The market capitalization of companies quoted on the New York Stock Exchange now averages 2.5 times book value. Further assessment suggests that approximately 40 per cent of market value of the average American corporation is missing from the balance sheet. For knowledge intensive companies, the average can be as high as 100 per cent. What proportion can be accounted for by reputation and brand capital?

A simple measure of intangible assets is the difference between the market value and book value of a company. So if a technology company's market value is estimated at $85.5 bn and its book value at $6.9 bn, intangible assets account for $78.6 bn. Comparing book values with market valuations suggests that the intangible assets of public companies in the US and UK constitute, on average, some 55 per cent of their market valuations – a proportion that has grown steadily over the past 40 years. These intangibles are made up of intellectual capital such as patents, competencies and innovation, and reputational capital – the strength of a company's stakeholder relationships. One way of estimating reputational capital, according to Professor Charles Fombrun of New York University's Stern School of Business, is to ask how much a third party might pay to lease a corporate name. Licensing arrangements are actually royalty rates for corporate names. The more a licensee is prepared to pay, the greater the drawing power of the company's reputation. Royalties on corporate licences generally range between 8 and 14 per cent of sales. Therefore, one estimate of the value of a company's reputation is the present value of all expected royalty payments over a given period.

Fombrun also suggests that companies which manage their relationships with stakeholders invoke a number of core principles that contribute to effective reputation management:

> - A sense of **distinctiveness** in the minds of stakeholders (*Intel*, *Virgin*, *Microsoft*)
> - A tendency on the part of successful companies to **focus** on a core theme (*Johnson & Johnson* as a nurturing, caring and therefore trusting organization; *Disney* as offering a magical experience)
> - A perception of **consistency** in performance and communication (Berkshire Hathaway, General Electric, Singapore Airlines)
> - A focus on **integrity and authenticity** in the contact and communication between an organization and its stakeholders (*Harvard Business School, Fortnum & Mason, Chateau Rothschild*)
> - A commitment to **transparency** as a prerequisite for effective financial and social performance which encourages contact with and support from stakeholders (*Shell, BP*)

Other research that has sought to quantify the value of reputation, implies that economic premiums are associated with strong reputations. Some suggest that reputational capital may generate higher returns. A 1990 study by Srivastava implied that against a cohort of companies with similar levels of risk and return, a higher reputation score could be associated with a higher market value.

Two titans of the financial community think there is much in this. Warren Buffet, Chairman of investment firm Berkshire Hathaway, told investment banking firm Salomon: "If you lose money I will be understanding. If you lose reputation I will be ruthless." He also told his staff in an internal memo: "Our reputation is our only asset – without it we are worthless." Alan Greenspan, Chairman of the Federal Reserve, said to a Harvard University audience, "In today's world, where ideas are increasingly displacing the physical in the production of economic value, competition for reputation becomes a significant driving force, propelling our economy forward. Manufactured goods often can be evaluated before the completion of a transaction. Service providers, on the other hand, can offer only their reputations."

For most corporate boards, shareholder value measured by share price is a key indicator of a CEO's success. A study completed by management consultants Towers Perrin, identified 25 companies that excelled at managing relationships with five types of stakeholder – investors, customers, employees, suppliers and the communities in which the companies operated. The companies included Shell, Coca-Cola, General Electric, Johnson & Johnson and Procter and Gamble. A combination of publicly available information such as *Fortune* magazine's Most Admired Companies rankings, and proprietary data about corporate activities, was reviewed over time and in comparison with the stock market. The analysis showed that these companies, referred to as 'stakeholder superstars', had doubly outperformed the Standard and Poor's 500 index over the past 15 years. The total shareholder return was 43 per cent over the 15 years, while the total shareholder return from the S&P 500 was 19 per cent (Schmidt, 2000).

Corporate reputation typically is driven by the price, features, and quality of the goods and services that a corporation produces. But more and more, it is also driven by the corporation's commitment to integrate economic and social considerations into competitive strategies.

A new development in recent years is the emergence of socially responsible investment funds (SRIs). Although it is still early days, companies that are responding to the new agenda of social and environmental performance and reporting may, in time, be rewarded by the financial markets. The New York-based Dow Jones Sustainability Index has outperformed the Dow Jones Index by 36 per cent over the past five years. Corporate social responsibility issues are covered in the portfolio screening for major SRIs. According to some estimates, the SRI sector is now worth more than $2 trillion in the United States and more than $25 bn in the UK. However, these figures still only represent a very small percentage of total fund management.

Reputation has always mattered, but the assault on corporate reputation has intensified as a result of some compelling trends that are placing new pressures on companies.

What's changed?

The erosion of traditional authority

Our respect in the judgement of experts has taken a nosedive. Twenty years ago we were expected to hang on every word that sprang from the lips of a doctor, accountant, lawyer or priest. Even politicians were assumed to have a sense of duty in looking after public interests. The United States and other industrialized societies are currently experiencing some of the lowest levels of confidence in government ever recorded, despite the fact that economic and political conditions have been relatively good in recent years. Trust in government is at an all time low, characterized by a pervasive decline in deference to authority. Findings from the World Values Surveys, conducted since 1981, clearly indicate declining deference to authority (World Values Surveys, 2000). Social scientists suggest that a combination of unprecedented economic growth over the last few decades, underpinned by the safety net of the modern welfare state, have produced exceptional levels of economic security. This has contributed to shifting authority away from religion and the state to us as individuals, and our growing preoccupation with the quality of our lifestyles, our opinions, our values and our own autonomy.

So today, we reject conventional authority, preferring to believe in our own sense of identity and individuality. We no longer talk about what is desirable, but instead use the language of rights, where every view and opinion is considered to hold the same weight, regardless of the credibility of its source. For public officials and business managers alike, disregard of such opinion can quickly trigger claims of discrimination or exclusion, reinforced through the media and consumer action.

A decline in trust

For many people in western societies today, the new century is not a source of hope – the predominant mood is one of fear. Many of us are anxious about the future and the heritage we will leave for our children. There is great concern about the human impact on the environment, as the simultaneous growth of material consumption and population generates greater pollution and resource degradation. In a modern media world we are able to witness poverty, famine and conflict and some of us question whether material wealth is a real substitute for quality of community life. The traditional model of economic and social progress, based on free trade, is beginning to be questioned. The economic and political structures of global and national development are, in some people's minds, starting to develop cracks and encourage inequality. The costs for some are becoming ethically unacceptable.

Table 1.2 *Questions about trust*

1. First of all, I would like to begin by reading out a list of different types of people. For each, would you tell me whether you generally trust them to tell the truth or not?			
	Tell truth %	Not tell truth %	Don't know %
Doctors	89	8	3
Teachers	88	7	5
Clergymen or priests	86	9	5
Television news readers	75	17	8
The police	70	23	7
The ordinary man or woman in the street	58	26	16
Civil servants	52	35	13
Trades union officials	40	39	21
Government scientists	38	46	16
Business leaders	35	49	16
Politicians generally	19	73	8
Government ministers	17	71	12
Journalists	10	82	8

2. Thinking now about pollution, which two or three, if any, of these sources would you trust most to advise you on the risks posed by pollution?	
	%
Pressure groups (e.g. Greenpeace/Friends of the Earth)	61
Independent Scientists (e.g. university professors)	60
Television	25
Government scientists	23
Friends or family	15
Newspapers	14
Government ministers	6
Private companies	5
Politicians generally	4
Civil servants	3
Other	*
None of these	2
Don't know	2

Source: Better Regulation Task Force/MORI, January 1999: Base 1,015 adults aged 16+

Seven out of ten Europeans don't trust others, according to the European Values Survey, representing the sharpest decline in social trust since the survey began in 1959. Ten years ago, 44 per cent said that most people could be trusted. By 1995, the figure had dropped to 38 per cent and it has remained at this level for the last five years.

The cumulative effect of a succession of highly publicized public health and food safety risk issues in the UK in recent years has contributed to a culture of blame and uncertainty. We've become better informed, educated and sophisticated as consumers, investors and constituents, with rapidly rising expectations in relation to product and service quality, value and access. However, we've also become more anxious about the complexity and remorseless pace of technological and scientific change that both drives and serves these demands. Business is pushing forward innovative changes which raise complex issues about choice, control, equity, ethics and need, and which must be accompanied by reassurances of responsibility and accountability in managing any risk – whether real or perceived – that may accompany associated benefits and safeguards. Each time a new risk is perceived to be mismanaged by government or industry, our scepticism and uncertainty over who to trust increases. These legacy issues are fuelling calls for greater transparency, spawning a raft of corporate governance guidelines and disclosure legislation. They also encourage feelings of public mistrust over the relationship between regulatory authorities, scientific experts and business. These changes are creating demands for more and better information generated by public concern over who to trust. Business has to be in the forefront of responding to these demands if it is to stave off further costly regulation.

A more intrusive, simplifying and sensational media

Many of our ideas and opinions are forged or reinforced by the media. In the '24/7' real-time world of global, electronic information exchange and reporting, the media are past masters at identifying and structuring issues that we need to be worrying about. They may not tell us what to *think* (although that's changing through media advocacy) but they do tell us what to *think about*.

Our emotions are also exploited by alarmist media reporting designed to amplify feelings of concern and examine questions of blame. The media plays on our anxieties and feeds off human interest stories – usually negative. So-called investigative reporting encourages speculation on alleged secrets and attempted cover-ups by business and government; journalists draw links with other high profile issues to compound a particular threat, amplifying conflicts of interest and opinions among experts to create a sense of uncertainty. Perceived unfairness or undue risk exposure to vulnerable groups such as the elderly and children, reinforced by predictions of even greater doom for future generations, do wonders for newspaper circulations. Needless to say, anything to do with celebrity status, sex or money, has a good chance of hitting the headlines (Fischhoff, 1985).

In January 1991, at the start of the Gulf War, CNN was not exactly an international household name, being available only to a few million viewers outside the United States. Today, that's all changed; CNN has access to around 160 m households and an array of commercial and leisure outlets. This is in part due to the fact that for more than two weeks during the Gulf War, CNN provided the only American reporting from Iraq and its coverage completely redefined live satellite television news. This was more recently demonstrated in the coverage of the terrorist attacks on America in September 2001, the ensuing military action in Afghanistan and ongoing conflict in the Middle East. According to one observer: "Television imagery transmitted by satellite is irrevocably altering the ways governments deal with each other, just as it makes traditional diplomacy all but obsolete in times of crisis … Instant access from the battlefield to the conference table and back again has enormous political implications both good and bad." (McNulty, 1993). Satellite news coverage now has a huge impact on policymaking, military operations, and on business performance.

We're also seeing a merger of what constitutes news reporting and what constitutes factual documentary-making with entertainment. 'Fly-on-the-wall' and docudramas are representative of this development, as has been the remorseless rise of daytime chat shows, led by Oprah Winfrey, which now address every conceivable social taboo and have huge influence over millions of consumers' attitudes and, importantly, purchasing patterns. Her weekly book club, for example, where she selected a new publication of her choice, could generate instant sales of half a million. "Many unknown American authors would crawl naked over broken bottles for this literary jackpot", according to journalist Robert McCrum, writing in *The Observer* (4 November 2001). Media and entertainment have not only become blurred, they have become big business. At its height, Vivendi, the French media conglomerate, had estimated annual revenues of $46 billion; AOL Time Warner had annual revenues of $44 bn; Disney $27 bn; Viacom $26 bn; and News Corporation $15 bn. Their interests span TV, cable and Internet services, publishing, theme parks and music.

The Internet

The impact of the Internet on reputation has been and will continue to be formidable, reducing geographic constraints, access, time and resources. In 1993, the Internet had some 90,000 regular users. By 2000, it had well over 300 m regular users. Five years from now, some industry estimates predict that the number of users worldwide will pass the billion mark.

"By creating newly accessible channels of communication and organization, the Internet has shifted the balance of power of 'voice'. The result is that corporate reputations are increasingly defined not by what companies do or say, but by how others perceive and respond to their actions and words." (Bunting and Lipski, 2000)

So big companies can no longer expect to make themselves heard above the noise levels of others. According to Internet specialist Infonic, opponents, however small, can make themselves noticed in quite disproportionate ways. First because access to the Internet doesn't require much money or resources; second, because the Internet has facilitated the proliferation of alternative information sources and authorities; and third, because they have become past masters at online communications. These factors are enabling individuals and NGOs to challenge corporate practices through the establishment of alternative web sites, through which they can successfully galvanize and co-ordinate direct action on a range of social, environmental and economic issues. Amid the growing hubbub of consumer, media and activist dissection of corporate behaviour, it is increasingly difficult for companies to assert their positions.

It's not all bad for business, however. Better access to, and sharing of information electronically, fuels demands for greater corporate transparency and facilitates communication between disparate stakeholder groups. Changes to company law will improve Internet-based shareholder communication, including distribution of electronic annual reports and accounts, AGM notification, news releases and a range of other institutional investor information through to electronic proxy voting.

In times of external scrutiny and pressure, companies can distribute stakeholder information with great speed, establishing themselves as authoritative sources of information on the issue in question and maintaining dialogue through news groups, bulletin boards and tailored web sites to provide information and encourage public support on specific topics.

The emergence of a victim culture

Since the late 1980s, central and northern European government policy has been increasingly oriented towards identifying and protecting victims, or potential victims, in the form of new 'rights'. In the late 1980s/early 1990s, the right to compensation and the recognition of a formal complaint was given an emotional dimension by a growing concern about the needs of victims.

The political desire to be seen to support victims was shaped by the apparent cluster of large-scale disasters around this time, including the Zeebrugge ferry disaster in 1987 when 192 people died; the Pan Am Lockerbie airplane crash in 1988 which left 286 dead; and the fire on board North Sea oil platform Piper Alpha in 1988, in which 167 people died.

Because the Piper Alpha was owned by American oil corporation Occidental, legal actions were intense and set new precedents: lawyers from 142 firms, representing 135 families and 50 survivors, formed the Occidental and Piper Disaster Group. They achieved a private settlement estimated to be worth £100 m, more generous than any previous settlement in the UK.

From these experiences and others, it became the norm to form a victim's group, not only for compensation purposes, but to carry the mantle of demands for better safety and associated regulation. Promoting victims' rights and promising to hold public inquiries in the immediate aftermath of disasters has become commonplace. It is now routine procedure for new policies – from criminal justice legislation and fire regulations, to transport spending and education matters – to be proposed in the name of victim protection, often on the wave of sensitivity immediately following an adverse incident. Typically, much of this type of policy change places a greater regulatory and cost burden on business.

The media has been quick to fuel this sensitivity to the victim in both policy circles and the public mind. The focus of news features has increasingly been on the experience of victims – on bereavement, fear, injury and suffering – in the most intimate detail. The events of 11 September 2001 in America provided a vivid example. This emphasis on personal tragedy is evident even among those who are ostensibly successful; there is a burgeoning interest in footballers with addictions, journalists with terminal illnesses and actors going through messy divorces.

Whether desirable or not from a social viewpoint, companies who fail to recognize the elevated social and political status accorded to victims do so at their peril. Reinforced by tougher occupational health and workplace legislation, policing, blaming and punishing companies has become a populist theme for governments as they seek to distance themselves from corporate interests. This has been seen in France in recent years following scandals about financing and influencing connections between the government and oil giant, TotalFinaElf.

A decline in the reputation of science

Society's relationship with science is in a state of change in Western democracies, particularly in Europe. While science today is exciting, full of opportunities, read about and popularized more than ever before, confusion over who to trust and scepticism over the role of science in policymaking have probably been the most profound outcomes from the BSE crisis. Peer-reviewed data no longer seems to count as an antidote to a piece of unpublished junk science promoted by an activist group through the pages of the tabloid press. Yet no matter how distinguished or independent an expert working group or advisory panel investigating the environmental health effects of dioxins in milk or botulism in cheese may be, the perception is one of corruption in the link between scientists working for business or government.

Survey data in Europe reveals negative responses to science associated with government or industry, and to science whose purpose is not obviously beneficial. These negative responses are expressed as a lack of trust. Recent trends identified in a UK House of Lords Select Committee on Science and Technology report, *Science and Society, 1999–2000*, highlight some key points, namely that:

- The perceived *purpose* of science is crucial to public response
- People now question all authority, including scientific authority
- People place more trust in science which is seen to be 'independent'
- There remains a culture of institutional secrecy which invites suspicion
- Some issues currently treated by decision-makers as scientific issues in fact involve many other factors besides science. Framing the problem wrongly by excluding moral, social, ethical and other concerns invites hostility
- What the public finds acceptable often fails to correspond with the objective risks as understood by science. This may relate to the degree to which individuals feel in control and able to make their own choices
- Underlying people's *attitudes* to science are a variety of *values*. Bringing these into the debate and reconciling them are challenges for the policymaker.

Developments in the new biosciences, the human genome map,

artificial reproduction, xenotransplantation and the use of animals in research, raise questions about the social and ethical impact of science on progress.

According to official estimates exposed in the media, the European Commission's plan to test the toxicity of 30,000 chemicals found in everyday products to make sure they are safe for human health and the environment will require the use and death of at least 50 million animals, creating outrage among animal welfare and environmental groups. When it comes to science, many of us are losing faith.

The remorseless rise in anti-business/anti-technology activism

Uncertainty over who to trust and intense scrutiny of government and business by the media has fuelled a meteoric rise in activism. Sophisticated, well organized, media- and Internet-literate, activists now operate in diverse coalitions across national and ideological boundaries. Their ability to galvanize public opinion and influence consumer attitudes was amply demonstrated in the debate in Europe on the safety of GMOs in 1999, where in the UK over 70 consumer, civil liberties and environmental groups joined together to vote for a ban on GM crops. One of these groups included the Federation of Womens' Institutes – a bastion of conservative, middle class and middle age attitudes. It was, according to *The Guardian* newspaper, like a missile despatched from middle England into the cold breast of government. The same group gave the British Prime Minister, Tony Blair, a disapproving slow hand-clap over his policies on public service investment at an annual conference in 2000.

In 1900, there were only 20 International Government Organizations (IGOs) and 180 international NGOs. There are now over 300 IGOs and 26,000 NGOs with operations in more than one country. This trend in consumer activism has been boosted by the Internet, facilitating information sharing and planning through the use of well-structured e-mail databases enabling groups with diverse interests to maintain contact and plan direct action. In addition, the Internet massively extends the scope and range of communication by reducing the constraints of time and space. Now, through newsgroups, web sites, bulletin boards, chat rooms, e-mail and mailing lists, anybody with access can have a worldwide presence and find a worldwide audience.

Protestors at the World Trade Organization meetings in Seattle and Washington DC and the G8 summits in The Hague, Genoa, Barcelona, Prague and Kananaskis in Canada expressed concern about growth of big

corporations, environmental degradation and the widening global gap
between the haves and have-nots. Anti-capitalism campaigners have
targeted, increasingly violently, leading consumer brands, especially
those which generate annual turnover greater than the poorest 20
countries' total wealth, such as McDonald's, Coca-Cola, Nike and
Starbucks. Some large corporations are getting their act together to
respond to this new and increasingly aggressive wave of anti-
corporatism, by involving NGOs in consultation processes. Others are
setting themselves up to be the targets of the future. Activism is an
established feature of modern-day society and must be factored into
reputation risk planning.

The new corporate social responsibility agenda

The twenty-first century has brought profound changes in the
relationship between business and society. Business has moved centre-
stage bringing many benefits, but also attracting new risks which will
determine prosperity or extinction. These changes – impact on the
environment, and on society in general – have created new challenges
for modern managers, and have powerful repercussions for financial and
reputation performance.

Corporate social responsibility is based on the emerging belief that
trade brings obligations and that companies should be responsible for
their use of resources. It covers a number of core issues:

- **Employment** – ensuring workforce diversity and suitable
  workplace conditions and practices
- **Environment** – minimizing environmental impact (ground, air,
  water and ecosystems) from any stage throughout product and
  process lifecycles
- **Human rights** – upholding basic human rights wherever a
  company may have commercial operations, including child
  labour, security, privacy, minimum wage levels
- **Communities** – support for and involvement in the communities
  of which a company is, or intends to be a part
- **Commercial relationships** – operating fairly with customers,
  partners and suppliers

Source: ABI, 2001

are coming to regard a company's 'social' performance as a core attribute of the business. The Conference Board surveyed 1000 Americans in 1999 and found that almost 89 per cent agreed that large companies should do more than focus only on achieving profitability within the law. Forty-two per cent said that they held companies completely or partly responsible for helping to solve social problems like crime, poverty, and lack of education. Thirty-three per cent said that companies should focus on setting higher ethical standards, going beyond what is required by law, and actively helping build a better society for all.

The survey found that consumers are willing to back up their expectations with action as well. Forty-six per cent of respondents said that they had carried out a purchasing decision in favour of a company, or decided to speak out in favour of a company because of a positive perception of its social responsibility. Forty-nine per cent of respondents said that they had decided not to purchase a product or service from a company, or had spoken critically of a company, because it did not meet their standard for being socially responsible (The Conference Board, 1999).

A plethora of voluntary but increasingly influential accreditation schemes has emerged relating to CSR performance and reporting. These include:

- ISO 14001 international standard for environmental management systems
- UN Global Compact and Global Sullivan Principles which focus on human rights, social and economic justice
- Global Reporting Initiative which aims to provide global application guidelines for corporate reporting on economic, environmental and social performance
- FTSE4Good index which assesses members of the FTSE All-Share Index (excluding tobacco, nuclear and weapons systems) against a range of social, environmental and management criteria
- Ethical Trading Initiative which seeks to encourage use of a widely endorsed set of standards on sourcing policies
- Association of British Insurers guidelines on investing in social responsibility
- OECD guidelines designed to evaluate and improve the legal, institutional and regulatory framework for corporate governance in member countries
- Social Accountability 8000, a monitoring and certification standard for assessing labour conditions in global manufacturing operations

Achieving a balance between commercial success, environmental quality and social justice means that the stakes are becoming much higher for companies in their dealings with the outside world. Society expects more from business. Transparency and accountability have become the watchwords of modern business, and external perception of the way in which companies are seen to be behaving now has material consequences for corporate reputation.

Governance and liability

Over the last ten years or so, the quest for greater institutional and business accountability, in response to a perceived decline in trust, has affected every aspect of our lives. It is increasingly taking the form of detailed and costly controls *via* an unending stream of legislation and regulation. Central planning may have failed in the former Soviet Union, but it is alive and well in many Western democracies! Government institutions and companies face new standards of accounting practice, more detailed health, safety and environmental guidelines, more complex employment and pensions legislation, copious provisions for ensuring non-discrimination, a welter of new product and consumer protection measures and a proliferation of complaints and compensation procedures. Today, the cost of regulation in the United States is estimated to be around $700 bn a year, representing 8 per cent of GDP.

These new pressures for transparency and accountability are increasingly becoming enshrined in corporate governance guidelines and disclosure legislation, turning the heat up on publicly-quoted and privately-run firms alike. Some of these developments are being led by the UK. Rules introduced in the summer of 2000, for example, require pension funds to declare how far they take social, environmental and ethical considerations into account when choosing stocks for investment. Trustees are required to make an annual statement of investment principles, which sets out for scheme members their approach to investing the fund's money. This development has contributed to the growing SRI movement. The Dow Jones Sustainability Index and FTSE4Good index can be used by fund managers to create SRI products which may appeal both to retail and wholesale investors. Eligible companies must be able to demonstrate a commitment to environmental sustainability, human rights and 'positive' relationships with stakeholders. Similar guidelines are under review in other European countries and by the European Union.

The UK government's Company Law Review, published in July 2001 and designed to overhaul British statutes that hark back to Victorian times, has considered the nature of directors' duties for non-financial matters and to non-shareholders. Significantly, the review has proposed that for public companies with a turnover of £5 m, and private companies with a turnover of £500 m, provision for a non-mandatory Operating and Financial Review (OFR) will be introduced. The OFR will take account of wider business relationships and will include reporting on social, ethical, environmental and reputational impacts. The essence of the Review's recommendations is to place emphasis on an 'inclusive' approach to directors' duties, in all relationships and through wider accountability brought about by improved company reporting. Directors are responsible for the long-term health of the company; not just the short-term interests of current shareholders. It concluded that directors:

> "... must recognize, where relevant, the importance of relations with employees, suppliers, customers and others, the need to maintain a reputation for high standards of business conduct, and the impact of their actions on the community and the environment."

Risk management and internal control have moved firmly onto the boardroom agenda. Following the lead of US regulators, when the London Stock Exchange published its Combined Code on Corporate Governance in the summer of 1998, the emphasis on control-related aspects of governance shifted from internal financial control to the broader concept of internal control. The Turnbull working party's report completed the construction of the current corporate governance infrastructure in the UK by providing implementation guidance on those aspects of the Code dealing with internal control and internal audit. It is designed to give companies a framework for setting up robust systems of risk management and, in doing so, they should consider emerging types of risk, such as those arising from branding and reputation.

In the last decade, more than 30 per cent of directors and officers of large companies in the US and Europe faced litigation. The issues responsible for 75 per cent of these liability claims were wrongful termination of employment, domestic marketing issues, discrimination, dishonesty, fraud and financial reporting (Green, 1999). In Europe, directors face even greater vulnerability to litigation with the incorporation of the European Convention on Human Rights.

In the late 1990s, US courts awarded punitive damages against cigarette manufacturers, including Philip Morris, R J Reynolds and Brown & Williamson. Punitive awards for public health cases could be extended to consumer goods generally and apply to European companies operating in the US. In addition, the EU product safety directive is being revised to include new provisions to allow consumer groups to take class actions. Increasing use of class actions in the US has set a precedent for EU law. The critical risk issues will be the scale of potential liabilities and the scale – and availability – of financial security.

In the wider context of corporate responsibility, other trends and legislative developments place new pressures on business to review operational and communication practices. The European Commission published a new communication in February 2000 clarifying that the precautionary principle should be applied when scientific evidence is insufficient, inconclusive or uncertain, and where there is a potentially dangerous effect on the environment, human, animal or plant health. This has major implications for the pharmaceutical and food industries, for example, and companies failing to apply this approach may find themselves subjected to individual as well as corporate liability.

So what do you need to do?

Today, more than ever before, the key to any company's success is its intangible assets of which reputation forms an important component. This is characterized most dramatically in the shift to a knowledge-based economy. Although intangible assets are difficult to quantify in traditional accounting terms, this new environment demands a radical change in risk management and reporting systems. While boards will feel comfortable in assessing operational risks, they may find it more difficult to assess less familiar risk icebergs associated with reputation. However, stockmarket volatility can be reduced by identifying and valuing unrecorded intangible assets such as reputation.

A more inclusive framework for reporting, together with a process for accounting for broader social and ethical business practices, is likely to improve transparency and accountability with stakeholders. In turn, this can provide a better mutual understanding of expectations and future returns. In its recent study, *Towards a Market-led Reporting Model,* the Institute of Chartered Accountants in England and Wales lists a number of features of the 'old' (that is, current system) and the way they will need to change in a possible 'new' system, which embraces the principles and value-based returns associated with improved dialogue and reporting. I think these features are applicable as a universal and international model.

Table 1.3 *A more inclusive framework for reporting*

Old System	New System
Shareholder focus	Stakeholder focus
Paper-based	Internet-based
Standardized information	Customized information
Company controlled information on performance and prospects	Information available from a variety of sources
Periodic reporting	Continuous reporting
Distribution of information	Dialogue
Financial statements	Broader range of performance measures (not just financial)
Past performance	Greater emphasis on future prospects
Historical cost	Substantial value-based information
Audit of accounts	Assurance of underlying system
Nationally oriented	Globally based
Essentially static system	Continuously changing model
Preparer-led regulations	Satisfying market-place demands

Source: ICA, 2001

With these trends and developments in mind, here are my guiding principles for avoiding the icebergs and charting a course towards effective reputation risk management. I shall explore them in detail in the following chapters, using real-life examples and guidelines on how to enhance the value of your reputational assets.

1. *Acknowledge that reputation is a valuable intangible asset and needs to be actively managed in the boardroom*

The practice of reputation management is about understanding and managing your responsibilities to your different stakeholders. Risk is a constant theme in managing reputation. The objective is to recognize that uncertainty around current and emerging risks poses threats and also opportunities. Sound reputation management seeks to reduce the former and increase the latter. There is a growing evidence base that reputation can be valued as an intangible asset so don't treat it as a Cinderella asset! Grab the opportunities that building support and trust can provide and proactively manage reputation in the boardroom and across your organization through openness and accountability. Building goodwill in your reputation bank account will earn interest in good times and provide a safety blanket if you are faced with pressure-cooker decision-making. The key emphasis here is on effective information sharing and engagement with stakeholders.

2. *Develop a finely tuned radar and become a listening company*

The chances that a head-in-the-sand approach to navigating your way around external events is going to work for long in today's 'see through' environment are remote. Assuming that the icebergs caused by adverse scrutiny will melt away is unlikely. Don't, whatever you do, resort to the 'Decide, Announce, Defend' school of communication. Companies faced with controversy often tend to decide on a policy stance without any external validation, let alone consultation, announce the policy and then stubbornly defend it in the face of adverse public scrutiny without any acknowledgement of perception factors. Most badly handled crises are representative of this style. Being a listening company can protect your future and enhance the potential for better financial returns. But it isn't just about clever market research and focus groups. The need for a finely tuned radar that can scan for icebergs and track individuals, groups and organizations which may have an interest – positive, neutral or negative – in your business now or downstream, is critical to future proofing. Shell and BP have each experienced the wrong end of NGO campaigning and associated negative media scrutiny over environmental mismanagement and human rights abuses. Today they consult with environmental, human rights and consumer groups alongside contact programmes with employees, policymakers, technical and social science experts, community leaders, journalists and customers. This isn't simply about remedial action, nor is about succeeding every time; but both are becoming more experienced reputation management organizations. Innovation in energy production and conservation are exciting commercial enterprises which will create next generation income. Although effective operational performance drives market sentiment, companies have the potential to benefit financially from the way in which institutional communities are valuing their assets in the light of improved transparency and reporting.

3. Develop clear and robust reputation management systems that integrate with your routine risk management procedures

Managing reputation risk is as critical to a business as managing any other facet of the risk management portfolio – in fact, it should be treated as a priority when a new risk emerges, there is a change in the degree of an existing risk or a new perception of risk occurs. The burden of proof responsibility for managing risks to reputation falls firmly on the shoulders of senior management. That means that you have the task of understanding, assessing and managing your company's response options against a backdrop of complex, confusing and often incomplete information. This is compounded by a lack of trust in information sources, selective reporting by the media and the many psychological, social and economic factors that affect how information about reputation risks are processed. Most importantly, start this process early and don't dither!

A well tuned radar will enable you to identify emerging and developing risks and opportunities. Prioritization, in terms of financial and reputational impact, should follow, along with an analysis of the gaps between your performance and stakeholder expectations. This activity will provide the ground work for avoidance and mitigation strategies and for establishing support systems and processes for communication, from which appropriate strategies and action plans can be charted and flow.

4. Create your own code of good behaviour and assure your licence to operate

Trade brings obligations and companies will have to put back into society – one way or another – some of what they take out. There is no getting away from it and in any case, behaving responsibly shouldn't be that difficult! Corporate social responsibility is being seen to be the new moral code for business and plays to a realization that finite resources need to be preserved.

Global fast food brands that encourage poor nutrition, environmental and workplace practices will need to deliver counter-weighting benefits to the communities of which they are a part. Purveyors of the global coffee shop experience will need to square up the consumer benefits and attributes they promote, with the demise of the subsistence coffee farmer in western Africa who is being squeezed out of the supply chain. 'Fat cat' remuneration policies, cosy boardroom relationships with non-executive directors and attempts to tinker with politics will have to become a thing of the past. Closer to home in the back yard of your organization, you can reappraise your attributes in the light of existing and potential vulnerabilities with the help of your employees, customers, opinion formers and investors. You also need to connect with the people who might, until now, be considered to be trenchant enemies of your company's success – journalists and activists!

Don't wait to be asked and don't try and deliver everything in one go. Adopt a stepwise approach based on openness but commit to deliver in a realistic timeframe. Establish or reaffirm your own set of business principles, but make sure they are manageable. You must be confident that your code of conduct is easy to define and explain, can be owned up, down and across your organization, and can be implemented and assessed for consistent delivery at all times. Don't speak weasel words – instead, decide through appropriate management systems, auditing and assessment processes what your business and employees stand for and move forward from there.

5. *Treat your stakeholders intelligently*

It is totally wrong to assume your customers are stupid. The financial services sector is riddled with this attitude from pensions mis-selling to mortgage lock-ins and unjustifiable insurance premiums and interest rates. Monsanto had the arrogance to assume that UK consumers would fall over themselves to buy the apparent innovations associated with genetically modified food. Not a single thought was given to an embedded anxiety and sense of confusion over who to trust about the safety of food production in the aftermath of a string of public health scares associated with food consumption. More recently, Nintendo's new president, Satoru Iwata, got in hot water by claiming that people are becoming bored with computer games. Pinning hopes of greater profitability on a new games console, the GameCube, Mr Iwata said, "no matter what great product you come up with, people get bored. I feel like a chef cooking for a king who is already full." The gaff will remind many of Gerald Ratner describing his jewellery products as 'crap' at a UK business leaders' forum in 1991. The perceived patronizing swipe at the customers who had made him a multi-millionaire, still holds resonance as one of the most dramatic reputation collapses of all time.

Consumers want to be informed, in order to make purchasing decisions – whether on choice, convenience, value, quality, authenticity, safety, innovation, need, ethical or other grounds. They are also getting much smarter through access to the Internet, consumer watchdog programmes and comparative product and service surveys. How an organization treats its employees, suppliers, communities and customers forms an increasing part of the purchasing decision and consumers will vote with their feet if the criteria don't stack up. Treat your customers (and everyone else) with respect and give them the information and options they need to decide.

6. Work as though everything you say and do is public

Even if you haven't got to the organizational change piece on new ways of working in an open-plan, 'touch-down', no-paper-storage-or-personal-effects-all-electronic-no-directors'-dining-room-ergonomically-fueng-shui'd environment, work to encourage openness and communication inside your company as well as outside. Consider yourself, however reluctantly, in a goldfish bowl which can viewed from all angles, attractive and not so attractive.

Action checklist

- Understand the potential risks to reputation and acknowledge that they may exist
- Put in place early warning and monitoring systems
- Consider ways to improve operational and organizational processes
- Establish a clear process for policy development and communication
- Identify stakeholder groups and establish their information needs
- Utilize third party allies to build credibility
- Be responsive and communicate in ways that relate to the differing concerns of each stakeholder group
- Build investment, product and service benefits separately from the risks
- Monitor, evaluate and fine-tune, and remember that progression is better than perfection!

Appendix 1

Corporate reputation criteria

Publication	Criteria used to assess reputation	Audience researched	Criteria for inclusion
Fortune Magazine	• Quality of management • Quality of products and services • Innovativeness • Long-term investment value • Financial soundness • Ability to attract, develop, and retain talent • Community and environmental responsibility • Use of corporate assets • Global business acumen	Business executives and analysts are asked to rank companies within their own industry group	Largest companies in *Fortune's* directories of US industrial and non-industrial corporations
Financial Times	• Strong strategy • Quality of products/services • Maximizing customer satisfaction • Successful change management and globalization • Business leadership • Innovation • Robust and human corporate culture	CEOs	Major global corporations
Asian Business	• Quality of management • Quality of products and services • Contribution to the local economy • Being a good employer • Potential for growth • Being honest and ethical • Potential for future profit • Ability to cope with the changing economic environment	Senior executives, CEOs and company board members	Largest listed companies, by turnover, in each of nine Asian countries: Hong Kong, Indonesia, Japan, Malaysia, the Philippines, Singapore, South Korea, Taiwan and Thailand, plus a variety of high-visibility multinationals and a small number of mainland Chinese companies

Publication	Criteria used to assess reputation	Audience researched	Criteria for inclusion
Management Today	• Quality of management • Ability to attract/retain talent • Quality of marketing • Financial soundness • Value as a long-term investment • Environmental responsibility • Quality of products and services • Capacity to innovate • Use of corporate assets	CEOs and opinion formers	UK companies listed in London Stock Exchange
Far Eastern Economic Review	• Quality of products/services • Long-term management vision • Innovation • Financial soundness • Whether others try to emulate the company	Readers of *Far Eastern Economic Review*	Asian multinationals and 20–40 local companies in Australia, Hong Kong, India, Indonesia, Japan, Malaysia, the Philippines, Singapore, South Korea, Taiwan and Thailand

Appendix 2

Fortune magazine – America's most admired companies

Companies most frequently cited in the Top Ten (1983–2001)

Company	83	84	85	86	87	88	89	90	91	92	93	94	95	96	97	98	99	00	01	Number of appearances
Merck	●	●	●	●	●	●	●	●	●	●	●	●	●	●	●					15
Coca-Cola		●	●	●	●		●	●	●	●	●		●	●	●		●			13
3M	●	●	●	●	●		●	●	●					●	●	●				11
Procter & Gamble		●		●	●		●	●	●					●	●	●				10
Rubber maid							●	●	●	●	●	●	●	●	●	●				10
Wal-Mart Stores								●	●	●	●	●	●					●	●	9
Johnson & Johnson	●	●								●	●					●	●	●	●	8
Boeing			●		●	●	●	●	●		●									7
Hewlett-Packard					●			●	●				●	●		●				6
Microsoft														●	●	●	●	●	●	6
Intel										●			●	●	●			●	●	6
Dow Jones					●	●							●				●	●		5
IBM	●	●	●	●	●															5
J. P. Morgan							●	●			●	●	●							5
Liz Clairborne					●	●	●	●		●										5
General Electric		●												●	●		●	●		5
Berkshire Hathaway															●	●	●	●	●	5
Pepsi Co									●	●						●	●			4
Southwest Airlines															●	●		●	●	4

■ = featured in the top ten

Top ten companies 1996–2001

Ranking	96	97	98	99	00	01
1	Coca-Cola	Coca-Cola	General Electric	General Electric	General Electric	General Electric
2	Procter & Gamble	Mirage Resorts	Microsoft	Coca-Cola	Microsoft	Cisco Systems
3	–	Merck	Coca-Cola	Microsoft	Dell Computers	Wal-Mart Stores
4	Johnson & Johnson	United Parcel Services	Intel	Dell Computer	Cisco systems	Southwest Airlines
5	Intel	Microsoft	Hewlett-Packard	Berkshire Hathaway	Wal-Mart Stores	Microsoft
6	Merck	Johnson & Johnson	Southwest Airlines	Wal-Mart Stores	Southwest Airlines	Home Depot
7	Mirage Resorts	Intel	Berkshire Hathaway	Southwest Airlines	Berkshire Hathaway	Berkshire Hathaway
8	Microsoft	Pfizer	Disney	Intel	Intel	Charles Schwab
9	– –	Procter & Gamble	Johnson & Johnson	Merck	Home Depot	Intel
10		Berkshire Hathaway	Merck	Disney	Lucent Technologies	Dell Computer

Appendix 3

Financial Times – World's Most Respected Companies

Companies in the top ten

Company	1997	1998	1999	1999
General Electric	■	■	■	■
Microsoft	■	■	■	■
Coca-Cola	■	■	■	■
IBM		■	■	■
Sony			■	■
Toyota		■	■	■
DaimlerChrysler/ Daimler-Benz	■	■	■	
Nestlé	■	■	■	
ABB	■	■		
Ford		■		
Intel	■	■		■
Dell			■	
Wal-Mart			■	
Cisco Systems				■
3M				■
General Motors				■
British Airways	■			
British Petroleum	■			
L'Oreal	■			
Royal Dutch Shell	■			

■ = featured in the Top Ten

Top Ten companies 1997–2000

Position in top ten	1997	1998	1999	2000
1	Microsoft	General Electric	General Electric	General Electric
2	General Electric	Microsoft	Microsoft	Microsoft
3	Coca-Cola	Coca-Cola	Coca-Cola	Sony
4	ABB	IBM	IBM	Coca-Cola
5	British Airways	Toyota	DaimlerChrysler	IBM
6	Nestlé	Daimler-Benz	Sony	Toyota
7	Intel	ABB	Dell	Cisco Systems
8	British Petroleum	Nestlé	Nestlé	Intel
9	Daimler-Benz	Ford	Wal-Mart	3M
10	L'Oreal Royal Dutch Shell	Intel	Toyota	General Motors

Appendix 4

Asian Business – Asia's Most Admired Companies

Companies cited in the top ten (1994–2000)

Company	1994	1995	1996	1997	1998	1999	2000
Singapore Airlines	■	■	■	■	■	■	■
Jollibee		■	■	■	■	■	■
Samsung Electronics	■	■	■	■	■		■
McDonald's	■	■	■	■	■		
Sony Corp	■	■		■	■		
San Miguel Corp	■	■	■	■	■		
Charoen Pokphand	■	■	■	■			
Pohang Iron & Steel		■	■		■	■	
Toyota Motor Corp	■	■				■	■
Hewlett-Packard			■	■	■		
Siam Cement	■	■	■				
Coca-Cola		■				■	■
Microsoft			■			■	■
Acer			■	■			
Taiwan Semiconductor Manufacturing					■	■	
General Electric							■
Ayala Corp						■	
Creative Technology of Singapore						■	
Unilever						■	
Hang Seng Bank					■		
Honda Motor					■		
Boeing				■			
Hong Kong Telecom		■					
Singapore Telecom	■						
Shangri-La Hotels	■						

■ = featured in the Top Ten

Top ten companies 1994–2000

Position in Top Ten	1994	1995	1996	1997	1998	1999	2000
1	San Miguel Corp	Singapore Airlines	Singapore Airlines	Singapore Airlines	Singapore Airlines	Singapore Airlines	General Electric
2	Singapore Airlines	Samsung Corp	Samsung Corp	San Miguel Corp	Sony Corp	Sony Corp	Microsoft
3	Samsung Corp	San Miguel Corp	San Miguel Corp	Samsung Corp	Hewlett-Packard	Jollibee	Jollibee
4	Singapore Telecom	McDonald's	Siam Cement	Jollibee	Pohang Iron & Steel	Taiwan Semiconductor Manufacturing	Singapore Airlines
5	Sony Corp	Siam Cement	Charoen Pokphand	McDonald's	Toyota Motor Corp	Creative Technology of Singapore	Toyota Motor Corp
6	Toyota Motor Corp	Pohang Iron & Steel	McDonald's	Charoen Pokphand	Jollibee	Toyota Motor Corp	Ayala Corp
7	Shangri-La Hotels	Jollibee	Acer	Sony Corp	McDonald's	Pohang Iron & Steel	Sony Corp
8	Siam Cement	Charoen Pokphand	Jollibee	Acer	Taiwan Semiconductor Manufacturing	Coca-Cola	Pohang Iron & Steel
9	Charoen Pokphand	Toyota Motor Corp	Hewlett-Packard	Hewlett-Packard	Hang Seng Bank	Unilever	Samsung Electrics
10	McDonald's	Hong Kong Telecom	Coca-Cola	Boeing	Honda Motor	Microsoft	Coca-Cola

Resource list

Websites

Asian Business: 'Asia's Most Admired Companies' surveys	www.tpl.com.sg/timesnet/navigatn/ab.html
Financial Times: 'The World's Most Respected' surveys	specials.ft.com/wmr2001
Fortune: 'America's Most Admired' surveys`	www.fortune.com/lists/mostadmired
Harvard Business School	www.hbs.edu
Interbrand	www.interbrand.com
Management Today: 'Britain's Most Admired Companies' surveys	www.clickmt.com/britain/index.cfm
Market and Opinion Research International (MORI)	www.mori.com
Reputation Institute (RI)	www.reputationinstitute.com
Results of RI-sponsored studies conducted with Harris Interactive	www.harrisinteractive.com/pop_up/rq
Rotterdam School of Management, Erasmus University	www.fbk.eur.nl
Stern School of Business, New York University	www.stern.nyu.edu
World Bank	www.worldbank.org
World Values Survey	wvs.isr.umich.edu

Articles and reports

Black, E., Carnes, T. and Richardson, V., 'The Market Valuation of Corporate Reputation', *Corporate Reputation Review*, 3 (1), 2000

Brouillard Communications and Yankelovich Partners, *Building Corporate Reputation*, Council of Public Relations report, 1998

Bunting, B. and Lipski, R., 'Drowned out? Rethinking Corporate Reputation Management for the Internet', *Journal of Communication Management*, 5 (2), 2000

Fischhoff, B., 'Managing Risk Perception', *Issues in Science and Technology*, 2, 1985

Green, R., 'Reputation and Directors' Liabilities', in Institute of Directors (eds.), *Reputation Management: Strategies for Protecting Companies, their Brands and their Directors*, IoD /Kogan Page, London, 1999

House of Lords Select Committee on Science and Technology, *Science and Society*, 1999–2000

Inglehart, R., 'Postmodernization Brings Declining Respect for Authority but Rising Support for Democracy' in Norris, P. (ed.) *Criticial Citizens: Global Support for Democratic Government*, Oxford University Press, Oxford, 1999

Interbrand/Citibank, *World's Most Valuable Brands Survey*, 2000

Knight, R.F., *Value Creation Among Britain's Top 500 Companies*, The Oxford Executive Research Briefings, Templeton College, Oxford, 1996

Knight, R.F. and Pretty, D.J., *The Impact of Catastrophes on Shareholder Value*, The Oxford Executive Research Briefings, Sedgwick Group, 1996

Lewis, S., *Reputation Matters*, MORI, 1999

McNulty, T.J., *Television's Impact on Executive Decision Making and Diplomacy*, The Fletcher Forum of World Affairs, 17, 1993

Schmidt, J.A., *Stakeholders' Perspectives: A Key to Success in the New Economy*, Presentation for the International Leaders' Conference, Towers Perrin, Washington DC, 2000

Weber Shandwick and Fombrun, C.J., *Understanding the Consumer Mindset in Brand Selection*, Weber Shandwick, 2001

Books

Andriessen, D. and Tissen, R., *Weightless Wealth: Find Your Real Value in a Future of Intangible Assets*, Financial Times/Prentice Hall, London, 2000

Clifton, R. and Maughan, E. (eds.), *Future of Brands: Twenty-Five Visions*, Macmillan, Basingstoke, 1999

Fombrun, C.J., *Reputation: Realizing Value from the Corporate Image*, Harvard Business School Press, Boston, 1996

Peters, G., *Waltzing with the Raptors*, John Wiley, 1999

CHAPTER 2

How to manage reputation risk

"To be rather than to seem"

CICERO

Risk management and change are linked and convergent, and yet few organizations appear to adopt a holistic approach to their integration in an operational context. Risk management involves avoiding, reducing or controlling potential or current hazards. Much of risk management is concerned with assessing and mitigating the effects of financial volatility, bad debt and liquidity problems but it also entails assessing risk specific to the markets or industries in which a company operates. Operational risks accrue as part of the functioning of routine business processes and as part of the way in which people associated with those processes behave.

Earlier, I highlighted classic operational disasters like Bhopal, Lockerbie, Exxon Valdez, Piper Alpha, Chernobyl and the Herald of Free Enterprise, where fundamental failure in management systems occurred compounded by poor or absent communication. Looking at the financial services sector, where transparency and accountability have traditionally been in short supply, the failures of BCCI, Credit Lyonnais, Barings, Morgan Stanley, the Korean banking collapse and Sumitomo bank are further testimony to such failure. No surprise then that tougher, costlier and more conservative regulation is mushrooming, in spite of claims from industry that most sectors are already heavily penalized in anticipation of possible product failure or consumer abuse.

With the exception of environmental protection and taxation constraints, health and safety has more legislation attached to it than any other risk issue. In the United States, the Bureau of Labor Statistics reported that in 1998 the number of fatal work injuries exceeded 6000. Approximately six million injuries were reported in private industry work places, and in the same year, the National Safety Council of America reported that work-related injuries cost $125.1bn – a little over 1 per cent of GDP. More regulatory authorities in Western countries are threatening to exploit the power of public humiliation by 'naming and shaming' companies that disregard health and safety law. No company is immune from the possibility of product or service flaws, but in the case of injury, companies can now face compensation bills running into billions of dollars.

Europeans are following the United States in becoming more aware of their rights or possible rights in product and consumer liability cases and are much less willing to tolerate business mistakes. EU product liability and consumer protection legislation is designed to make it much easier for people to bring claims against suppliers of defective products. Product liability claims are increasing at a rapid rate, not because products are becoming more defective or dangerous but because technological advances and safety standards are generally making it easier to identify defects and protect against environmental health hazards. The main reason for the upturn in claims is that social attitudes have changed and consumers are becoming much more conscious of their ability to bring claims against business, encouraged by legal advertising and conditional fee arrangements ('no win/no fee'). In the United States during the 1980s, companies faced a crisis over product liability and consumer protection with compensation costs spiralling out of control. The availability of insurance became scarce with numbers of insurers actually failing, offset only by rising premiums and the fact that businesses chose to self-insure against such risk. Post 11 September 2001 and recent corporate failures in the United States, employer and public liability insurance premiums have soared.

Reputation risk management involves anticipating, acknowledging and responding to changing values and behaviours on the part of a range of stakeholders. Greater scrutiny and demands for transparency are key drivers of reputation management. According to Stephen Pain, Group Corporate Affairs Director of international financial services group, Aviva, "CEOs today, like it or not, are public figures. They must expect that everything they do and say is in the public domain, and they must expect to be scrutinized accordingly." These trends are driven by a global 24/7 media environment and the Internet. Democratization of opinion through electronic communication means that companies have to deal with reputation risk issues in real time and on a consistent basis, globally. Anyone can create a share of voice that is disproportionate to the financial or administrative resources required. This is reflected in the plethora of anti-corporate and complaint-based websites, just two mechanisms exploited to great effect by activists campaigning through the Internet, and explored in more detail in Chapter 4. "Corporations have become the media's bogeymen", says Dominic Fry, Group Director of Corporate Communications at Scottish Power. "The volume of business stories has increased dramatically so scrutiny and the ability to respond and pre-empt damaging editorial are critical to reputation. The quality of management and a company's ability to avoid surprises are key drivers for effective reputation risk management."

According to leading researcher, Robert Worcester, behaviour is what people do; knowledge is what they know – or think they know. The responses of stakeholders can be better understood if you divide them roughly into *opinions*, *attitudes* and *values*. "Opinions are the ripples on the surface of the public's consciousness, shallow, and easily changed; attitudes are the currents below the surface, deeper and stronger; and values are the deep tides of public mood, slow to change, but powerful." (Robert Worcester, MORI, 1999).

Values are about beliefs and levels of trust – they are embedded in our development and approach to life, reinforced by the influence of others and our conduct in, and relationship with, society.

The evidence base of public opinion polling is telling us that in many Western democracies today, there is scepticism and mistrust of government and business. Judgements about scientific developments are made in the context of their end purpose. Ignorance about the way in which technological development is regulated leads many consumers to assume that it is insufficient. Significant numbers of people are prepared to use their power as consumers to put pressure on those involved to object to innovations or to demand changes in behaviour associated with the management of businesses. What do these trends mean for reputation risk management? What is meant by corporate reputation today, how significant is its value and why is there so much talk about stakeholder perspectives of reputation?

In this chapter, I'll start to answer these questions and present some planning and management models that have successfully enabled organizations to anticipate and manage reputation risks. These models provide a valuable way forward when there is an urgent need to develop and resource from scratch a reputation risk management strategy, or when systems and strategies may be in place but need validation or fine-tuning through auditing or testing. I will examine the case for reputation as a commercially valuable asset using opinions and experiences from senior practitioners interviewed on the subject, and I will argue that it needs to be actively integrated into operational risk management processes, and owned at board level not in the PR department.

Finally, I'll provide some guidelines on what to do under intense pressure – when there is no turning back from the onslaught of a crisis situation, and I will illustrate these with a case study which is a model of good crisis and reputation management.

What do we mean by reputation?

The question of what we mean by corporate reputation is often overlooked. It might seem the answer is obvious from the pages of the business news and especially the frequent stories of reputational failure. But it's worth digging a little deeper. How can we make sense of something which can take years to establish, has enormous value, although is difficult to quantify precisely, but which can be destroyed overnight – even by factors entirely outside a company's control? Unfortunately this is one area in business where research is lagging behind the concerns of business managers and reputation specialists. There is certainly no single or dominant definition or theory of corporate reputation. Part of the problem is that the academic research is still in its infancy, and rather inconveniently reputation straddles different disciplines, each with a distinct perspective and research approach.

According to Balmer (1998), the reputation story is unfolding in a series of phases. In the 1950s to 1970s, the focus was corporate image – part psychology and part marketing, looking at associations and mental images as well as people's actual experiences of the company. Graphic design was also part of this mix – company names and visual representation were deemed a vital part of the corporate reputation. The focus then shifted inside the company, looking initially at corporate identity, culture and corporate personality into the early 1980s, and more recently at corporate reputation and corporate marketing as broader-based concepts. Today, accounting (intangible assets as the gap between reported earnings and market valuation), strategy (assets which offer competitive advantage and act as a barrier to mobility), marketing (drawing on social and cognitive psychology to explain the pictures of an organization, a product or a brand in people's heads), organizational behaviour (culture and organizational identity, values, and the general perceptions of internal stakeholders), sociology (the interactions between the organization, stakeholders and intermediaries) and finally corporate communications all have something to say on corporate reputation – but none speaks the same language (Fombrun et al., 2000; Fombrun and van Riel, 1997). An awareness of these different perspectives is a key step in making sense of corporate reputation and thinking through how it can be managed.

There are two key conclusions emerging from recent research and discussion in this field. Firstly, researchers in corporate reputation are no longer looking for links between reputation and some measure of improved organizational performance, whether financial, competitive

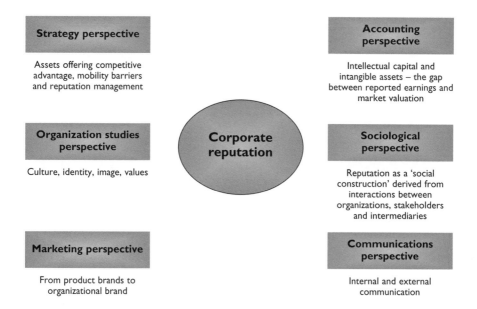

Figure 2.1 *Corporate reputation: converging ideas*
Source: Adapted from Schultz *et al.*, 2000

differentiation, employee motivation, access to cheaper capital or a favourable treatment from stakeholders. Instead, the focus is on recognizing corporate reputation management as a strategic construct in its own right – one that goes to the heart of what the company is about (Schultz *et al.*, 2000). Corporate reputation is not an add-on, but a fundamental aspect of business performance.

From a strategic reputation risk management perspective, this implies that the company's vision and leadership, strategy, HRM (human resources management), marketing, corporate communications and customer service all directly influence how the business expresses itself to the outside world. The goal of effective reputation management is therefore to align these activities.

Secondly, researchers now agree that a key feature of reputation is effective management of stakeholder relationships. The idea of stakeholders as "any group or individual who can affect or is affected by the achievement of the organization's objectives", for example, customers, investors, employees, suppliers, analysts, regulators, the media and so on (Freeman, 1984) is now part of common business parlance across corporate governance, strategy, marketing and public policy.

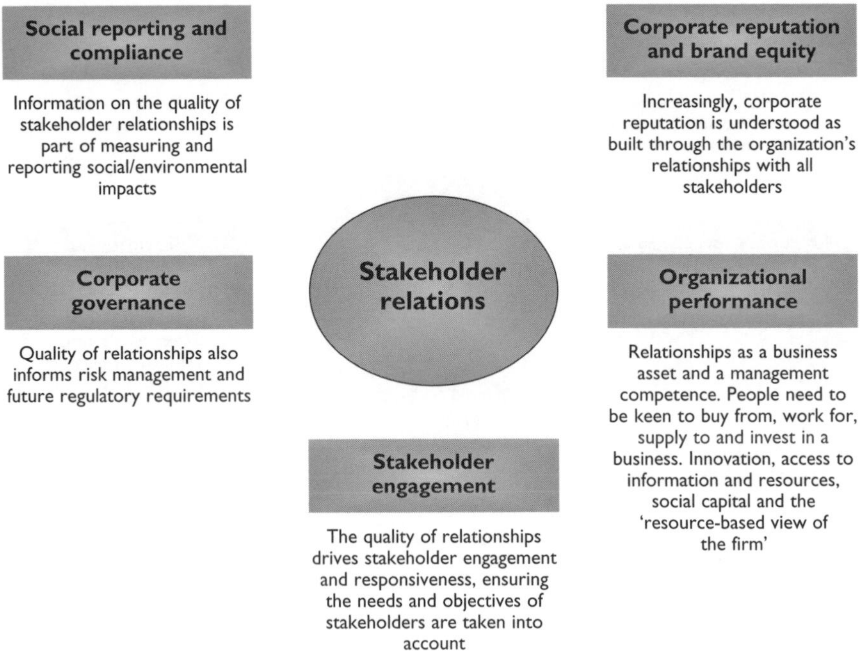

Social reporting and compliance		Corporate reputation and brand equity
Information on the quality of stakeholder relationships is part of measuring and reporting social/environmental impacts		Increasingly, corporate reputation is understood as built through the organization's relationships with all stakeholders

Stakeholder relations

Corporate governance		Organizational performance
Quality of relationships also informs risk management and future regulatory requirements		Relationships as a business asset and a management competence. People need to be keen to buy from, work for, supply to and invest in a business. Innovation, access to information and resources, social capital and the 'resource-based view of the firm'

Stakeholder engagement

The quality of relationships drives stakeholder engagement and responsiveness, ensuring the needs and objectives of stakeholders are taken into account

Figure 2.2 *Why stakeholder relationships matter*
Source: Williams, Henley Management College, 2002

From a reputation point of view, stakeholding has two important dimensions which tend to be muddled together. Stakeholding clusters people into groups who are likely to hold similar perceptions of a business, but different stakeholder groups will assess each organization using different criteria. The perceptions held by individuals are formed through their direct experience of a company's activities and employees, more general perceptions of the character of the business, and from other people's information and influence through social networks (Bromley, 2000). So a business is likely to have various different reputations with its multiple internal and external stakeholder groups, and an overall reputation emerges through a dynamic process.

This is somewhat at odds with the thinking that corporate reputations are also enduring and built over time. Corporate reputation is now very much defined in stakeholder terms, for example, as the "aggregate perceptions of multiple stakeholders about a company's performance" (Fombrun *et al.*, 2000).

"Reputation is not a homogenous commodity", says Tim Sharp, Head of Corporate Communications at international construction company, Balfour Beatty. "Different groups have different needs and objectives so it is important to understand the range of constituents that you are dealing with, although some prioritization is inevitable".

The stakeholder approach to understanding corporate reputation accommodates the new diverse and complementary approaches to measuring reputation which are designed to capture the views of all stakeholders. Because we cannot measure reputation directly, researchers have to use a proxy of some kind. Henley Management College in the UK measures reputation within the quality of an organization's relationships with its stakeholders, and links past business behaviour and the current stakeholder relationships to future organizational performance (Macmillan *et al.*, 2000). Henley is also researching how reputations are built up within the networks of stakeholders surrounding a business. This relational approach to understanding and measuring reputation is a key research direction. The Reputation Quotient (RQ), highlighted in Chapter 1, is a different approach – a sophisticated perceptual measure of the type popularized by *Fortune* magazine's America's Most Admired Companies rankings.

The RQ measures public perceptions across 20 items within six dimensions – emotional appeal, products and services, vision and leadership, workplace environment, financial performance and social responsibility which this model identifies as the constituent parts which together make up corporate reputation (Fombrun and Gardberg, 2000). Manchester Business School uses a third approach, capturing the emotional attachments stakeholders hold toward a business by measuring the 'corporate personality' (Davies *et al.*, 2001)

The relational and stakeholder approach to both measurement and reputation management holds much promise. Understanding corporate reputation in terms of what stakeholders perceive and expect is fundamental to reputation risk management which must include active monitoring and managing relations with the company's stakeholders.

The second aspect to stakeholding and corporate reputation is the debate around corporate social responsibility. Reputation and corporate social responsibility have long been linked. On the one hand, corporate social responsibility has been identified as a driver of reputation and indeed included within the RQ (*via* three variables, 'environmentally conscious', 'supports good causes', and 'maintains high standards in the way it treats people') and *Fortune* magazine rankings. On the other hand, reputation is widely put forward as part of the enlightened self-interest

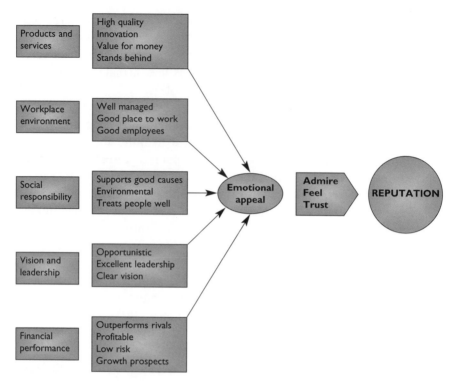

Figure 2.3 *Constituents of corporate reputation*

Source: Fombrun, Charles, *The Reputation Institute: Who, What, Why?* Presentation by The Reputation Institute, 2000. The model is based on extensive empirical research conducted by the Reputation Institute and Harris Interative.

or 'business case' for corporate social responsibility. Companies consistently assume reputational benefits with stakeholders, and current and prospective employees in particular, although a clear link with employee motivation and retention is often not made. Corporate social responsibility and related concepts are themselves complex and difficult to measure, as I discuss in Chapter 6. Unravelling the links between reputation, a corporate social responsibility stance, demonstrable corporate social performance, the communication of this activity to stakeholders (an issue in itself) and other measures of business performance, especially financial, has not been achieved but is a key research direction. Leading European business schools are now co-operatively researching the overall business case for corporate social responsibility and corporate reputation will certainly be captured within this. A much clearer picture of the value of a 'reputation for doing good' will emerge.

Reputation risk matters

Trying to define and measure reputation is difficult. It is tempting to look at reputation from different viewpoints forgetting that the total picture is much more complex and fluid. This brings to mind the story of the six blind men describing an elephant. One man feels the trunk and likens it to a snake, while another feels a leg and associates it with a tree. Each of the blind men manages to say something that is, strictly speaking, correct and yet none can create a description that correctly captures the complete animal.

Considering reputation risk is not dissimilar to looking at operational or financial risk. Conventional risk management can increase value in different ways – it can reduce a company's regulatory and tax burden, minimize potential for financial volatility, increase debt capacity and help to maintain a particular risk profile that enables investors to assess performance. Traditionally, risk management has not been undertaken in a co-ordinated way across a business. While managers have always been involved in some form of risk management, risks have tended to be dealt with separately. Treasury or Finance manages exchange-rate exposure and credit risk. Operations managers assess risks associated with production, distribution and supply chain management. Corporate insurance and health and safety functions focus on property, environmental and casualty risks. Human Resources examines risks associated with employee and workplace policies and practices, while marketing and product management functions consider brand risks.

Today, this rather tactically driven approach to risk is changing with the evolution of group risk and internal audit functions, responding to new governance and reporting guidelines that assist managers in analysing and controlling a range of risks – not just financial – as part of an integrated risk management policy. It is now a vital role within senior management to decide which risks are essential to the profitable performance of the company, to ensure its licence to operate and to develop appropriate strategies to manage those risks. As organizations are beginning to initiate wider internal controls, the need to factor in risks to reputation must be better understood.

Describing reputation risk is not a matter of starting from ignorance; most of us can understand some elements that indicate the importance and value of reputation, even if it helps to relate the subject matter to our own reputational experiences. And yet senior managers seem unable to present a complete picture of one of the most vital assets of their business.

The quest to find a formula for financial risk management has been forced by regulatory agencies in the aftermath of major financial disasters, fed by a growing support industry in consulting and auditing, all closely associated with identifying a single number, Value-at-Risk (VaR). VaR is a percentage of a profit and loss distribution over a specific horizon.

For example, a portfolio of currencies, bonds, equities and derivatives could be assessed in risk terms over a period of three weeks. The objective is to consider the maximum that could be lost on the portfolio over the period – a worst case scenario would be a 100 per cent loss but that would be unlikely to occur. Perhaps a figure of 90 per cent would be more reasonable, that is, the assumption is that losses would not exceed that amount. In other words, it is the VaR for a three-week period and a 90 per cent confidence level. However, in spite of various international banking agreements and risk metrics systems, neither markets, portfolios, nor levels of volatility remain 'normal'. Calculating VaR remains extremely difficult in financial risk management terms but it has, at least, brought greater awareness of the fundamental risk issues associated with market risk management and of the data, systems and expertise needed to monitor risk. While I am not advocating a formula like VaR for measuring reputation risk, because of the complexity of organizational and stakeholder relationships, and volatility associated with risk perception, I am certain that a more rigorous and integrated approach to anticipating, assessing and managing risks to reputation does have a tangible contribution to make to overall performance. And what is increasingly clear is that one of the most formidable icebergs confronting managers in capital markets is the predisposition of markets to a company's operational *and* reputational performance. The ability of a company to articulate its current and future performance in relation to investment and other operational risks and opportunities in a consistent and credible manner does impact on Value at Risk.

Furthermore, regulation of business and risk management are closely linked, because regulation endeavours to manage risks in contemporary society while corporate risk management is a form of self-regulation. Governments are under increasing pressure to regulate risks as a result of the legacy of public perception of mismanaged environmental health and consumer service failure in areas such as food processing and distribution, financial services mis-selling, public transport systems, information disclosure and e-commerce. Coupled with the changing dynamics of global economics, environmental pollution and conflicting cultures and value systems, risk now permeates every facet of modern day regulation.

What constitutes compliance often is not clear, as regulation may be vague or inconsistent, with significant discretionary powers being delegated to regulatory and public officials, as Chapter 5 highlights. Regulation is designed to be flexible in the face of changing technologies and circumstances, so it intentionally leaves scope for interpretation. Finding a balance between the purpose of regulation – protecting public health, the environment or attempting to create an equitable framework for doing business – and its cost, is a constant challenge, particularly as our understanding and tolerance of current or emerging risks changes. Compliance is also determined by regulators' knowledge about particular industries or organizations, so a good or bad reputation can influence what constitutes compliance or acceptable behaviour.

Although we can't determine what the future holds, we know quite a lot about the likelihood of unpleasant things happening and we are increasingly proficient at learning how to manage their consequences. Nonetheless, many smart companies continue to take very poor decisions. In the 1980s, US long-distance operator AT&T turned down a free offer to take control of the Internet, and successive decisions by a string of CEOs to reposition the company as a global technology company have seen its market capitalization plummet.

Scenario planning expert, Peter Schwartz, believes that some decision-makers often carry with them an 'official future', an accepted view of the way things are and the way they will turn out to be. Too often, he argues, organizations will assess risk through a lens of collective self-delusion (Schwartz, 1998). Scenario planning involves challenging that future by creating convincing and detailed alternatives. Tuning the corporate risk radar is a first important step in attempting to identify, assess and manage the potential for change and associated commercial and reputational impacts.

Virtually anything an organization says or does can enhance or destroy reputation value, which is why I believe reputation risk management is becoming the natural successor to brand management – good reputations enhance the potential to sell goods and services while badly managed ones can rapidly destroy shareholder value. Companies are now held accountable and responsible for all sorts of actions by a variety of stakeholder groups, not just a brand's make-up or promotional claims. History, operational locations, senior management profiles, environmental record, workplace and recruitment practices, manufacturing processes, sourcing and supply chain management all have the potential to be scrutinized. Public perception of whether a business is responsible is increasingly based on how the business is seen to behave and whether it applies a clear set of values in its day-to-day conduct. Nike's decision to sponsor the growth of basketball in China through building and branding basketball courts in major cities as an investment in a huge emerging market was initially seen as perfectly reasonable. However, when it emerged that the cost of an average pair of Nike trainers was well beyond the financial reach of the majority of Chinese consumers and that the company was allegedly using sweatshop labour, then some people at least started listening to the complaints by activists that Nike may be instituting a new form of corporate imperialism for manipulating potential consumers.

Reputation risk management can generate considerable material benefit for a company and this may explain why it is becoming a fashionable subject for senior management analysis. In my experience, however, reputation risk management continues to be ignored as a central part of operational management. It is not sufficiently recognized as a valuable intangible asset and it is not managed in a way that acknowledges that reputation risks can and do emerge from across the business – both internally and externally.

"Few companies appear to be formally assessing and integrating reputation, including behaviour, within risk management frameworks", comments Roger Hayes, Director of the International Institute of Communications. "Nevertheless, companies can no longer operate from behind a moat with the drawbridge up. We are living in an interdependent world where interaction between different communities is becoming a commercial imperative".

My general recommendations to managers are as follows:

- Corporate reputation must be taken as seriously as brand management has been over the last 20 years. It is essential that both corporate reputation and brand reputation are actively managed and in a way that acknowledges each has a significant impact on the other. There is growing evidence in market economies that consumers are assessing the wider behaviour and performance of companies which own consumer brands as part of their purchasing decision. Chris Major, Head of Public Relations at AstraZeneca, has this advice: "invest as much time in corporate reputation as in product brands – don't assume that corporate reputation will manage itself. Be in touch with the levers that influence perception and recognize that Pavlovian responses to critical scrutiny no longer work." Brands were once considered a characteristic of packaged goods marketing, based on quality, value, fashion, desirability, accessibility and so on. Today more or less everything and any kind of organization is considered as a brand – even individuals are brands whether they are high profile politicians, rock stars, entrepreneurs or celebrities, and whether they are dead or alive. Most organizations have some form of brand association, ranging from academic and artistic institutions looking for sponsorship, to professional services organizations – law firms, accountants, doctors, dentists, alternative therapists, through to manufacturers of basic household goods and associated tradespeople such as plumbers, builders, electricians, garbage disposal firms and corner shop suppliers. Corporate reputation represents a holistic view of business, influenced by financial performance and reporting, strategy, marketing and brand management, risk management, organizational behaviour, relationships and communication. Corporate reputation management should be integrated with business planning and strategy development.

- Reputation is a valuable asset. Just as protection and enhancement of major consumer brands are considered to be essential to global consumer-marketing companies, corporate reputation often exceeds the value of conventional tangible or physical assets. Furthermore, as the sum of the parts of a corporation – characterized through management strength, knowledge, expertise, innovation, quality, staying-power and share price stability – corporate reputation can not only protect the long-term value of prized consumer brands, it can add considerably to the overall asset base. The value of brands like Coca-Cola, McDonald's and Nike can represent over 90 per cent of all their corporate assets. When there is a real or perceived failure associated with an established brand, the cost of restoring confidence can be considerable, as each of the three companies has experienced. It requires active, senior level management.

- Because every part of the organization plays a part in reputation management, each employee is a reputation ambassador. This must be acknowledged and responded to by management. Ensuring that everyone in a company understands the importance of a good reputation – what it stands for in their particular workplace, how to behave in a way that is consistent with it and how to articulate it outside when meeting customers, suppliers, potential recruits and other third parties, is of paramount importance. A chief executive may be the most charismatic, dynamic and communicative individual on the planet, but if he or she cannot instil the values and beliefs associated with the distinctive reputation of the business

Who pays to restore the brand?

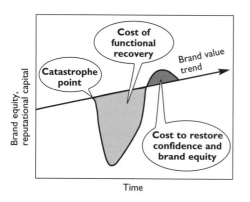

What *you* pay to restore (trust and confidence in) the brand

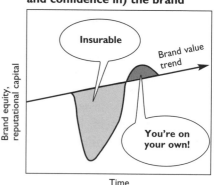

Figure 2.4 *The cost of brand restoration*
Source: Regester Larkin

across and down the corporation, there is little hope of achieving consistent and long-term reputation value. "Reputation cannot be fitted into a box or a specific function", says Michael Broadbent, Director of Corporate Affairs at international banking group, HSBC Holdings. "It needs to be embedded into everything that a company does, which is why there isn't one reputation manager at HSBC. Every single member of staff is expected to adopt this role, and so it should be for any corporation."

• Reputation management requires collective responsibility on the part of management and must be driven by every part of the organization. Reputation cannot be owned solely by one individual or department. "You cannot 'ghettoize' the communications function in any organization", says Matt Peacock, Director of External Relations at telecommunications company H3G. Some senior practitioners that I interviewed on the subject believe that the CEO is synonymous with a strong reputation. Quality of leadership undoubtedly equates to enhanced reputation value. A difficulty here, however, is that when that individual leaves, a vacuum can be left which may be hard to fill even by the most competent successor. General Electric, immediately post Jack Welch, is a case in point. There is no question in my mind that leadership from the top of the organization is a critical ingredient of successful reputation risk management. However, because reputation risks and opportunities can emerge from a host of different sources, locations and events, a multi-functional approach to management is essential. "Don't depend solely on narrow commercial arguments", says Simon Lewis, European Managing Director of utilities group Centrica. "It is essential today to address the wider context associated with business strategies and corporate behaviour. Always find a moment to pause and think about how others would perceive your actions."

Figure 2.5 *They're all Reputation Risk Managers*
Source: Regester Larkin

Reputation management must be properly embedded into the culture of an organization. People are a core asset in any business. Reputation is an important asset too because it can help to attract and motivate the best employees. However, neither should be treated as easily replaceable machine parts. Poor communication, insufficient understanding of how an organization works and what it stands for, and too much emphasis on short-term results can result in low levels of commitment and reduced performance.

• Reputation can only become an effective driver of high performance if it is properly integrated into HRM and general workplace practices, and implemented across the organization. This requires the senior management team to reach a clear consensus on what reputation management is, why it is important and what it represents in terms of KPIs (key performance indicators), values and behaviour. Implementation through regular and open communication and consultation, for example, *via* workshops, team meetings, interactive cascade information processes, and qualitative opinion surveys should be designed to familiarize everyone with the concepts, the reality for their business, delivery processes and expected outcomes. Clearly, this needs management commitment, investment and time to take effect. Only when the value of effective reputation management is really integrated into the mindset of every employee at every level can it be translated through behaviour into operational reward.

Equivalent processes have worked successfully for many corporations in the areas of quality assurance, supply chain management and health and safety. Morgan Stanley clearly embedded its HSE policies across the business, otherwise it would never have managed to safely evacuate all but seven of its 2700 staff from the South Tower of the World Trade Centre on 11 September, 2001. According to Jan Shawe, Director of Corporate Relations at food retailer, J Sainsbury, "managing reputation must be a core management competence. It is far too easy in big companies to operate in functional silos and this can be a disaster for reputation management. Everyone has to own the reputation of the business – it cannot just be a pimple on the face of the organization!"

That is why my guidelines for effective reputation risk management are critical to survival and success.

- **Acknowledge that reputation is a valuable asset and needs to be actively managed at board level**
- **Develop a finely tuned radar and become a listening company**
- **Design clear and robust management systems that integrate with routine risk management processes**
- **Create your own code of good behaviour and assure your licence to operate**
- **Treat your stakeholders intelligently**
- **Work as if everything you say and do is public**

A framework for planning and managing reputation risk

Risk issues typically have a *lifecycle* and pass through several stages as the example model below indicates. Some issues are extremely difficult to predict. When they occur, they can move rapidly through to the crisis stage, become highly politicized, particularly in the case of environmental health, product failure or consumer protection risks, and impose severe constraints on what can be said and done by the company or industry at the centre of scrutiny. Often this position is compounded by competitive conflicts between government agencies, NGOs and industry, with damaging consequences for reputation.

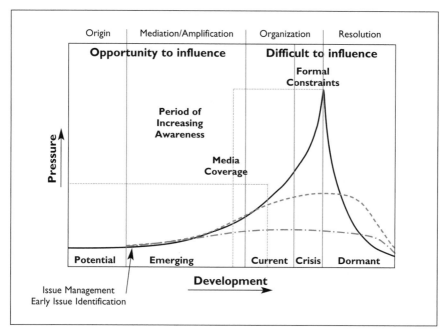

Figure 2.6 *Risk issue lifecycle*

Source: Regester Larkin adapted from Hainsworth and Meng, 1988

Early identification, assessment and prioritization of risk issues – potential threats and also opportunities – are, therefore, critical success factors in helping to anticipate and plan for change, validate company positions and facilitate share of voice in contributing to, or shaping the debate over the evolution of an issue. The ultimate aim is to avoid escalation up the solid curve to the crisis issue stage where there is little space to navigate and where formal constraints through financial or regulatory penalties are inevitable. By starting to take action during the potential and emerging stages, even though the nature and shape of the issue may be unclear and difficult to assess in formal risk management terms, there is more room to manoeuvre around potential icebergs. Early monitoring and assessment can also help to head off the issue or influence its course in a mutually constructive way, both for the organization involved and its stakeholders.

In real life, the shape of the issue curve is never a tidy continuum. Some risk issues can emerge and move through the formative stages in a matter of days, creating rapid escalation to the crisis stage; others can evolve over months or years, and are only revealed when a particular event occurs and suddenly draws attention to the seriousness of the underlying risk issue. And sometimes managers appear to resolve the problem even at this late stage, only for it to re-emerge in a different shape or form further downstream. Examples include public concerns over food safety issues in Europe through the 1990s, the evolving profile of tobacco litigation in the United States, the changing profile and impact of environmental campaigning since the 1970s, and the emerging challenges for corporations associated with human rights abuses, corruption and bribery. A case study illustration follows here, and more are provided throughout the book.

Ford and Firestone: a management and communication failure

Ford, and tyre manufacturer Firestone, badly handled a product recall in the United States in 2000/2001 after it emerged there was a fault with the Ford SUV Explorer. Because of the poor way the issue was managed and communicated, both companies are still suffering from the repercussions of their actions.

Both companies were slow to initiate a product recall of SUV tyres in the United States, despite evidence from international markets that there was a problem. As claims and statistical evidence mounted, the media started to cover the issue actively, retail stores suspended tyre sales and the US National Highway Traffic Safety Administration (NHTSA) began to investigate, a recall of 6.5 m Firestone tyres began in the US in August 2000.

However, tyre tread separation problems on Ford Explorers had been reported as far back as October 1989 and both companies were aware of specific problems in Middle East markets from 1999. At that time, and at Ford's direction, Firestone developed tyres with a nylon cap for countries with hot climates and rough roads. Ford replaced Firestone tyres in Saudi Arabia in August 1999, in Malaysia and Thailand in February 2000 and in Venezuela in May 2000. Tyres had been replaced on nearly 50,000 vehicles outside the USA before any consolidated action was taken. This led to criticism from the media, NGOs and the public that the companies were putting profits before customer safety.

Neither company acknowledged the risk potential of the initial incidents overseas, and when faults began occurring in the US, the problem was not linked to what had happened elsewhere – each case was treated in isolation. By the time the NHTSA opened its preliminary investigation into Firestone tread separations in May 2000, the agency had received 90 complaints involving 27 injuries and 4 deaths. The companies adopted a unified response initially – they had had a successful and close working relationship going back over many decades. It was agreed that Firestone tyres produced at its Decatur plant in the United States were causing the problem and this led to the August 2000 recall.

Accidents continued to occur, however, at which point Ford and Firestone began blaming each other. Ford emphasized the problem was with the tyre while Firestone pointed to customer error, heat exposure and design flaws on the SUV Explorer. The lack of agreement and consistency intensified media coverage and campaigning for comprehensive recall programmes and more stringent safety regulations.

Firestone's Japanese parent company, Bridgestone, became involved in the communications response by sending Japanese officials over to run a press conference. Although this was perceived to be the right response in Japan, the American public and media were furious at what was perceived to be such a late-in-the-day, superficial response.

Ford's CEO, Jac Nasser, achieved some success in communicating Ford's concern and care towards its customers, but other actions led to accusations of insincerity. Although Nasser featured in two television commercials reassuring customers that SUV Explorers were safe, he ill-advisedly refused to testify at Senate and House Commerce sub-committee hearings on the tyre recall in September 2000 stating he was 'too busy' to attend.

Neither company behaved in a way that recognized the value of reputation or the importance of treating stakeholders intelligently. The initial recall appeared to be the rational thing to do, but when this didn't stem the flow and the companies started to publicly disagree on the causes and subsequent actions to be taken, such as the need for and nature of further recalls, mitigating liability became the over-riding message to the public. Problems with the tyres and Explorer vehicles had been occurring in different markets for at least three years prior to the emergence of the issue in the North American market. If the risk radar was turned on, either it wasn't tuned in or it wasn't acknowledged. The links were eventually made by a Texan TV station report which raised the alarm, exposing a major safety hazard to US consumers.

Ford and Firestone's poor handling of the evolving crisis led to a dramatic fall in share price and profits for both companies – and the end of a long-term commercial partnership at a time when both were struggling in highly competitive markets. The recall resulted in major internal change and restructuring within both companies; Masatoshi Ono stepped down as CEO of Bridgestone in October 2000, and Nasser resigned as CEO of Ford in October 2001. Over 200 lawsuits have been filed against the companies. On 9 January 2001, American victim Donna Bailey was awarded $100 m in damages, making the case the largest vehicular liability settlement ever. In November 2001, Bridgestone/Firestone agreed to pay $51.5 m to settle claims by American state attorneys.

The Ford and Firestone case also led to new legislation in the US. On 11 October 2000, the House and Senate passed the Transportation Recall Enhancement Accountability and Documentation (TREAD) bill. The bill was designed to ensure that the Department of Transportation would receive the information it needed to detect defects, including information about foreign recalls, and increased penalties for manufacturers that fail to comply with the statute and its regulations. All automotive manu-facturers in the US now have to report any recalls that they issue in any part of the world, together with warranty information. A year on, public opinion polling by Gallup indicated that Ford had finally mitigated further reputation damage. Firestone, however, didn't recover.

What went wrong? Mike Palese from Daimler Chrysler's Global Issues Management group highlights four fundamental points of failure on the part of the companies involved. First, they were unable to identify the risk early on in spite of the fact that incidents had been reported going back over several years. Failure to 'connect the dots' and alert appropriate senior management was a big mistake. Second, when they did finally recognize they had a problem "they had their eyes wide open but continued in denial". The companies failed to talk to each other, share information or acknowledge they had a problem although they had a working relationship dating back over 100 years. Neither demonstrated an open culture or a corporate environment with appropriate systems and processes in place. The issue was managed in isolation. Third, when the story broke there was no evidence

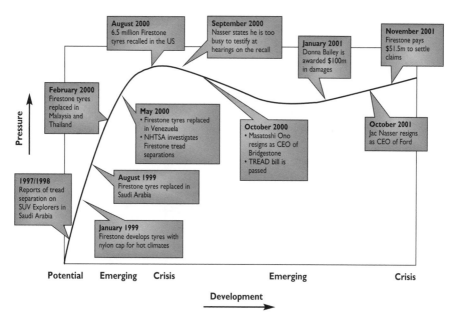

Figure 2.7 *Risk issue lifecycle: Ford Firestone*
Source: Regester Larkin

of responsible behaviour or of working in partnership. Resorting to blame was a recipe for disaster, creating public fear and then outrage. They missed their chance to make their case by pointing fingers at each other. Fourth, a basic failure in leadership proved to be each company's undoing. When Firestone's parent company finally woke up and decided to hold a press conference belatedly in the United States fronted by Japanese management, they got roasted by the media and made a rapid retreat.

How to manage reputation risk

1. Establish early warning and monitoring systems – the reputation risk radar
2. Identify and prioritize risks (and opportunities)
3. Analyse the gaps; identify response options
4. Develop strategies and action plans
5. Implement
6. Keep the radar tuned

Establishing early warning and monitoring systems – the reputation risk radar

Step 1 in the reputation risk management model is to establish appropriate early warning or surveillance systems designed to routinely scan commercial, political/regulatory, social, economic, technological and other trends, developments and changes that may have the potential to impact on business strategies. Anticipate and assess the likely evolution and impact of emerging risk issues.

Figure 2.8 *Reputation risk radar screen*
Source: Regester Larkin

The overall aim is to gather, interpret, forecast and manage information and opinion in such a way that a sustainable and non-volatile business profile can be maintained. Activities may include *stakeholder profiling* (of NGOs, public officials/public policies, media and Internet interest/activity, other opinion formers and expert commentators, and so on) in relation to a specific risk issue – to identify and assess their levels of interest, potential positions and influence (see Chapters 3 and 4); *qualitative and quantitative opinion polling* of customers, employees, investors, politicians and other stakeholder groups, consultation initiatives; examination of *look-alike* and *legacy* issues that may provide indicators of likely outcomes against current or historic action, particularly in the context of influencing regulation and litigation; and assessment of websites, chat rooms, scientific, public health, consumer and other relevant databases.

Establishing and maintaining a risk radar system will facilitate more informed tracking of a risk issue through the stages identified in the lifecycle diagram and provided in this 'traffic lights' escalation model (see Appendices).

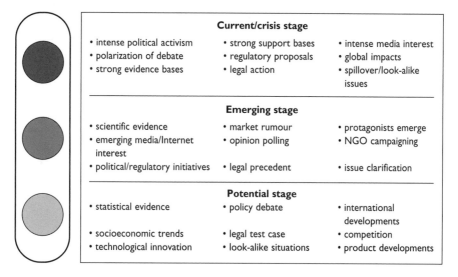

Figure 2.9 *Traffic lights escalation model*
Source: Regester Larkin

Identify and prioritize the risks

Step 2 in the reputation risk management model provides the basis for developing and validating risk issue management strategies, both for short-term action and in taking a longer-term strategic view on how to clarify and enhance understanding of a company's objectives, operations, values and behaviours.

The aim is to identify all the risk issues that may have current or potential impact on the business according to, for example, (a) cost to commercial operations and reputation through impact on stakeholder relations, and (b) likelihood of occurrence. This is about factoring in the reputational risk dimension to integrated risk management and internal audit policies and procedures – part of the routine formal mapping process that should occur within an integrated risk identification, assessment, management and communication process. Different industries and corporations have varied approaches to risk management but I believe that the essential point is to ensure that reputation risks are included at operational and strategic planning levels. While a few companies are starting to include reputation risks in an operational 'risk register' or as part of regular operational reviews, for the most part, my research suggests this is still, largely, an *ad hoc* process, often an after-thought. Actions to consider include facilitated scenario planning, auditing and benchmarking designed to prioritize reputation risks and gathering qualitative and quantitative data that can assist planning.

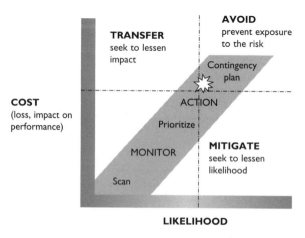

Figure 2.10 *Prioritizing risk issues: the risk issue matrix*
Source: Regester Larkin

Gap analysis and identification of response options

Step 3 involves analysis of any gaps between current performance and stakeholder expectations to provide a basis for determining anticipatory or response options that can contribute to closing the gap. Questions to ask are: *Is there a gap between performance and expectation? If so, what is it and why is there a gap? Is our risk evaluation effective? Do we really deliver the standards and values we claim? Which people determine how we behave? Which stakeholders can influence our reputation and performance on these issues?* This helps an organization to identify differences between how it sees its own objectives, values, competencies and priorities relative to the perceptions of its key stakeholders, and to assess and validate company policies, codes of practice and positions on priority issues: *Do they exist? Are they credible? Will they gain support and acceptance? Do the words match the deeds, that is, the associated operational/systems delivery? Can they be supported now and over time? Do they respond to stakeholder expectations? Do appropriate contingency plans exist in the face of rapid change? Can they be articulated by senior managers and employees alike? Are they transparent and measurable?* Understanding the agendas and support bases of individual activists, more sophisticated NGOs, opinion-formers and decision-makers provides vital intelligence for strategic response – both defensive and offensive – including assessment of the organization's own support base and potential for coalition-building.

Develop strategies and action plans

Step 4. I have emphasized the importance of integration and a cross-functional approach to reputation risk management. Planning, developing and implementing risk issue strategies, according to Malcolm Williams, Head of Global Issues Management and Resource Development for Shell International, must feature the following principles:

- Ownership is a line responsibility
- It is an integral part of normal business management, assessment and challenge processes
- A central co-ordinating function can add value in tuning the risk radar and intelligence gathering, providing issue management expertise to operating groups, validating priorities for escalation, co-ordinating stakeholder contacts and monitoring effectiveness (for example, corporate/external affairs)
- It requires a systematic approach (processes, owners, management, and so on)
- It is a strategic process – systemic, early warning, prioritizing and objective setting
- Risk issues drive stakeholder engagement
- A 'prudent over-reaction' policy is good practice
- Transparency can be balanced with a respect for confidentiality

Developing risk issue strategies follows naturally from the previous steps through selection of the most appropriate response option and associated company position, resource assessment and approval, identification of stakeholders to be targeted, development of an action plan highlighting steps to be taken, responsibilities, timelines and measurement criteria. A standard, bullet point template which describes the risk issue and a risk assessment, objectives, potential scenarios, strategic approach, key messages and summary operational and communication actions can help to filter out all but the most salient information for implementation purposes.

Implementation

Step 5 is about putting the strategy approved by appropriate management into action, consulting with and/or communicating the response effectively to relevant stakeholders, in such a way that negative impacts to the company's position are avoided, and support, or at least acceptance, of operational policies can be secured.

Consulting with and then testing positioning information and engagement techniques may be essential early steps. Building a support base and utilizing trusted third parties for stakeholder research and communication will also be important considerations. Supporting materials may include position papers, Q&As, backgrounders, specially developed web sites and press statements, together with assigned and properly briefed spokespeople. Throughout this process, the reputation risk radar must be tuned – tracking media, Internet, trend and event data influencing the issue, both locally and at an international level as appropriate. Internal communication and networking are also essential. Mike Palese believes that the process must be a "relentless reality check" designed to connect all the dots.

Keep the radar tuned

Step 6 involves evaluation and ongoing vigilance. *Has the issue moved from the top right quartile of the risk issue matrix (Fig. 2.10) towards the lower left quartile? (page 60) Is there support/acceptance among key stakeholder groups? To what extent has the issue faded from the radar in the media/on the Internet/among NGOs? Can the company fulfil its objectives more easily/effectively? What input can be provided to future strategies? What learning can be disseminated and built upon as part of this process?*

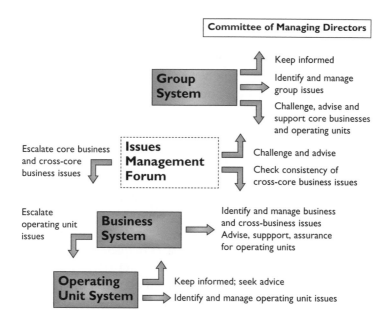

Figure 2.11 *Roles and relationships between issues management systems*
Source: Shell, 2000

And if things really do come unstuck?

From the many crisis situations I have been involved with over the years, the key to effective crisis management is crisis prevention, whether vigilance and preparation is self-motivated, or enforced by legislation. But if the ultimate iceberg comes into sight, comprehensive contingency planning can minimize the catastrophe; and clearly a policy of rapid, open communication – aligned with my other key guidelines – can reduce damage to corporate reputation. In some cases, although there is limited evidence to date, it can actually enhance reputation. As history shows, some crises are unavoidable.

However, whether many events or developments become crises is largely in the hands of senior management. Moreover, management action – in interfacing with stakeholders – plays a defining role in either exacerbating or reducing the effects of a crisis, as the Ford and Firestone case study demonstrated.

Crises that have traditionally created the greatest public interest are those commonly described as disasters; airplane and rail crashes or public health failures involving tragic loss of life. The scrutiny of those perceived to be responsible for such events is intense and unforgiving. Crises are not confined to disaster events and, like icebergs, come in many shapes and sizes. They can occur for reasons as diverse as safety lapses, inadequate training, unethical behaviour, critical media commentary, threat of litigation, poor systems and internal controls. The costs of a crisis also vary. Damage to reputation can have far-reaching implications beyond an initial financial loss associated with clean-up and reparation costs. Product boycotts, share price collapse, loss of competitive advantage, exposure of legacy issues and the ultimate imposition of costly regulation and litigation often have more damaging consequences for a company or a whole sector.

The definition of what constitutes a crisis is changing. As I have already described, public perception of risk is frequently out of kilter with the evidence base. Often, emotive and negative publicity and campaigning carries far more weight than an objective appraisal of risk probabilities. If corporate activities are regularly perceived to be damaging, badly managed, secretive or insensitive, an adverse issue is easily turned into a full-blown crisis. A global 24/7 marketplace, subject to intense scrutiny and demanding greater transparency, requires a much more sophisticated approach to safeguarding reputation, and one which recognizes that *perception is the reality*.

Acknowledging mistakes quickly also can help to neutralize public concern and anger. According to Mark Goyder, Director of think-tank The Centre for Tomorrow's Company, "If you acknowledge mistakes or failure, you often find that you can create a more loyal customer – the customer who is turned around after a mistake. A company can be perceived as more trustworthy if it demonstrates integrity with dealing with problems." A crisis often doesn't suddenly manifest itself but can creep up on a company over a period of time. Developments which appear minor can reach crisis proportions with extraordinary speed. Awareness and anticipation are, therefore, key. 'Outside-in' thinking – a company's ability to view itself from the many different perspectives that stakeholders have of it – can help to pre-empt worst case scenarios. Having in place a practical and robust crisis management plan, regularly tested through senior management communication training and combined operational and communication simulations, is an essential building block for reputation risk management. Managers are, nevertheless, often unaware or complacent about their responsibilities for taking the initiative in preventing potential crises. They may come up with comments such as:

"We're not exposed to that type of risk"
"We could manage our way through"
"Reputation can't be accurately valued"
"Reputation management = media training and crisis management (that is, training)"
"The media can be managed"
"It's the responsibility of the PR department"

These remarks show that management's perception of reputation risk management is fatally simplistic, represented in the left-hand of Figure 2.12 below. The reality is much more complex, interconnecting every facet of a company's risk exposure as the right-hand part of the figure indicates.

Figure 2.12 *Managing reputation risk – perception and reality*
Source: Adapted from AON, 2000

There is an increasingly good international literature and case study database to guide senior managers through appropriate crisis planning and management processes. The rest of this chapter contains:

- A checklist for preparing a crisis management plan if none exists, or there is a need to refresh current structures and content
- A template for developing a crisis response strategy
- An escalation checklist
- A case study on how to get it right.

Even so, according to my business partner and crisis management expert, Michael Regester, the best-laid plans can be worthless if they cannot be communicated. Speed is of the essence. A crisis simply won't wait. "Tell it all, tell it fast, tell it truthfully – and stay constantly on the alert. It's like wrestling a gorilla: you rest when the gorilla rests!" So:

- **Ensure all key players keep a summary copy of the crisis management plan with them at all times**
- **Have background information prepared**
- **Set up a press centre**
- **Ensure executives are trained to manage communication and operational responses against pretested crisis scenarios**
- **Establish trained telephone response teams to cope with media, relative, customer and other calls**
- **Keep press releases and web-site updates coming thick and fast; date, time and number them**
- **Don't forget employees – they are the company's ambassadors**
- **Co-ordinate the response of the company and third parties**
- **When it's all over, review the organization from top to bottom in the light of lessons learnt – lightning *can* strike twice**

I The crisis management plan

Table 2.1 Crisis management plan: contents checklist

Content	Description
Introduction	• Short description of objectives and scope of plan and how it fits with other operating/business/location plans • Best practice principles (business principles/values)
Definitions and escalation process	• Explanation of different levels (severity) of crisis with a clear explanation of the escalation process and likely triggers
Crisis management team structure	• Explanation of CMT structure; outline composition, roles and responsibilities
CMT member action checklist	• Covering the roles of the CMT chairman/team leader; technical/ operational; corporate affairs; human resources; HSE; legal; customer liaison; regulatory/compliance; administration

Table 2.1 (continued)

Content	Description
How to manage the media response in a crisis	• Best practice guidelines • Guidance on key messages • Briefing a spokesperson • Preparing for and managing a press conference • *Pro forma* holding statement
How to handle next-of-kin in a crisis	• Best practice guidelines
Information management in a crisis	• Guidance on how to prioritize, manage and disseminate information in a crisis
Facilities and equipment	• Facilities and equipment to be used by each team • Guidelines for setting up rooms
Out-of-hours contact list/stakeholder database	• Regularly updated and easily accessible database

2 The crisis response strategy

This template provides outline guidance on developing a crisis response strategy.

Table 2.2 *Crisis response strategy*

Objectives
For example: • Minimize risk to public/environment • Minimize commercial and reputation damage to the business • Maintain credibility with and trust of customers/others affected • Maintain credibility with and trust of authorities/communities • Minimize potential for litigation • Respond in line with company business principles/values
Business risk assessment
This section should outline the probability and impact of: • The situation escalating • Other business/locations/markets being impacted • Linkages being made with other company or external issues • Litigation, regulatory and insurance issues
Potential scenarios
This section should outline the most likely as well as worst case scenarios in

▶

▶ terms of the crisis/issue evolving. Operational and communication activity that would be necessary to respond to the worst case scenario needs to be factored into a separate stakeholder plan

Strategic approach
This section should outline the current situation and overall response strategy; what operational actions are to be taken and the degree to which communication activity will be proactive or reactive

Key messages
Identify priority messages and, if appropriate, tailor for key stakeholders, such as customers, local communities, employees, investors

Summary of operational actions
Prioritized list of actions taken/underway/to be taken

Summary of communication actions
Prioritized list of actions taken/underway/to be taken

3 Escalation check list

What to do if it happens

Being seen to take immediate, responsible action in the aftermath of a crisis is often critical to people's overall perception of how a company has managed a crisis. The first 48/72 hours shape how the media covers the ongoing story and often dictate how long the story stays at the top of the news agenda. If a company is perceived to be responding inadequately, journalists will be motivated to dig deeper and scrutinize more closely for new angles. Equally, if a company is seen to be doing everything 'right' in terms of helping those involved and cleaning up the 'mess' often the story ceases to hold the same attraction to the media and falls off the agenda relatively quickly. It is therefore essential to act and communicate immediately after a crisis has emerged.

The priorities should be as follows:

- Mobilize the appropriate Crisis Management Team; inform senior management
- Take immediate action to help people affected
- Express concern and sympathy from the outset

- Proactively establish contact with key stakeholders (ensuring dialogue)
- Brief the media proactively; keep the flow of information fresh and regular
- Establish the company as *the* credible source of information on the situation

Ask and consider the following questions:

- How serious is the situation?
- How quickly could it escalate?
- What are the likely triggers?
- What is the worst case scenario?
- What will people directly/indirectly affected make of it?
- What is actually at stake?
- Where and from whom can we obtain support?
- Who else is involved?
- Can the situation be contained?
- If so, what resources will be needed?

Then consider:

- What will be the demand on company/operating unit resources?
- What is the potential financial impact?
- Does the situation warrant further escalation of internal plans?

Once the first 48–72 hours are over it is important to remember to:

- Monitor reactions of key stakeholders; ensure dialogue
- Correct misconceptions and rumours; challenge inaccurate reporting
- Conduct critical self-evaluation of strategies adopted; adapt and fine-tune where necessary
- As far as possible, maintain consistency of team members but have relief teams available
- Avoid complacency

Also bear in mind the following legal considerations:

- Consider legal advice in the context of potential impact on reputation
- Avoid concern over liabilities becoming a public issue
- Never speculate on the cause but defer to the inquiry

- Don't be afraid to say 'sorry' and express sympathy/concern – this should not impact on liability
- Ensure quick legal sign-off for communication materials
- Ensure compensation issues are handled quickly and sensitively

When preparing internal communication materials, briefing spokespeople and considering the overall strategic response, always bear in mind:

- Science and technical data do not address or change emotionally charged perceptions
- Perceptions become people's reality, so respond accordingly
- Perceived 'victims' automatically occupy the moral high ground
- Every move the company makes anywhere in the world could come under the spotlight
- The prevailing political, public and media climate must be factored into strategic and tactical decisions.

Case study: Thomas Cook gets it right

On 27 September 1999, a bus carrying 34 elderly holidaymakers, two tour guides and a driver, lost control and careered off the Long Tom Pass in the Drakensburg mountains, South Africa. Twenty-six elderly British tourists and their South African tour guide were killed instantly, one tourist died two weeks later as a result of her injuries. Seven British tourists, a tour guide and the driver of the coach survived the crash, many with broken bones and head and chest injuries. The company at the centre of the tragedy was tour operator Thomas Cook, a subsidiary of Thomas Cook AG.

As soon as Thomas Cook received news of the accident, it initiated its crisis response plan. Thomas Cook's then Director and General Manager, Simon Laxton, was contacted immediately and made his way to Thomas Cook's UK headquarters north of London. Within an hour, an Incident Control Team was mobilized to manage media and relative response teams and to deal with all other aspects of the accident.

The Incident Control Team focused first and foremost on the needs of the victims and survivors of the crash, and their relatives. A team of trauma counsellors, mortuary technicians and legal and customer advisors was immediately sent to South Africa to counsel survivors, and to communicate with the police and the media. A coach engineer accompanied the group in order to initiate an independent internal investigation into the crash. In addition, Thomas Cook consulted its insurance provider, Axa, which also sent representatives to the scene to assist in co-ordinating insurance claims.

A Relative Response Hotline was established to deal with the thousands of calls expected from concerned friends and relatives. The Incident Control Team used the media to communicate the hotline number to the public, using international newswires and all major UK television bulletins. Despite the fact that the full details of the incident were not yet known, the Incident Control Team recognized that friends and relatives needed reassurance that Thomas Cook was doing everything possible and that everyone involved was being treated with the utmost care.

The company received over 2000 calls in the first 24 hours after the crash. Simon Laxton worked with the team and answered a number of calls himself. Additional staff were drafted into the relative call centre to cope with the growing enquiries from concerned friends and relatives. Thomas Cook made sure that all staff (in over 700 high street branches and all bureaux de change) were contacted, briefed and updated regularly to deal with members of the public who called or visited stores for information.

Immediate contact was made with South African Airways to make arrangements for relatives to fly to Johannesburg. The terms of Thomas Cook's insurance policy included costs for one relative to fly to the scene. However, Thomas Cook immediately recognised the need and importance of being totally flexible with this policy and in many cases allowed more than one relative to fly to the scene. The company made contact with the Foreign Office, the South African government, the British High Commission in South Africa and the South African Police to ensure that relatives were kept informed and those who flew to South Africa were protected from any intrusion or invasion of privacy that could have occurred. All the necessary practical and financial arrangements were made to ensure that relatives were given all the support and information they needed while there.

Those flown to Johannesburg were 'fast tracked' through the airport and a member of Thomas Cook's team was assigned to each family to ensure that they had a single point of contact and were constantly in touch with updated information.

Thomas Cook proactively contacted all customers booked on the same tour two weeks after the accident and offered them the opportunity to cancel their trips without charge. Only six chose to cancel, demonstrating the high levels of confidence felt in the company at the time.

Media management and victim response

Media attention around the world was immediate and intense. Over 500 media inquiries were received by the media team in the first 24 hours of the crash. TV crews arrived at the company's head office within two hours and 'camped' in the car park outside the building. Statements were issued to the press as frequently as possible, as new information was received. Broadcast interviews were given as far as practically possible. Simon Laxton was head of the Incident Response Team as well as primary spokesperson for Thomas Cook and interviews were tightly scheduled around the activities of the team.

All the media statements issued by Thomas Cook emphasized concern about the care and wellbeing of victims, survivors and relatives affected by the accident, and explained the company's commitment to finding out the cause of the accident as soon as possible. Initial media speculation about the cause of the crash and safety record of the coach operator was immediately quashed and senior management took care to reiterate the company's strict health and safety assessment of contracted operators and its confidence in the coach company, Springbok Atlas.

Teams flown to the scene of the accident were briefed to handle media enquiries and to protect the privacy of survivors and relatives. A Thomas Cook representative was later based at the Millpark hospital, Johannesburg, in order to deal with inquiries that might have been too intrusive for relatives and survivors.

The core Incident Response Team relocated to Johannesburg on Wednesday 29 September, three days after the crash. The volume of calls from both relatives and the media had subsided, the team felt it was important to address issues in South Africa directly, and also wanted to give relatives direct and personal support and to make absolutely sure that the victims' bodies were correctly identified prior to their repatriation to the UK. Teams at Thomas Cook's headquarters remained to sustain the incident response in the UK.

The nine survivors had been transported by air ambulance to a private hospital in Nelspruit, Lyndenburg, for immediate treatment. As soon as they were fit to travel, air ambulances transported them to a specialist trauma unit in Millpark Clinic. A few days later, a second air ambulance was called into service to repatriate the injured from South Africa back to the UK. Even though doctors at the Millpark Clinic were confident that it was safe for survivors to return to Britain by commercial airline, Thomas Cook decided to use air ambulances to ensure maximum comfort for those flying back to the UK. One survivor later died of injuries suffered as a result of the crash, increasing the number of victims to 28.

Thomas Cook also recognized the vital role that the people of Lyndenburg played during the accident; many drove to the scene of the crash to provide assistance to emergency teams dealing with the crash. A memorial service was organised by the South African authorities and attended by senior management who wanted to thank the townspeople "for their overwhelming compassion and support".

Overall, relatives felt that they were handled well at an extremely difficult and stressful time. Compensation issues were addressed immediately, with Axa acting as a universal point of contact for all relatives, many of whom were represented by different organizations.

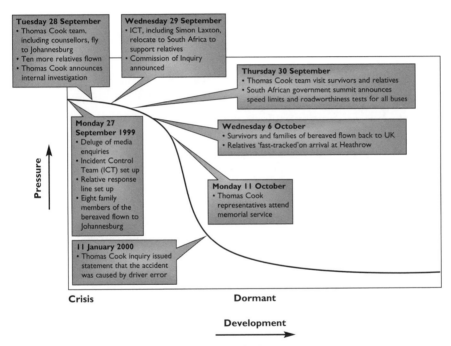

Figure 2.13 *Risk issue lifecycle – Thomas Cook*

Source: Regester Larkin

Investigations

Thomas Cook announced an immediate internal investigation as soon as the expert team arrived at the scene the day after the crash (Tuesday 28 September). South Africa's Transport Minister announced a commission of inquiry the following day. Thomas Cook publicly pledged to do everything possible to co-operate with the government's inquiry but refused to speculate on the cause. Within a week, the coach wreck had been transported to South Africa's Council for Scientific and Industrial Research for forensic investigations into the cause of the accident. The driver, severely injured as a result of the crash, later claimed the accident was due to faulty brakes, though subsequent investigations pointed towards driver error. Investigations by Thomas Cook and the South African government were completed in January 2000. Both revealed that the cause of the crash was not mechanical failure, as originally thought, but driver error. Despite these findings, neither organization wished to prosecute the driver or engage in any official action against Springbok Atlas.

Calls for tougher legislation

Recognizing the growing potential impact of the negative international media coverage on the country's tourism industry, the South African Minister for Transport organized an emergency road safety summit three days after the Lyndenburg accident. As a result, an immediate enforcement of a 100 km per hour speed limit for all buses on South African roads was introduced. The minister also announced with immediate effect, the introduction of roadworthiness tests for all South African buses. Longer term changes to the National Road Traffic Act to enable on-site safety inspections at bus companies are due. The decisions came in the wake of six bus crashes in South Africa within the week of 23–30 September, which killed 60 people and injured 184. During the months of September and October 1999, over 424 people were involved in South African road accidents, resulting in 98 deaths and 326 injuries. Road safety in South Africa became the overriding issue in the international media. The South African Minister's speedy action was undoubtedly driven by the shift in public focus from the isolated accident in Lyndenburg to the wider issue of public health and safety on South Africa's roads and highways.

Thomas Cook managed both its operational and communication response to the South African coach crash effectively and sensitively. This resulted in:

- No immediate or long term damage
- No material backlash from friends and families of the victims
- Largely neutral media coverage

- Sustained public confidence in the company
- Maintenance of good relationships between Thomas Cook and its operators and contractors
- Heightened public and employee confidence in management

Source: Thomas Cook, Shell International, 2001

In summary, corporate reputation management is not an isolated add-on located in the PR department, but a fundamental aspect of business performance. The value of reputation as an important intangible asset justifies integration with operational and risk management strategies. A company's vision and leadership, business strategy, HRM, marketing, relationship management and communications all directly influence how the business expresses itself to the outside world. The goal of effective reputation management is to *align* these activities. 'Outside-in' thinking – a company's ability to view itself from the many different perspectives that stakeholders have of it – can help to pre-empt worst case scenarios and exploit competitive opportunities. Understanding corporate reputation in terms of what stakeholders perceive and expect is fundamental to reputation risk management. Senior management have an obligation to actively anticipate, engage and co-ordinate relations with stakeholders.

Greater scrutiny of business performance, amplified by the media and the Internet, has created a mirror image environment where it is now easy to find out a company's true profile. This should reinforce the importance of anticipating and responding to change and aligning business practices with the new values-driven priorities of stakeholders. Ensuring the reflection in the mirror is true and clear underpins successful reputation risk management.

Appendix

Risk radar screen – in more detail

I. Potential stage

Statistical evidence: examples

- R&D/technical/clinical trial(s) – preliminary results published
- Illnesses reported among general populations *re:* specific products/ procedures (such as asthma and vehicle emissions, radio frequency emission rates, salmonella in poultry, glue sniffing among teenagers)
- Customer complaints increase (*re:* defects, misinterpreted product information, misleading pricing, advertising campaign, and so on)
- Research establishes causal relationships (for example, childhood cancers and electro-magnetic fields, environmental damage and processing plant/products, and so on)
- Media tracking spots occasional reference to potential risk issues
- Consumer survey data indicates background opinions impacting on potential risk issues (such as product safety and environmental protection)
- Economic statistics indicate potential risk issues (such as inflation, (un)employment and interest rate rise prospects)
- New monitoring scheme initiated to produce league table(s) at future date

Socio-economic trends: examples

- Socioeconomic trend data and forecasts indicate potential changing attitudes to product/service/procedures and emergence of potential risk issues, such as
  - Demographics (for instance, ageing populations, single person homes and cultural mix)
  - Public health trends
  - Economic trends forecasts
  - Lifestyle choice data
  - Consumer trends surveys
  - Household survey data

Technological innovations: examples

- New commercial innovations launched with public health/environ-mental risk implications
- Technological solutions proposed to address current risk issues
- Public opinion moves in favour/against specific technological develop-ments (such as biotechnology)
- New technology changes communication of risk issues (such as Internet privacy/information disclosure)
- New technology produces new monitoring/data collection mechanisms – and potential need for new legal requirements

Political/policy changes: examples

- New international/EU product, corporate or legal liability proposals/laws
- New code of practice (statutory or voluntary, national or sector/product specific)
- Another neighbour country/state/EU member state adopts more stringent controls on the issue
- Legislative proposals require qualified majority rather than unanimous approval
- Legislative proposals change burden of proof principles and attitudes to risk defined in public policy (for instance, precautionary principle adoption)
- Insurance companies increase premiums/caveats to cover the risk issue
- Inadequacies of existing legislation revealed (such as in interpretation, enforcement or penalties)

Legal test cases/precedents: examples

- Test case initiated through national/federal/international legal system
- Legal institution(s) threatens to establish new legal precedent for example, extends definition of individual director's personal liability
- Courts expected to award new high in compensation to litigant/costs to defendant company
- New legal provisions anticipated allowing collective representations (such as class actions)
- Increased use of civil law by individual campaign activists

- Increased recourse to criminal activity by activists seeking prosecution regarding the issue
- Activists increase use of libel laws to provoke company defence and public debate (media coverage) of an issue

'Look-alike' situations: examples

- Legal precedent anticipated on similar product, service, procedure or risk issue
- Stringent legal outcome anticipated on a similar risk issue at a later stage in the risk issue lifecycle
- Analogies, previously not associated with a product/risk issue (such as *via* media coverage, public policy/regulatory debates, scope of new policy proposals)

International developments: examples

- New international laws/proposals anticipated addressing/impacting on product/service/corporate policies or procedures
- International changes anticipated which would stimulate a risk issue or a crisis (such as rising oil prices, successful international litigation)
- International mass actions anticipated impacting on the company's operations in key/multiple markets (such as in new precautionary policy approaches)
- Threatened political activism about conditions in developing countries and their impacts on product/service supply (such as child labour, international trade talks, and so on)

Competition: examples

- Market competitors take commercial and/or political action in relation to the potential risk issue, for instance:
  - Initiates research
  - Makes public statement
  - Withdraws product
  - Issues new product information addressing the risk issue
  - Changes procedures
  - Joins public policy/ advisory groups
  - Launches commercial solution for example, CFC-free aerosols; phthalate-free toys for babies)
  - Receives 'best practice' award/ tops league table

- Activists attack competitor premises in protest at specific practices (such as pharmaceutical company laboratories over use of animals in research, McDonald's over anti-globalization protests)

Product development: examples

- Increase in customer complaints
- Company/independent research reveals defect/causal link to environmental, safety or public health issue
- New legal requirements/political pressure on safety testing
- Testing methods expected to attract increased public opinion (such as animal testing, GM crop trials, food traceability)
- Activists threaten to sabotage R&D/supply chain partners/locations
- Activists expected to launch campaign for moratorium ban or 'burden of proof' evidence of no adverse environmental health effects

2. Emerging stage

Scientific evidence: examples

- Clinical trial results published
- Research initiated in response to reported increased incidence of illness/environmental/consumer damage/abuse
- Regulatory agencies/standards bodies report unfavourably on the company and initiate action
- League table(s) published
- Increased academic/scientific research on causal relationship between product/service/procedures and damage to public health or environment

Specialist/local media coverage: examples

- Media tracking reports increased incidence of risk issue coverage
- Specialist/expert/independent opinions sought on the subject and subsequently reported
- Local public officials and opinion-formers reported to be taking an active interest in the issue, in response to public concern
- Sector/industry representatives' views sought and reported
- Media invites company to comment on the alleged risk issue

Political initiatives: examples

- Product/trade/sector/professional associations formally begin to consult memberships and opinion-formers on the subject
- Utilization of federal/state/national/regional government/regulatory procedure to raise the profile of the risk issue
- Policymakers initiate preliminary discussions with interested parties on the subject

Market rumour: examples

- Analysts begin to comment on the risk issue
- Competitors exploit potential uncertainty over risk issue
- Concerns expressed that the risk issue could have share price implications
- Concerns mount that market/consumer confidence will be damaged by the risk issue

Public opinion polling: examples

- General public opinion polls begin to include questions relevant to the risk issue
- Opinion polls report increasing interest in the issue
- Protagonist organizations initiate public opinion polling on the subject (consumers/members and so on)
- Opinion polling on the issue begins to reveal distinct unfavourable trend towards the company
- Polling moves up a gear from expression of concern about the risk issue to calls for stringent responsive action

Legal precedent: examples

- Courts establish legal precedent which impacts on the risk issue directly or indirectly regarding:
  - liabilities (corporate, personal, product and so on)
  - increase in high profile individual and class actions
  - award of (unprecedented) compensation/costs

Protagonists emerge: examples

- Local campaign groups formed
- National campaign organizations begin to take up the issue (such as environmentalists, consumers, industry, professional and general business associations)
- Key personalities (spokespeople) emerge, including individual direct action campaigners

Active campaigning: examples

- Challenges issued to company to produce counter-evidence, open governance, and so on
- Threats issued by campaign activists regarding direct action targeted at the company (for instance, boycotting, occupying/sabotaging property/products or services, shareholder activism tactics)
- Local associations formed to petition opinion-formers on the issue

Issue clarification: examples

- Campaign messages clarified (such as charges, defences and proposed actions)
- Campaign positions identified

3. Crisis stage

Intense political activism: examples

- Direct action intensifies ranging from:
  - symbolic (media stunts), such as custard pies at CEOs/government ministers, boycotts, occupations; activists at AGMs, direct targeting of shareholders and fund managers, and so on, to...
  - serious damage to people or property (such as US anti-abortionists, tampering with foods, death threats)
- Senior political personnel become engaged/embroiled in the issue
- Company 'blows budget' on reputation damage-limitation exercise
- Calls are made for independent inquiries/scapegoats in political/ litigation/compensation arenas
- See 'Intense media interest' on page 83

Polarisation of debate: examples

- Campaign messages polarize around 'for' and 'against' positions; difficult to arbitrate
- Protagonists unite, forming ideologically disparate but high impact coalitions, for instance, anti-globalization demonstrations
- Company becomes isolated through emergence of clear 'no-comment' element, for example, parties involved, competitors, politicians seeking to depoliticize the issue

Strong evidence bases: examples

- Main protagonists and independent sources produce 'evidence' for and against the main campaign positions
- Evidence (scientific/public opinion, and so on) reaches a 'critical mass' in favour of some action: legal, regulatory, commercial and/or political

Strong support bases: examples

- Main protagonists claim strong support bases (in numbers or status)
- Public opinion polls reveal strongly held views on both sides of the argument

Formal political proposals: examples

- Federal/state/regional/international policymakers initiate public consultation to discuss proposed solutions
- Campaign activists highlight precedent in other countries/sectors
- Defendants initiate minimum voluntary action to offset case for new statutory controls

Legal action: examples

- Individual campaigners initiate civil actions against company
- Campaign group(s) initiate mass actions against company
- Regional/international authorities initiate legal proceedings against countries/member state(s) for failing to effect appropriate laws
- Company initiates legal action to defend its position through national/ regional/international courts
- Outcome of a related legal case changes the dynamics of the current risk issue
- Campaigners in other countries win legal case against the company on the same issue

Intense Internet/media interest: examples

- Internet/media tracking reports and advocacy editorial on the risk issue
- Escalation of risk issue to top broadcast/print media slots
- Internet news groups/anti-corporate web-sites and media adopt 'blame and shame' approach to reporting the risk issue, supported by key activist groups
- Media challenge senior political personnel to comment/act on the issue
- Different Internet/media channels take sides and actively campaign on the issue
- Leading current affairs/documentary programmes cover the crisis issue

Global ramifications: examples

- Crisis initiates call for international measures to address the risk issue or wider issues raised (such as trade laws, competition policy, corporate governance, public health controls, environmental protection, employment laws)
- Regulatory penalties ramp up adverse cost infrastructures for sector(s), threatening licence to operate
- International treaties/conventions are deployed by activists in their case against the company, for instance Global Reporting Initiative, Universal Declaration of Human Rights

Spillover issues: examples

- Some senior political figures and campaign activists present the issue as illustrative of their case for wider controls on an industry/ sector/practice in the interests of public safety, consumer protection, and so on
- Other senior political personnel and industry bodies seek to 'ring-fence' the issue – scapegoating the company to prevent wider controls
- Crisis issue debate/investigations reveal/trigger underlying risk issues, i.e. 'tip-of-the-iceberg' scenarios, such as safety controls, privacy, financial product mis-selling
- Crisis in one country/region spills over into other markets/regions encouraging government-sponsored product recalls, company closures, and so on.

Resource list

Websites

Centre for Tomorrow's Company	www.tomorrowscompany.com
Henley Management College	www.henleymc.ac.uk
International Institute of Communications	www.iicom.org
Journal of Brand Management	www.henrystewart.com/journals/bm
Manchester Business School	www.mbs.ac.uk
MORI	www.mori.com
Regester Larkin	www.regesterlarkin.com
Reputation Institute	www.reputationinstitute.com

Articles and reports

Balmer, J.M.T., 'Corporate Identity and the Advent of Corporate Marketing', *Journal of Marketing Management*, 14, 1998

Bromley, D.B., 'Psychological Aspects of Corporate Identity, Image and Reputation', *Corporate Reputation Review*, 3 (3), 2000

Davies, G. Chun, R., da Silva, R.V., and Roper, S., 'The Personification Metaphor as a Measurement Approach for Corporate Reputation', *Corporate Reputation Review*, 4 (2), 2001

Fombrun, C.J. and Gardberg, N., 'Who's Tops in Corporate Reputation?', *Corporate Reputation Review*, 3 (1), 2000

Fombrun, C.J., Gardberg, N. and Sever, J.M., 'The Reputation Quotient: A Multi-Stakeholder Measure of Corporate Reputation', *Journal of Brand Management*, 7, 2000

Fombrun, C.J. and Van Riel, C.B.M., 'The Reputation Landscape', *Corporate Reputation Review*, 1, 1997

Hainsworth, B.E. and Meng, M. 'How Corporations Define Issues Management', *Public Relations Review*, 1988

MacMillan, K., Money, K.G. and Downing, S. 'Successful Business Relationships', *Journal of General Management*, 26 (1), 2000

Shell, *Roles and Relationships Between Issue Management Systems*, 2000

Books

Financial Times, *Mastering Risk*, FT, 2000

Freeman, R.E., *Strategic Management: A Stakeholder Approach*, Pitman, Boston, 1984

Schwartz, P., *The Art of the Long View: Planning for the Future in an Uncertain World*, Wiley, Chichester, 1998

Schultz, M., Hatch, M. and Larsen, M. (eds.), *The Expressive Organization: Linking Identity, Image and the Corporate Brand*, Oxford University Press, Oxford, 2000

CHAPTER 3

Perception or reality?
A risky business

"Perceptions are truth because people believe them"
EPICTETUS (FIRST CENTURY SLAVE PHILOSOPHER)

By every objective measure, from infant mortality to life expectancy, Westerners are healthier today and are exposed to fewer hazards than ever before. However, living longer and having few immediate, material concerns now seems to mean that we have more time to contemplate all sorts of long-term theoretical risks. A catalogue of surveys demonstrates that we worry so much about the future that we believe new technologies and innovative products and services should not be permitted until it is known for certain that they won't endanger our health or the environment (Wildavsky, 1988).

Managing risk depends on understanding it, measuring it and assessing its consequences. For much of human history, we have relied on gut instinct in the face of uncertainty. Our biological legacy means that we take risks by nature, whether we like it or not. Indeed, *homo sapiens* has been such an evolutionary success because our ancestors were prepared to risk life and limb developing fire as a means of cooking and keeping warm. In the seventeenth century, two mathematicians analysed a simple game of chance, creating the basis of probability theory. Other techniques consolidated the development of the insurance industry and enabled businesses to make rational assessments of risk and plan their operations accordingly. Today, risk is an essential part of competitive markets, driving our insatiable appetite for new products and services that reflect a host of attributes and aspirations associated with modern and future living (Bernstein, 1996).

Communicating about the nature and consequences of environmental health is one of the most complex areas of public policy. Attitudes to risk vary enormously according to social, multi-cultural and economic factors. Traditional approaches to risk assessment and management are no longer adequate in dealing with the pace of technological change in knowledge economies. Assuming that risk can be managed at a global level is fraught with pitfalls – as the debate over the safety of GM food has illustrated.

Too often risk is treated as a vaguely connected set of disparate factors, with quite different definitions and scope. At its simplest, risk can be described as the likelihood of something unpleasant happening. In the financial community, it is about protecting earnings and capital, minimizing exposure to the degree of uncertainty over future returns. In the health and safety arena, risk is usually considered in terms of hazard to personal safety and associated physical and environmental risks. At a broad operational level, managers assess factors that may disrupt business continuity, driven by competitive, technological, supply chain, regulatory, employee or broader social and economic change.

Making decisions about risk is a highly subjective process. Communicating risk to consumers is, therefore, challenging. The principal objective of effective risk communication is to help stakeholders understand the reasoning behind risk-based decisions with the aim of making judgements that reflect the facts in the context of available options, interests and values.

This chapter looks at the damage that adverse public perception of risk can have on commercial goals, provides guideposts for effective risk communication and with it, reputation management. In a risk-averse, precautionary environment the twin spotlights of intense scrutiny and pro-consumer regulation mean that getting it wrong can carry a terminal cost burden.

Some of the areas I will explore include:

- The impact of low trust and uncertainty
- The difference between hazard and outrage
- The importance of critical performance assessment as part of an integrated approach to risk management and communication
- Media amplification of risk
- The need for tailored information and communication
- How to build a support base among diverse stakeholder groups
- Tuning the radar for improved performance through collecting feedback and assessing changing attitudes and behaviour

Who will guard the guards?

Confucius told his disciple Tsze-kung that three things are needed for government: weapons, food and trust. If a ruler can't hold on to all three, he should give up the weapons first and the food next. Trust should be guarded to the end: "without trust we cannot stand". Confucius' view is still convincing (O'Neill, 2002).

Reputation is built on trust and belief. Risk means being exposed to the possibility of a bad outcome. Risk management is about taking deliberate action to shift the odds favourably – increasing the odds of good outcomes and reducing the odds of bad outcomes! So, why are companies and government agencies such bad risk communicators? It should be widely understood that successful companies are those that are outward-facing and understand who their stakeholders are, what they think and what they want. This is a fundamental rule of thumb in anticipating where potential risk icebergs may be lurking and where and how to chart a course for a smooth and uninterrupted passage.

Why is it then, that companies are often surprised by controversy? I think much of it is to do with the fact that rational decision-making based on logic and supported by technical and other factual data, quite naturally, rules in the boardroom. Furthermore, until all the available facts are gathered, managers don't want to think about communicating with the outside world, and by the time they do it is often too late for any form of balanced debate. In the field of risk communication, however, it is an absolute fallacy to assume that information equates to understanding. Decisions about risk are values-based not technical! However, when the potential for danger emerges, senior managers frequently fail to understand that a risk issue can be viewed in many different ways – I used the distorted angles of a goldfish bowl as a metaphor in the first chapter. The key point is that emotion is an incredibly powerful change-maker and perceptions of risk are largely driven by a variety of less tangible influences which go some way to explaining why we don't react to risk in predictable ways. That is why organizations dealing with emerging risk issues need to tune the radar, listen and communicate in response to differing concerns and expectations – and actively manage the process from the outset.

Risk perception is one of the most destructive forces as far as reputation is concerned and each time a risk is perceived to be badly managed, public scepticism over who to trust increases. Risk perception is about fear. Fear is more emotional than rational and so we fear before we think. Billions of dollars and countless human-years of effort get wasted unnecessarily because we are frightened of the wrong things. The estimated annual expenditure associated with rabies prevention, which affects approximately five people a year in the United States, is over $300 m. Yet only $500 m is spent a year on programmes to reduce smoking, which accounts for approximately one in every five deaths in America.

Foot and Mouth – feeding public distrust

On 20 February 2001, Foot and Mouth disease was confirmed in sheep at an abattoir in the county of Essex in England. It was to be the start of the world's worst outbreak of the disease and brought about the slaughter of six million animals, costing the UK economy at least £10 bn. The crisis has left a permanent legacy, not only in compounding public anxiety over food safety but also adding to the further decline in trust as a result of the UK government's mismanagement of the catastrophe. The sight of pyres burning across the land created dramatic, ghostly images of a country seemingly retreating into the dark ages – a major deterrent for visitors and a crippling blow to a farming industry still recovering from the aftermath of BSE. Furthermore, the government's actions received widespread condemnation as it is now accepted that the countryside did not have to be 'closed down', with the related devastating consequences for the tourism industry.

An absence of properly co-ordinated and tested contingency plans, a retreat from animal vaccination – now widely regarded as the most effective deterrent – as a sop to British farmers in favour of mass culling and compensation and a decision to hold inquiries in private, resulted in legitimate accusations that the government put speed and 'white-washing' ahead of concerns about public confidence, thoroughness and accountability.

A commentary piece in *The Washington Post* in 2000 highlighted the frenzied panic that led to millions of dollars being spent protecting people against an outbreak of West Nile virus when only a fraction of that sum was invested in public education encouraging people to wash their hands before preparing food. This would eliminate far more disease transmission than killing every mosquito in America! The same article referred to a Boston suburb, where parents were so terrified that traces of a chemical were found in the air in just one room at their children's elementary school that they pressured the town school board to close the school, forcing 6 to 11-year-olds to be bused through treacherous snow-covered streets in rush-hour traffic to the local high school (*The Washington Post*, 6 August 2000).

Risks are vivid and memorable – characterized through personal experience, the experience of others, news, fiction, signals and symbols. Risk is also a reflection of inevitable scientific uncertainty. Individuals are now making significant choices in the context of incomplete and conflicting information amid growing cynicism over the competence and trustworthiness of experts. Ironically, even expert decision-makers can suffer from over-confidence, or bias in the interests of publicity and research funding, becoming fixated on a particular set of assumptions which ignore alternative views and uncertainties.

Risk managers will only succeed in protecting reputation when they recognize that any debate dealing with risk perception needs to consider alternatives through proper scenario planning and by addressing non-technical factors, such as values and emotions. Communicating about scientific and technical research is extremely complex – it is also much more than words and numbers. Scientific results couched in terms of aggregate populations are an absolute turn-off – individuals will primarily be concerned with risk to themselves. Together with effective internal risk management processes, formulating and presenting the message is vital and risk managers who overlook stakeholders' basic concerns can't assume a quick fix from standardized press statements.

We know that when we make decisions about risk we do not simply respond in a clinical, machine-like way to factual information. We want access to the data but we are also strongly influenced by instinct and intuition, feelings of concern or fear are amplified if a new risk is unfamiliar, difficult to quantify or is beyond our direct control. This process is difficult to characterize because:

- **Risk means different things to different people.** Some of us are avid risk-takers, enjoying extreme sports, gambling, travelling at speed or smoking like chimneys. We also tend to overestimate sensational, memorable risks like flying or contracting vCJD, and underestimate common risks like driving a car or jay-walking. I love to drive at speed but for many driving a car is an imposed risk. Afraid of flying, we drive, which dramatically increases our overall risk of injury or death (an estimated 40,000 to 50,000 Americans will die in motor accidents over the next 12 months compared with an estimated 500 lives lost in airplane crashes).

- **Basic attitudes are hard to change.** They are forged by a range of social and cultural factors, reinforced by our contact with and opinions advocated by relatives, friends, colleagues and others. Responses to risk are not only dependent on context, they are directly connected to individual values and beliefs – about society, our relationship with nature, our attitudes towards technological progress, our spiritual convictions and so on. These attitudes contribute to shaping the way we interpret, understand and act upon new risks.

The Swedish potato chip scare – communicating scientific complexity

In April 2002, Sweden's food watchdog declared that there were alarmingly high levels of acrylamide – believed to cause cancer – in starch-rich food cooked at high temperatures. According to the National Food Administration (NFA) in Sweden, a single bag of chips could contain up to 500 times more acrylamide than allowed in drinking water by the World Health Organization. One major Swedish food retailer said that sales of ships fell by 30–50 per cent in the days following the announcement. This wasn't, apparently, a one-off, poorly designed piece of research – it was coming direct from a Swedish government agency, supported by research from Stockholm University.

Critics of the announcement highlighted both the limited nature of the research (the product analysis was based on 100 random samples) and the controversial nature of the link between acrylamide and human cancers, accusing the NFA's alarm as being "disproportionate and exaggerated". The haste in which the research was presented was also criticised. The research was deemed so important that the NFA took the unusual step of going public with its findings before the research had been officially published in an academic journal. The NFA was subsequently accused of seeking publicity as a means to justify its role at a time of budgetary difficulties, and was criticised for not providing the public with alternative dietary recommendations.

Presenting sensitive and complex scientific research to the public in relation to health scares is incredibly difficult. Dr Leif Busk, head of research and development at the NFA, has defended the decision to present the information to the public at such an early stage. "If we had just informed the food industry or waited one or two years, how could we have later defended this to the public?" The Food Standards Agency in the UK, formed after public confidence in food regulation was shattered post-BSE, works from the principle that eating food is never a risk-free business and has adopted rigorous standards of openness and consumer-focus in its communication. Other national agencies in Europe as well as the European Union, are reviewing their approaches to policy development and consumer communication over food-related risks. In an environment of considerable confusion over who to trust on food safety, transparency and accountability must be the essential building-blocks of good practice.

Source: Adapted from *Financial Times*, 3 May 2002

- **Few of us expect zero risk in our lives.** Actually, a zero-risk life isn't even on the menu. However, we do want answers to two basic questions. What are the benefits and safeguards associated with the risk, and can we trust the people responsible for managing it?

- **Sources of information are crucial** to the way in which risk is perceived, understood and acted upon. This point plays to the issues of declining trust and respect for the authority of institutions, business and experts, outlined in the first chapter. We generally prefer to seek the advice of a trusted local community leader, medical doctor, family friend or well-regarded specialist. Information about risk is judged not by the content but by the source – *Who are they? Can I trust them? Are they qualified to sort out the problem? Are they competent, objective, fair, consistent, caring, responsible, able to acknowledge our concern?* Building trust is a painstaking and incremental process; there is no easy, short-cut way to manufacture goodwill and support.

Flexing local community muscles in Thailand

The Thai mussel-farming community of Klong Daan on the outskirts of Bangkok appears a tranquil and traditional remnant of a past era. It has, however, rocked the Asian Development Bank with a remarkably well-orchestrated campaign to stop a $750 m ADB-backed waste water treatment plant that residents say threatens to destroy their livelihood. The Samut Prakarn waste water plant, planned to be the biggest facility of its kind in South East Asia, is intended to clean chemical-laden waste water from the province's rash of leather-works, textile mills, battery plants and other dirty industries. But Klong Daan residents, supported by international environmental groups, believe the plant has a flawed design and will send toxic effluent into the sea. They also claim that the siting of the plant, in a relatively unpolluted area, is the result of influential landowners profiting from selling the land, and there are allegations of corruption. This David and Goliath clash has resulted in considerable soul-searching within the Bank about its cosy relationship with borrowing governments in Asia at the expense of proper public consultation around new projects. The controversy, together with a shifting focus towards poverty alleviation, is forcing the Bank to change its ways. It recently established a non-government centre to co-ordinate outreach efforts and has redrafted its independent inspection mechanism to make it more responsive to the public.

Source: Adapted from *Financial Times*, 10 May 2002

However, organizations that listen, act and communicate as a regular and integral part of doing business are more likely to influence – constructively – the overall impression people have. Trust is closely linked to accountability and transparency; this has almost become a clichéd expression of our time.

- **Emotion is the most powerful change-maker of all.** Symbols and images of disaster portrayed through the media and by activists can overwhelm and totally negate scientific fact. Film of the Challenger rocket exploding in 1996, cartoons of genetically modified monster crops, airplanes crashing into the World Trade Centre, carnage on the battle-field, the mangled wreckage of train disasters feed our imagination and risk aversion. Technological complexity and scientific uncertainty compound the potential for anxiety.

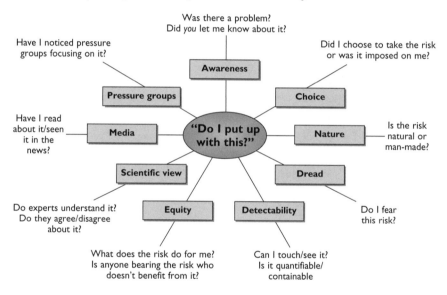

Figure 3.1 *Risk perception wheel*
Source: Regester Larkin

There is always a strong desire for certainty in making judgements about risk, but only uncertainty can be guaranteed in technological and scientific innovation. Experts and policymakers who highlight the gambles associated with risk benefit decisions are resented for the anxiety they provoke. Where very high levels of certainty are sought the costs are likely to be high and, in any case, some risk is inevitable. Eliminating uncertainty can mean losing a technology and its associated benefits, as Chapter 5 highlights.

Furthermore, questions are now being asked about the social and ethical impact of progress – is there a real need for every new product or process? Taking this a step further, there are factors that can provide quite good indicators of overall public response to risk as shown in the risk perception wheel. Can we choose whether or not we want them, or are they imposed on us? Are they man-made, or naturally occurring? What is the potential for a scary consequence associated with any risk? In examining the risk/benefit equation, do we all get to share the benefits and the risks equitably or do some benefit more while others are exposed to more of the risks? Is there consensus among the experts on claims that could affect our health or safety? What are the media and NGOs saying? Do these changes fit in with our basic principles and value systems? What effect do these questions have on the way we think about the organizations responsible for pushing forward the juggernaut of progress? Clearly, the potential for risk icebergs increases if people consider a risk:

- Has been imposed
- Is man-made
- Has a high dread factor
- Isn't easy to quantify
- Lacks equity, that is, some people have a greater exposure relative to the benefits
- Is the subject of disagreement among experts
- Has strong emotional appeal for media reporting and activism

Source: Adapted from Fischhoff, 1995

DVT causes free-fall in the airline industry

In November 2000, the death of 28-year-old Emma Christoffersen from a blood clot following a long-haul flight from Australia to the UK created widespread sensational media reporting and pressure for regulatory change around a possible connection between air travel and deep vein thrombosis (DVT). Links have been suggested since the 1950s but to date there is no substantive evidence to support these claims. Twelve DVT-related deaths out of the 31 m passengers flying through London's Heathrow airport each year suggests a very low 1 in 2.5 m risk. Furthermore, research published in the *Lancet* (October, 2000) found no causal link and a literature review by the US Aerospace Medical Association stated that the link between air travel and DVT is weak. The international aviation industry association, IATA, said that there is no reliable evidence of any difference between being immobile in an aircraft compared to being immobile on a train, a long car journey or lying in bed. Nevertheless, continued negative media reporting and campaigning for precautionary measures by consumer groups, such as the Aviation Health Institute, has elevated the issue from a minor health concern to a major, widespread public health risk issue. So much so, that the WHO is embarking on a two-year study into air travel and health effects, class action law suits have been initiated in Australia and New Zealand, and most major airlines have felt obliged to invest in passenger information campaigns designed to provide guidance on eating, drinking and exercising in-flight to minimize DVT risk.

Understanding probability and the law of averages

Risk is about chance, and probability is the accepted measure of the likelihood of something unpleasant happening. Probability obeys established mathematical principles, unlike the human brain which tends to manipulate, ignore or contradict them! Essentially, this is to do with simplifying the way that we manage information (called heuristics) which leads to common biases in dealing with probabilities, such as:

- Availability bias – events are seen to be more frequent when we can easily recall examples of them. This leads to an overestimation of the frequency of memorable events and hence the chance of something similar happening again

- Confirmation bias – once we have formed a view, new evidence is generally made to fit while contradictory information is filtered out

- Overconfidence – this bias seems to affect most of us including scientific experts. In judging the probability of being correct, our tendency is to apply a higher figure.

Table 3.1 Bias in judged frequency of death

Most overestimated		Most underestimated	
All accidents	Botulism	Smallpox vaccination	Asthma
Motor vehicle accidents	All cancer	Diabetes	Emphysema
Pregnancy, childbirth,	Fire	Stomach cancer	
abortion	Venomous bite	Lightning	
Tornadoes	or sting	Stroke	
Flood	Homicide	Tuberculosis	

Source: Slovic, *The Perception of Risk*, 2000

In responding to probability and risk it is possible to 'frame' a situation in different ways. The most common example is that outcomes can be measured against different starting points, for example, through lives lost or saved.

Imagine the country is preparing for an outbreak of a particularly nasty viral disease which is expected to kill 600 people. Two alternative strategies to combat the disease have been proposed. The exact scientific consequences of the programmes are:

Programme A: 200 will be saved

Programme B: There is a one-third probability that 600 people will be saved and a two-thirds probability that no people will be saved

Most people choose Programme A because it is risk averse – the prospect of any certainty becomes attractive. This can be repeated with the descriptions of Programmes A and B being changed as follows:

Programme C: 400 people will die

Programme D: There is a one-third probability that nobody will die, and a two-thirds probability that 600 people will die

In this case Programme D is chosen as a risk-taking strategy because the certain death of 400 is less acceptable than a 2 in 3 chance of 600 dying. Therefore the way a problem is framed (gains: A *vs* B; losses C *vs* D) affects how judgements are made and whether or not individuals act in a *risk averse* or *risk taking* manner. Choices involving gains tend to be risk averse and choices involving losses tend to be risk-taking.

Source: Fischhoff *et al.*, 1981

Just as gamblers bet more wildly to recoup increasing losses, people tend to make riskier choices if alternatives are framed as possible losses, while playing safe if choosing between alternative gains (Tversky and Kahneman, 1974).

There is much debate about the value or otherwise of risk comparisons in trying to understand risk probability and impact. Because of our ability to measure substances and effects much more accurately, scientists justify a small probability as, say, 'a risk of 1 in 10^8' or 'a probability of 0.0000013', but what does it mean? What of the scientific case for banning beef on the bone which could be BSE infected? In the UK, consumers were informed of a 1:600,000,000 chance of contracting vCJD. How does this compare in our minds with the 1:700,000 chance of being killed by the officially encouraged car airbag in the United States? Scales and 'ladders' are used

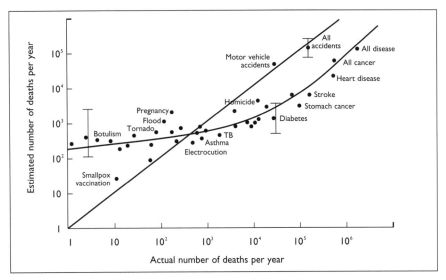

Figure 3.2 *Estimated and actual frequency of deaths from various causes*

Sources: Lichtenstein *et al.*, 1978, Slovic, 2000. If actual and judged frequencies were equal, the data would fall on the straight line. The points and the curved line fitted to them represent the averaged response of a sample of the US population. While people were approximately accurate, their judgements were systematically distorted. This is indicated by both the compression of the scale and the scatter of the results.

to compare the risk of death from acid rain with that of driving 50 miles over the speed limit. Calibrating public perception of risk against real data, especially mortality statistics is another mechanism as Figure 3.2 indicates.

The difficulty here is that we tend to apply availability bias, over-estimating death caused by unusual or dramatic circumstances like vCJD, and underestimating common killers such as heart disease. Table 3.2 overleaf provides another example using the criteria 'one in a million chance of death'.

Government health departments use risk averages to identify the likelihood of death or incidence of adverse events in given populations. The average risk of dying in a road accident in the UK is estimated at 1:15686, but the figure is useless for an individual making a risk decision based on it. Risk communication expert, John Adams, demonstrates this by trawling through the scientific literature. A young man is 100 times more likely to be involved in a severe crash than a middle-aged woman, someone driving at 3 a.m. on Sunday is 134 times more likely to die than someone driving at 10 a.m., someone with a personality disorder is 10 times more likely to die, and someone with two and half times the blood alcohol limit is 20 times more likely to die. He concludes that if these factors were all independent of each other, one could predict that a disturbed, drunken young man driving

Table 3.2 *Examples of risk 'estimated to increase the annual chance of death by one in a million'*

Activity	Cause of death
Smoking 1.4 cigarettes	Cancer, heart disease
Spending 1 hour in a coal mine	Black lung disease
Living 2 days in New York or Boston	Air pollution
Travelling 10 miles by bicycle	Accident
Flying 1000 miles by jet	Accident
Living 2 months in Denver (rather than New York)	Cancer (cosmic radiation)
One chest X-ray in a good hospital	Cancer (from radiation)
Eating 40 tablespoons of peanut butter	Liver cancer (aflatoxin B)
Drinking 30 12 oz cans of diet soda	Cancer (from saccharin)
Living 150 years within 20 miles of nuclear power plant	Cancer (from radiation)

Source: Wilson, 1979

at 3 a.m. on Sunday would be about 2.7 million times more likely to be involved in a serious road accident than would a normal, sober, middle-aged woman driving to church seven hours later!

The insurance industry uses past accident rates to estimate the probabilities associated with future claim rates. However, this doesn't ensure that the cost of insuring against a risk provides an effective measure of that risk for *individuals*. The figures that insurance analysts need to get right in order to make money are the risk *averages*. For the risks listed in the table above and the diagram on the previous page, variation around the average will range over several orders of magnitude, which is why insurers ignore variability so that insuring against 'good' risks can subsidise the 'bad' risks. It will be interesting to see what impact the greater precision with which individual risks can be specified through the identification of genetic predisposition to fatal illnesses has on the insurance industry's performance in the future (Adams, 1999).

Although quite interesting, risk comparison tables and averages should be treated with great caution as they do not allow for individual value judgements or any of the criteria identified in the risk perception wheel. As one expert put it "use of these comparisons can seriously damage your credibility!" (Morgan and Hennon, 1990).

Hazard and outrage

A key principle for managers facing risk decisions is that public perception of risk has a much broader and variable definition. While risk managers and technical experts have traditionally focused on quantifying *hazard* – the physical risk and the likelihood of it happening through statistical analysis, members of the public also factor in a wide range of preconceived attitudes, biases and values which, collectively, can generate *outrage* – public anger and indignation. The risk perception wheel identifies some of them. The dilemma is that while the experts respond to hazard, the public respond to outrage. When hazard is high (for example, with smoking, alcohol or drug abuse, fatty diet) and outrage is low, the experts will be concerned and the public will be indifferent. When the hazard is low (as with radon, GM food, MMR vaccine) and outrage is high, the public will be concerned and the experts won't be worried. Clearly, when a hazard is very high everyone focuses on the emergency; but a 1 in 3000 hazard may be tolerable if outrage is low, while a 1 in 3 bn hazard may not be tolerable if outrage is high (Sandman, 1993). In a high outrage situation, no amount of convincing by the experts will do any good. Events that suggest a 'tip of the iceberg' scenario generate disproportionate public concern and outrage.

Silicone breast implants – what constitutes acceptable risk?

Breast augmentation began in the United States in 1962. Since then, it is estimated that about two million women in the US have undergone surgery to have silicone breast implants. Eighty per cent of these implants were for cosmetic reasons, the remaining 20 per cent for breast reconstruction following cancer surgery. Although breast implant products represented only 1 per cent of sales (but 30 per cent of all surgical implants) by 1995, Dow Corning Corporation announced it was filing for bankruptcy in the face of a potential global settlement of $4.5 bn against implant manufacturers involving over 440,000 women. The class action settlement involved unprecedented punitive damages for which there was, and remains, little reliable scientific evidence. It proved to be a potent example of the extraordinary mismatch between scientific and public risk perception that mismanagement of risk and risk information can create.

There is no conclusive scientific evidence that silicone materials in breast implants increase the risk of developing breast cancer or connective tissue diseases. A study published in the *New England Journal of Medicine* in 1992 examined the potential for breast cancer in over 11,000 women who had received silicone breast implants and did not find an increased risk of cancer. Based on the research performed and statements issued by the Food and Drug

▶

Administration (FDA) and National Science Panel on the safety of silicone breast implants, it was deemed unlikely that any of the systemic health problems, such as connective-tissue disease, experienced by the women suing Dow Corning and others, related to silicone. Furthermore, the overwhelming majority of women with breast implants have had no medical problems at all. Only subsequently, through an independent review conducted by the US Institute of Medicine in June 1999, were local complications with silicone breast implants found to be the primary safety issue.

Some early toxicological research conducted in laboratory animals into the potential health effects of silicone and the breast implants did suggest that silicone might not be biologically inert and that it could enter the immune system of rats and mice. Following a 1984 lawsuit, Dow Corning informed surgeons of these findings but concluded that no convincing evidence existed of a causal relationship – a not untypical situation for a health risk assessment, where organizations involved will tend to emphasize the low risk indicators.

The company came unstuck over its perceived failure to conduct more thorough risk assessments through research. Although there was a lack of evidence that implants were dangerous, there was little consolidated evidence that they were safe. The killer blow for Dow Corning came with the discovery, associated with the 1984 litigation, that it had suppressed and misrepresented scientific data. Internal memos highlighted complaints from doctors over defective and ruptured implants and associated health effects, and failure to make public data from a study of implants in dogs that at the end of a two year trial period showed one dog had died and the remaining three had severe chronic inflammation.

Whilst the company repeatedly claimed that it had been open and communicative with physicians at all times, and that it had become the victim of greedy lawyers and victim groups, plaintiffs' defence successfully argued that not enough effort was made to rigorously examine the data for evidence of insufficient safety, the internal company memos showed a less than satisfactory attitude to developing risk data and the company had withheld and, potentially, tampered with the dog study results. Today's precautionary environment demands a constant and proactive approach to risk information disclosure.

Source: Adapted from Brunk, C.G., 'Silicone Breasts: The Implant Risk Controversy', in Powell and Leiss, 1977.

The nuclear malfunction at Three Mile Island in the United States in 1979 didn't cause a single death but had a huge effect in creating public anxiety about the scary possibilities of nuclear fall-out. By contrast, when reactor number four at Chernobyl in the former Soviet Union exploded on 26 April 1986 and killed 31 people in the immediate aftermath, it sent shock-waves through the international community but government secrecy and geographic remoteness dampened down understanding of the real impact and the associated outrage. By 1992, it was estimated that there were 187 instances of acute radiation sickness as a result of involvement in the accident and its clean-up, and 5237 people were unable to work for the same reason, while 15,000 had contracted radiation-related diseases. The rate of thyroid cancer in children has risen from 1 per million in 1984 to 100 per million in 1991. The incidence of throat cancer in Ukraine as a whole has doubled. Imagine the level of public outrage such a disaster would have created if it had occurred in North America or Europe.

Our love-hate relationship with the pace of technological change and inherent associated risks is reflected in an article in the *New Yorker* magazine following the widely reported Bhopal tragedy in India in 1985:

"What truly grips us … is not so much the numbers as the spectacle of suddenly vanishing competence, of men utterly routed by technology, of fail-safe systems failing with a logic as inexorable as it was once – indeed right up to that very moment – unforeseeable. And the spectacle haunts us because it seems to carry allegorical import like the whispery omen of a hovering future"

Source: New Yorker magazine, 1985

Dealing with outrage is largely common sense but it is remarkable how counter-intuitive to corporate culture it is! Companies all too often have no radar or tune it in only on an *ad hoc* basis. First, because corporations find it difficult to accept responsibility for a problem and to say "sorry". By doing so, stakeholders and members of the public are, more often than not, prepared to give an organization some latitude in fixing the problem.

Second, companies that insist that a risk is small usually find the public thinks the opposite. Experience suggests that outrage can be reduced or avoided by acknowledging the full potential or possibility of a problem upfront. Third, using the language of trade-offs, for example: "living by this landfill site is better than being next to the highway" is a high-risk

Salomon Brothers – acknowledging failure and rebuilding trust

Financial institutions deal in risk – credit, interest rate, market, operational, liquidity and reputation risk. In 1991, Salomon Brothers in New York was charged by the US Justice Department with rigging its bids in the regular government bond auctions. Salomon had a fearful reputation in the US bond markets and as a primary dealer was one of only 40 investment banks allowed to bid directly for new issues, not only on behalf of customers, but for its own book. Under the rules, no bank was allowed to bid for more than 35 per cent of an issue but as bids are often submitted on behalf of clients too, an individual bank could end up controlling more than 35 per cent of the issue, as either principal or agent.

In May 1991, the Treasury received complaints from other dealers that Salomon had squeezed them out of the latest two-year note auction. It emerged that the government bond desk at Salomon had submitted false bids in the name of uninformed customers, resulting in them controlling more than 94 per cent of the issue. Subsequently, Salomon admitted that it had placed illegal bids in 30 of the 230 auctions of government securities since 1986.

In August, the US Treasury Department suspended Salomon from bidding on behalf of clients. This threatened the very existence of the firm as many of its institutional clients decided not to deal with it at all. Some thought it might lose its status as a primary dealer.

In the face of the reputational risk that this posed, the Salomon board reacted quickly. The head of the bond desk and several others who had been involved in submitting the bogus bids were sacked. When it emerged that both the chairman and president of the company had been aware of the auction rigging since April, they left too.

The interim Chairman, respected in the business community as a conservative, long-term investor, understood the importance of restoring client trust as the basis for retrieving the reputation of the bank. He candidly acknowledged failure with the media and discussed the results of his investigations before undertaking a drastic purge of Salomon's top management aimed at correcting the over-aggressive, 'greed is good' culture. An executive committee was established to manage the firm on a day-to-day basis, as was a compliance committee of the board to monitor trading activities. In the longer term, the company's compensation scheme was changed with a larger proportion of bonuses being paid in shares.

Salomon's prompt acknowledgement of failure and regret, combined with major operational and compliance change to remove a divisive and dishonest corporate culture, enabled it to salvage its reputation. Although taken over by the Travelers Group in 1997, and later Citigroup, the Salomon brand continued to evoke respect as demonstrated by the unpopularity of the decision to rebrand Salomon Smith Barney to Citigroup in 2001.

Source: British Bankers' Association, 2000

strategy. Suggesting a risk is worth taking receives no public sympathy. Ignoring tradeoffs and letting people find them is a better route to mutual decision-making and resolution.

Addressing these three points actively and early by:

- Acknowledging concern and saying sorry
- Accepting that different people have different attitudes to risk, so it is counter-productive to downplay the perceived size of the risk
- Avoiding the language of trade-offs and facilitating shared debate and decision-making

will help to establish credibility and understanding, and so reduce the potential for the media and activists to amplify public outrage and, ultimately, put pressure on regulators to intervene. Any serious hazard requires hazard mitigation – it is just the same for dealing with outrage (Sandman *et al.*, 1998).

The cost of apathy at Snow Brand

In June 2000, over 13,000 people living in the Osaka area of Western Japan fell ill with food poisoning after drinking Snow Brand milk powder. The cause of the outbreak was enteroxin, a toxin secreted by the staphylococcus aureus bacteria. The Health and Welfare Ministry discovered that Snow Brand's Tiaki plant in Hokkaido had experienced a three hour power failure during March, which could have caused the bacteria to develop. Failing to take swift action or to communicate in response to growing public alarm, the company was instructed by Osaka's municipal government to institute a total product recall, including placement of advertisements in local newspapers. Snow Brand was slow to respond, ignoring government deadlines for action and giving rise to media speculation that the company had recycled milk returned from stores which had passed its sell-buy date for use in other dairy products. Media reports also alleged that the company adopted poor hygiene standards at its manufacturing plants. Such was the reluctance of senior management to take action that the company became the subject of a police investigation later in the year for its failure to manage such a widespread public health risk. Public outrage forced Snow Brand to temporarily close all its 21 milk-producing plants in Japan, significant litigation ensued and heads rolled at the top of the company. It wasn't until December 2000 – nine months after the crisis – that a new President of Snow Brand apologized at a public meeting in Osaka.

▶

▶

Public confidence in Snow Brand plummeted, forcing additional 'precautionary' product recalls, 1300 redundancies and a dramatic decline in market share from around 45 per cent to single digits. In March 2001, the company reported a consolidated loss of 52.9 bn yen, rising to 71.9 bn yen by March 2002. Performance has been slow to recover, compounded by further scandals relating to product contamination and mislabelling. Snow Brand has failed to find appropriate commercial trading partners and was forced to spin off its milk operations into a separate entity in June 2002. The company is routinely cited in the business and financial media as a company struggling to survive.

Even in a country where deference to authority remains a powerful influence, the impact of risk perception on politics in Japan is challenging many established norms. In April 2002, the Japanese government came under fire for ignoring a World Health Organization recommendation that could have prevented the outbreak of BSE, and suppressing a European Union report highlighting the risks a year earlier. Public outcry over the blunder has undermined trust in the Japanese administration and the scare has been compounded by other food scandals, involving Snow Brand's milk-related and beef-mislabelling incidents. The bureaucratic bungling echoes the negligence and cover-ups that enabled the infamous Minamata mercury poisoning scandal to remain unchecked for years, and which also led to the deaths of haemophiliac patients given untreated blood and being infected with AIDS in the 1980s. The perception of a long line of environmental health failures in Japan is underpinning a significant rise in critical media reporting and consumer activism – unheard of ten years ago.

Risk perception and media amplification

It is tempting to assume that media coverage of environmental health risks is routinely exaggerated, and there is certainly some truth in this! After all, most of us obtain risk information from the media and some media sources are highly trustworthy. However, different types of hazards are associated with very different types of risk reporting and the amount of coverage of a risk issue is rarely related to the seriousness of the risk. Traditional journalistic criteria to do with immediacy, human interest, vulnerable groups exposed, strong visual imagery, linkages with similar 'scary' issues and 'end-of-the-world' scenarios, the tendency to allocate blame rather than attempt to quantify available technical information, to imply secrecy, or conflict between experts tend to dictate the amount of coverage, *regardless of the seriousness of the hazard* (Fischhoff, 1984). Research also indicates that 'keynote' effects – such as headlines and images – which are often separate from independent or objective risk information, are more important in influencing the emotional style and, therefore, the risk perception of a hazard within a media report (Freudenberg *et al.*, 1996). Recent health scares treated in this way include phthalates, phytoestrogens in infant formula, antibiotic resistant bacteria, and dioxins and PCBs in breast milk.

Media coverage tends to play to emotional rather than technical criteria in risk reporting. Questions of *blame*, *fear* and *anger* which fuel public outrage outrank technical information about an existing or potential hazard.

Managers faced with the need to communicate around risk are justifiably frustrated by the fact that it is not only difficult to reproduce technical data about a hazard in newspapers, it rarely has any effect if any technical content actually gets printed. This is largely to do with the fact that journalists intentionally target their audiences by focusing on outrage rather than hazard.

And it follows that sensational, 'scary' content about risk is more common than reassuring content. For companies at the centre of wrestling with risk, it would be reasonable to assume that technical information would reassure us. At least we might feel that those responsible for managing the risk know what they are doing to contain it. This doesn't seem to be the case. Complicated language, the possibility – however slight – of scary consequences and a tendency to think the worst, plays more to increasing outrage than lessening it. Faced with the following 'balanced' news item, how would you feel as a consummate milk drinker?

"Scientists from a consortia of European universities have reported that a significant build up of dioxins and PCBs in milk poses a major human health risk.

Experts from the World Health Organization, however, have dismissed any possible risk as being extremely low."

Even if you believe the WHO response, you might pause to think before you poured milk over your cornflakes at breakfast. A neutral story can be alarming and, as a rule, opinion wins far more editorial space than data. Scary stories are more interesting than neutral or passive stories and motivate journalistic standards. While not all reporters are antigovernment or anti-business, many jealously protect their right to probe public officials and business executives 'in the public interest'. Ironically, business executives stereotype journalists more negatively than journalists stereotype them, acting defensively or being seen to be 'economical with the truth'. I think this is one of the main reasons why balance in the risk debate gets sidelined and provides a strong case for industry and government expert sources to dramatically improve their skills in communicating through the media.

Coca-Cola's failure to impress in Belgium and France

On 9 June 1999, 120 people in Belgium – 40 of them schoolchildren – became sick after drinking Coca-Cola products. A further 80 complained of similar symptoms – vomiting, dizziness and headaches – in France. The company launched an immediate investigation, which led to a partial withdrawal of some of its major brands including Coca-Cola, Coca-Cola Light, Fanta and Sprite. However, it took a further week for the company to establish that two separate contamination incidents had occurred. Defective carbon dioxide found in a small supply of bottles was discovered as the source at the Antwerp plant in Belgium, while at the Dunkirk plant in France, a fungicide sprayed onto wooden pallets was the culprit.

From the outset, Coca-Cola's Atlanta headquarters took responsibility for the response and for a week stated that bad odour was the cause and that there was no public health risk. Rather bland, technical statements were posted on the company's web site with no acknowledgement of responsibility or concern for the people affected. This was quickly seen to represent the arrogant, uncaring face of corporate America and triggered immediate public outrage. It was only when consumers stopped buying Coca-Cola and the Belgian and French authorities insisted on full product recalls that the company finally mobilized its chairman, Douglas Ivestor, for a visit to Europe and ran a costly advertising campaign apologizing to consumers. A major mistake by the company was its failure to have its reputation risk radar properly tuned and to empower local management to deal swiftly and sensitively with the situation. Atlanta was unaware that Belgium was trying to extricate itself from a major public health scandal caused by dioxin contamination of animal feeds that had affected supplies of pork, chicken and dairy produce – which resulted in bringing down the government and a bill of over $1.5 bn. In France, the government was sensitive in the aftermath of the BSE crisis in the UK and events in neighbouring Belgium.

> Coca-Cola's ponderously slow response to acknowledging public concern – even though events proved that there was no real public health risk – cost the company dearly. At the end of 1999, a 31 per cent drop in profits was announced; competitors took full advantage of using the empty shelf space presented by the recalls which cost the company $103 m; a major restructuring resulted in the loss of 5200 jobs in Europe; and Douglas Ivestor left. Media coverage for months after the incident referred to Coca-Cola as a company "struggling to rebuild itself".

Source: Regester and Larkin, 2002

The pill panic: a lesson in lack of planning and mixed messages

An example of how to generate widespread panic quite unnecessarily is illustrated by examining the handling of perceived health risk involving contraceptive pills in the UK in 1996 and 1997. The safety of contraceptive pills has been debated since they were first marketed in the 1960s. Over time, new formulations have been developed to try to remove potential negative health effects. Second generation pills, introduced in the 1970s, contained less synthetic progesterone than the first pills, but being chemically similar to the male hormone testosterone, caused side effects in some women, including nausea, headaches, irritability, acne, weight gain and water retention.

Third generation contraceptive pills, which contain a different form of synthetic progesterone, were introduced in the early 1990s to reduce these side effects. However, some studies indicated that third generation pills were more likely to cause thrombosis than second generation pills. The research found that second generation pills were associated with a lower incidence of thrombosis than previously thought, not that third generation pills posed an increased risk.

When the World Health Organization (WHO) issued findings in July 1995 that the second generation progestogen, levonorgestrel, was only half as likely to be associated with thromboembolism compared to third generation progestogens, desogestrel and gestodene, a new risk story hit the headlines. Sensational media coverage of the 'danger' associated with third generation pills spread across a number of European countries.

Smarting from accusations of a cover-up over BSE, the UK government was keen to be seen to be protecting public health and taking action, and accelerated a pan-European study on the subject, while the UK Committee on Safety of Medicines (CSM) conducted its own study using a national database of medical doctors. On the findings of these three unpublished studies, on 18 October 1995 the CSM faxed a letter to 190,000 doctors, pharmacists and directors of public health, alerting them that third generation pills could pose a higher risk of thrombosis. The CSM announced that the 1.5 m women in the UK taking third generation pills should be encouraged to use second generation pills or other forms of contraception.

At the same time as the CSM mail-out, a government press statement was issued *before* doctors had the chance to digest the results of the research. Although women were advised not to stop taking the pill until they sought medical advice from their doctor, the message conveyed in the media was one of increased health risk, compounded by the fact that the statement contained no tangible information on what the increased risk represented in terms of probability, patient susceptibility or numbers of women likely to be at risk.

Table 3.3 *Risks of non-fatal thromboembolism per 100,000 women per year*

Activity	Risk of death
Women not using oral contraceptives	5–11
All women using low dose combined oral contraceptives	30
Women using combined oral contraceptives containing desogestrel or gestodene	30
Women using combined oral contraceptives containing levonorgestrel or noresthisterone	15
Pregnant women and women post-partum	60

Note: As at 19 October 1995
Source: Mills A.A *et al.,* 1996

Furthermore, the manner in which information was conveyed to journalists – an emergency announcement at the end of a routine press briefing on another subject – emphasized its importance and urgency. The controversy filled newspaper pages for weeks.

Many doctors were angry that although they should have been alerted by the CSM, they heard the news from the media, as did their patients, some of whom stopped using their contraceptive pills immediately. Sales of third generation pills plummeted as an estimated 41 per cent of women stopped taking them. Figures from the Prescription Pricing Authority,

PACT, report showed that contraceptives containing desogestrel and gestodene, which had accounted for 55 per cent of usage and 70 per cent of cost in October 1995, had fallen to 12 per cent and 23 per cent respectively by June 1996.

The panic led to thousands of unplanned pregnancies, and was blamed for an additional 3000 abortions in the UK in the first quarter of 1996, a rise of 6.7 per cent. The British Pregnancy Advisory Service reported that 61 per cent of women requesting termination of pregnancy during this period claimed to have failed to finish their current course of oral contraceptives because of the scare. Maternity units around the country also reported higher than expected birth rates of up to 25 per cent.

Ann Furedi, director of the Birth Control Trust at the time, said: "Our research showed this was a needless panic. Other countries, having assessed the same data, concluded there was no need for immediate action. The action of the Committee on Safety of Medicines resulted in the misery of unwanted pregnancy for many women in the UK, and undermined the attempts of medical authorities in other countries to present a more objective assessment of the risks and benefits of the pill. We are not arguing that information should be held back from women – simply that it should be presented in an accurate, balanced way."

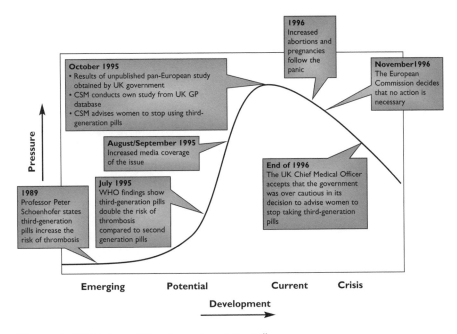

Figure 3.3 *Risk issue lifecycle: contraceptive pill scare*

Source: Regester Larkin

Analysis of the WHO data by the European drug safety and advisory committee in November 1996 concluded that no action was necessary other than informing women of the possible increased risk. The European Commission ruled that third-generation pills posed no higher risk to public health than other brands of oral contraceptives. As a result, only Germany and Norway followed the UK lead in advising women against taking the pills.

The actions of the UK government seriously undermined the actions of other national medicine control agencies who had chosen to interpret the new studies more cautiously. For example, in Cyprus, where the UK CSM announcement was widely reported in the press and discussed on television, it was claimed that around 10 per cent of the women who were on third generation pills stopped taking them (Ministry of Health, Nicosia, 1996). In the USA, there was less concern over third generation contraceptives as they were not used widely. However, the culture of litigation meant that many doctors were wary of prescribing them for fear of being sued.

The lesson that the Chief Medical Officer drew from this panic in his annual report (Department of Health, 1996) was that "there is an important distinction to be made between relative risk and absolute risk". A knee-jerk, reactive response to a real or perceived risk without a coherent process or strategy can cause more harm than good.

Managing for outrage potential

Each of us has a propensity to take risks. We do this consciously or subconsciously every day and the degree to which we take risks varies according to our individuality. Our tendency towards taking risks represents a balancing act between assessing the potential rewards of risk-taking *versus* our perceptions and experiences of associated losses.

As experience has been telling the agrochemical and bioscience industries, any new product or process needs to demonstrate some key criteria if public outrage, dread or stigma are to be avoided:

- It must offer consumers, not just producers, a tangible advantage
- The regulatory process for market acceptance must be rigorous and open
- Consumers must be able to make their own, informed decisions and be given choices

Because there are so many inconsistencies and vagaries attached to perceptions of risk, it is difficult to anticipate why some situations become major risk stories and others – often with much greater substance – don't. However, some of the points discussed here and, in particular, the drivers of outrage, including media amplification, should help reputation risk managers to prepare themselves for plotting a course in icy waters fraught with danger. When companies totally ignore the icebergs, however, by regarding their operations to be beyond accountability, then absolutely nothing can save a business from sinking, as Enron's navigation onto the rocks has demonstrated.

Arrogance, greed and dishonesty – no room to manoeuvre for Enron

Following the failure of a series of dubious accounting transactions, US energy giant, Enron, had to amend its profits for a number of years by hundreds of millions of dollars. This destroyed investor confidence causing a catastrophic drop in the company's share price and a downgrading of its debt rating. The result was immediate and spectacular bankruptcy. Enron employees, who had been encouraged to buy shares, could not sell and watched helplessly as their pensions were wiped out. Meanwhile, Enron executives were unloading the soon-to-be-worthless stock as fast as they could. Enron's accountants, Arthur Andersen, had approved the transactions that sealed the company's fate and were caught shredding volumes of Enron-related documents. The firm was indicted and clients jumped ship in droves. The ripple effect in the corporate world was, and continues to be, substantial. As the fateful story unfolded, a picture emerged of a corporation feeding on an arrogant free-market ideology underpinned by massive financial muscle. It appeared that Enron bankrolled and ingratiated itself with an enormous cadre of influencers and political decision-makers to support its push for deregulation in the sectors in which it operated, giving campaign contributions to nearly half the members of Congress. Enron CEO, Kenneth Lay, enjoyed a close personal relationship with US president, George W Bush, trading favours over many years and reaping benefits as soon as Bush entered the White House. Management guru, Gary Hamel, wrote enthusiastically about Enron's "genius for innovation" and its "capacity for revolution". Now, all the senior officers of the company feel able to do is to plead the fifth amendment.

A kick in the teeth for the beliefs and values of the new economy? It would seem so, and in spades. No transparency, accountability or caring culture here. As a result, this new corporate criminal has generated public outrage on a level

▶

normally reserved for the worst human atrocities. Fascination and fury over the devastating fall-out from the worst US corporate failure in history is reflected in opinion polling suggesting that more people followed the Enron scandal than the winter Olympics! Even though public confidence and trust in big business is higher in the United States than in other regions, perception of the extent of the greed and duplicity of Enron's management, compounded by subsequent failures at WorldCom, Xerox, Tyco and others, is likely to dent goodwill and feed public cynicism for years to come.

Source: Adapted from *The Nation*, 2002

For companies that create risks, the stakes for achieving public understanding, let alone acceptance, are high. And yet, risk communication is frighteningly *ad hoc*; it is often difficult to assess exactly what needs to be communicated and the extent to which messages have achieved their impact. Some stakeholders may simply want to hear from a trusted expert about what they should do; others may want detailed information in order to consider options, choices or to sort out their thinking. Choice is terribly important to many people. In the case of a new medical treatment, for example, information about costs, treatment process, likelihood of success, potential for complications such as adverse side effects, alternative treatments and the impact of doing nothing will influence personal value judgements and decision-making. The information provided could be based on statistical evidence and the experience of other patients. In other situations, for example, medical radiation waste or electromagnetic emissions, people may want to understand the science, how the potential risk is created and how it can be measured and controlled. In the adversarial climate of risk management, the reputation risk manager is faced with planning and developing risk communication strategies in the context of:

- Complex, confusing, inconsistent or incomplete messages
- Lack of trust in information sources
- Selective reporting by the media
- Recognizing compliance as a start point, not an end game
- Diverse psychological, social and economic factors that affect how information about risk is understood and processed

Managing and communicating about risk requires an understanding of a number of issues that combine to provide a framework for good practice, alongside some critical navigation marks.

> ### Risk communication navigation marks
>
> - First and foremost, acknowledge public concern and that a risk may exist; understand the emotional dynamics of risk perception and what makes a risk story
> - Establish an approach based on openness, listening, active communication and feedback
> - Recognize that it is better to own up to past or current mistakes and then move forward
> - Assess whether operational processes can be modified to improve risk management and operational performance — there's nothing like a wake-up call to prompt a critical look at the business
> - Find out what concerns people have; demonstrate commitment to respond and steps being taken to control, contain and reduce the risk
> - Work with trusted third parties and close the credibility gap
> - Understand outrage and that it is as important as hazard; it is real, measurable and manageable, so tune the radar and the risk perception wheel

Source: Adapted from Sandman, 1993

Step 1. Assess the type of risk

What stage in the risk management process has been reached and what type of risk has to be dealt with. Is the risk a potential issue, emerging more clearly, active and current, or maturing to the point that there is limited space to navigate an equitable course?

- *A routine risk situation* is quantifiable, the probabilities associated with related events are known and can be accurately assessed. There are few uncertainties. Communication is largely to do with reassurance that the risk is familiar, manageable and can be contained with confidence. Examples could be the use of food additives or the supervision of a manufacturing site.

- *Poorly defined risks* are less well known and contain uncertainties on potential impacts and outcomes. They require detailed and ongoing risk assessment and are susceptible to precautionary risk management policies. Examples include the possible effects of electromagnetic emissions from mobile phones and base stations or the long-term environmental consequences of genetically modified plants. Risk managers and communicators need to demonstrate neutrality to the science; the competency and openness of risk assessment and management processes; and be proactive in information sharing and stakeholder partnering.

- *Risks with high potential controversy* are likely to trigger strong emotional responses and the potential for significant public outrage. Typically, the experts do not agree on causal mechanisms or likelihood of effects, fuelling often sensational media debate and direct action, and pressurizing regulators to introduce more stringent, precautionary guidelines. BSE, endocrine disrupting chemicals, and the handling of Foot and Mouth disease are examples. Communicating in this environment requires acknowledgement that there is a risk, a process for quantification and mitigation, and the resources to elicit people's values and beliefs in relation to the hazard with detailed, tailored feedback and discussion processes.

- *Crisis* situations mean being firmly stuck between an iceberg and a hard place! Time constraints are enormous, options are limited and regulatory and legal liability loom large. This is precisely why a finely tuned radar is so critical in helping to detect the smaller ice flows before they build in size and momentum. It is also why it is so import-ant to have in place clear and robust management systems that integrate with routine risk management procedures. Demonstrating absolute transparency by describing what is being done to reduce, contain and prevent further risk is the only way that organizations at the centre of the crisis vortex can hope to re-establish their credentials.

Source: Adapted from Renn, *et al.*, 2002

Step 2. Carry out a detailed gap analysis

Assess the potential or emerging risk against the criteria described in the risk perception wheel. If the risk scores high in terms of potential outrage factors, it is likely that it is poorly defined and/or has high potential for controversy. Review experience from similar risks, if available. For example, international experience over public concerns about the health effects of electromagnetic frequency emissions from power lines has helped to inform the mobile telecommunications industry's responses regarding EMF emissions from mobile phones and base stations. And food scares abound, although identifying good practice is a depressing experience! In assisting strategy development and planning, profiling stakeholder concerns and attitudes ahead of programme implementation can help both to shape consultation approaches and communication materials as well as provide a benchmark for ongoing evaluation.

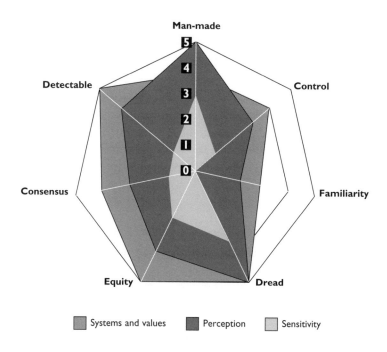

Figure 3.4 *Sensitivity gap profile*

Source: Adapted from Slovic, 1987

Consider the robustness of the company's risk management systems and business principles in controlling and reducing potential impact, and preliminary core messages in response to the criteria identified in the model; then conduct stakeholder opinion polling to gauge perceptions of the risk and classify against the criteria. The sensitivity profile will indicate where the smallest gaps exist between the company's current position and the perceptions and expectations of stakeholders, indicating reasonable compatibility and a good baseline for planning purposes. The widest gaps indicate the potential for disconnection between attitudes and behaviour, providing markers for focusing strategies and communication emphasis.

Step 3. Undertake a risk assessment and choose risk measures

Managers involved in risk communication must know enough to acknowledge valid criticisms and to determine whether available estimates of risk are sufficiently credible for stakeholders to develop a perspective on the potential dangers they may face and the decisions that need to be made. Some environmental health hazards, such as asbestos and radiation, are fairly well understood and for other hazards risk estimates are made on precautionary criteria. Although uncertainty is a fact of life, it is reasonable to believe that the 'true risk' is likely to exceed estimates resulting from such conservative processes. Uncertainty and subjectivity don't imply chaos! (Slovic, 2000). Defining the hazard type, deciding what consequences to measure, and determining the criteria for observation are an essential part of the assessment and planning process. In this context it can help to anticipate the types of questions that journalists may consider in verifying whether they have a good risk story.

Questioning risk analyses

Does the risk analysis:

- State the probability of potential harm and the degree of harm expected?
- Clearly explain to what extent it is based on assumptions and guesswork as opposed to an established evidence base?
- Describe uncertainties in the data and/or various interpretations of the data?
- Identify numbers of people predicted to suffer adverse effects?
- Explain the confidence limits for its projections and the method of arriving at those confidence limits?
- Include individual sensitivities, exposure to multiple hazards and cumulative effects?
- Consider questions of (a) involuntary exposure, (b) equity, and (c) alternatives to the hazardous activity?
- Respond to anticipated public concerns, values and beliefs?
- Facilitate public scrutiny?
- Indicate independent verification?

Source: Adapted from Fischhoff, 1985 and Slovic, 2000

Step 4. Design a risk communication strategy

Using outcomes from the earlier stages, some key marks for strategy development include the need to:

- Identify the costs and resources likely to be required and prepare a case to justify the overhead to senior management

- Ensure senior management buy-in from the outset and create an internal communication process that can deliver consistency of information and message across the organization

- Be clear about your own position – your commitment and your principles in delivering an outcome that you can live with and which provides a potentially credible solution

- Through research conducted under Stage 2, try and find a common theme to focus the risk communication on and, whatever else, understand the social and emotional context around which people are likely to assess and judge the risk. For example, if it's a routine risk situation (see above) public concerns may be neutralized by the provision of independently verified factual information. If the risk is poorly defined or subject to significant potential controversy, develop a wider range of information supported by and communicated through third parties who may have a chance of being trusted or, at least, given the benefit of the doubt

- Allow time to plan and rehearse against different role-play scenarios; public consultation processes are complex so don't steer ahead towards any icy blockage without reviewing all routes first

- Invest in some form of qualitative evaluation process that helps to assess, fine-tune and redirect the radar where necessary. Importantly, evaluation of effective risk communication programmes provides measures of progress, delivery and potential offset against larger-scale regulatory, insurance and legal liability cost burdens.

Step 5. Message development

Keep communication clear, consistent and credible. In an emergency or crisis situation, my essential markers are to express *concern* over what has happened, *commitment* to fix the current problem, and *control* in demonstrating that the company is involved at the highest level to assess the risk impact and to put in place safeguards to reduce the potential for future risk. The *three C's* provide an essential guide when all else fails. It is common sense and about being human! In preparing for stakeholder communication around an evolving risk issue, remember to:

- Treat stakeholders intelligently – understand who they are, what they think and what they want
- Keep messages simple, especially around technical information
- Tell the whole story and don't shy away from uncertainty
- Tailor information and contact processes against different needs
- Explain the decision-making process, the business principles and values used
- Relate risk to real-life situations and place it in a social and emotional context
- Try and avoid risk comparisons unless they are clearly seen as being comparable
- Distinguish risk from hazard by describing the relationship between exposure, dose and risk
- Emphasize the potential benefits of regulatory processes designed to take serious risk into account
- Provide choices where possible
- Be thorough and cover off all bases with quality information

Step 6. Involving consumers

Greater public participation in regulatory processes is now recognized as an essential step towards improving the quality of debate on risk. Successful delivery is complex and difficult to measure, but trying to build some form of structure and process for participation does facilitate an environment for more constructive dialogue. Emerging initiatives include:

- Appointment of consumer representatives on decision-making bodies such as expert advisory committees
- Public meetings
- Referenda
- Deliberative polling where a representative group of people are invited to listen to a debate on an issue before voting on it

- Citizens' juries, pioneered in Germany and the USA, where a group hear evidence on an issue before reaching a verdict
- Consensus conferences which are larger scale citizens' juries
- Internet forums

Citizens' juries are becoming more common as a mechanism to address a wide range of policy issues on healthcare, local planning, hazardous waste management, bioscience applications, nuclear energy, and privacy. A group of between 12 and 16 'representative' citizens, identified through social research techniques, are brought together over the course of few days with the objective of addressing one or more specific questions. Extensive written and oral background information is provided, and they can cross-examine a range of 'witnesses'. The issue is then discussed in detail, in sub-groups through plenary sessions with facilitation support. While a verdict is not necessarily the required outcome, their views and conclusions are recorded for delivery to the commissioning organization but only when the jury members have approved the report (McKechnie and Davies, 1999).

Australia and New Zealand are leading proponents of public consultation and participation in public policy decision-making. Whereas in some European countries regulators are based in government departments and their expert committees on environmental health and safety issues are constituted to report to government ministers, in Australia all regulatory bodies are independent and make their advice public without reference to ministers. In New Zealand, there is a statutory obligation to consult on any new public health policy.

Public participation is going to have a much greater role to play. The time and resources involved make it important for reputation risk managers to trial and refine the most appropriate models for dealing with different types of risk issues, and make it part of a coherent strategy. While there is limited evidence on systematic evaluation of different models, there is enough to support the two-way communication process of public involvement as a deterrent against icebergs!

Step 7. Don't forget evaluation

Risk communication strategies deal with important issues of public health and safety. They also deal with relationships and the existence of trust, so anecdotal information isn't enough. In order to help achieve objectives, research and evaluation are essential elements of the navigation plan as a means to:

- Demonstrate accountability and cost justification
- Identify whether and why strategies are working
- Provide an empirical basis for planning, the need to change course or fine-tune
- Support learning and improvement

Judgements about risk are frequently influenced by memories of past events and our imagination of future events. Any factor that makes a hazard unusual, memorable and visual to the imagination has the capacity to seriously distort perceptions of risk. Media coverage of hazards is biased in the same way. Recent vivid disasters such as the 11 September terrorist attacks on America and the following anthrax scare made the threat of global terrorism and biological warfare more imminent in our consciousness, and more concerning than serious health hazards such as heart disease, asthma and stroke. Because perceptions of risk are often inaccurate, reputation risk managers need to make the case for active and ongoing stakeholder engagement as well as public information and education programmes in the face of emerging risk issues. This is not a straightforward course to navigate. Risk information can confuse and further alarm people, merely by mentioning possible adverse consequences. If people trust the ability of the reputation risk manager and independent third parties to handle the broad operational implications of a risk, they may be less likely to react in ways that trigger outrage. Open communication that is not constrained by prejudice or bias and which is integrated as part of a cohesive risk management strategy has a remarkably good chance of success.

Resource list

Websites

Adam Smith Institute   www.adamsmith.org.uk

British Bankers Association   www.bba.org.uk

Articles and reports

Bernstein, P.L., 'Against the Gods: The Remarkable Story of Risk', John Wiley & Sons Inc., 1996

Fischhoff, B., 'Protocols for Environmental Reporting: What to ask the Experts', *The Journalist*, 1985

Fischhoff, B., 'Risk Perception and Communication Unplugged: Twenty Years of Progress', *Risk Analysis*, 15, 1995

Fischhoff, B., Watson, S. and Hope, C. 'Defining Risk', *Policy Sciences*, 17, 1984

Furedi, A. and Furedi, F., 'The International Consequences of a Pill Panic in the UK', Birth Control Trust, London, 1996

Lichtenstein, S., Slovic, P., Fischhoff, B., Layman, M. and Combs, B., 'Judged Frequency of Lethal Events', *Journal of Experimental Psychology: Human Learning and Memory*, 4, 1978

McKechnie, S. and Davies, S., 'Consumers and Risk', in Bennett, P. and Calman, K. (eds), *Risk Communication and Public Health*, Oxford University Press, 1999

Mills, A.A. *et al.*, 'Guidelines for Prescribing Combined Oral Contraceptives', *British Medical Journal*, 312:121, 1996

O'Neill, O., 'Spreading Suspicion', BBC Reith Lectures 2002 – A Question of Trust

Renn, Kastenholz, Leiss and Lofstead, *Draft OECD Guidance Document on Risk Comunication for Chemical Risk Management*, 2002

Sandman, P.M., *Responding to Community Outrage: Strategies for Effective Risk Communication*, American Industrial Hygiene Association, 1993

Sandman, P.M., Weinstein, N.D. and Hallman, W.K., 'Communications to Reduce Risk Underestimation and Overestimation', *Risk Decision and Policy*, 3 (2), 1998

Slovic, P., 'Perception of Risk', *Science*, 236, 1987

Tversky, A. and Kahnemann, D., 'Judgement Under Uncertainty: Heuristics and Biases', *Science* 185, 1974

Wilson, R., 'Analyzing the Risks of Daily Life', *Technology Review*, 81, 1979

Books

Adams, J., *Risky Business: The Management of Risk and Uncertainty*, Adam Smith Institute, London, 1999

Bennett, P. and Calman, K. (eds), *Risk Communication and Public Health*, Oxford University Press, Oxford, 1999

Covello, V., Sandman, P. and Slovic, P., *Risk Communication, Risk Statistics and Risk Comparisons: A Manual for Plant Managers*, Chemical Manufacturers Association, Washington, 1988

Fischhoff, B., Lichtenstein. S., Slovic, P., Derby, S.L. and Keeney, R.L. *Acceptable Risk*, Cambridge University Press, New York, 1981

Morgan, M.G. and Hennon, M., *Uncertainty*, Cambridge University, New York, 1990

Powell, D. and Leiss, W. (eds), *Mad Cows and Mothers Milk: The Perils of Poor Risk Communication*, McGill-Queen's University Press, Montreal, 1997

Regester, M. and Larkin, J., *Risk Issues and Crisis Management*, Kogan Page, 1997

Slovic, P., *The Perception of Risk*, Earthscan, London, 2000

Wildavsky, A., *Seaching for Safety*, Transaction Publishers, 1988

CHAPTER 4

The consumer awakes

"Global brand name recognition has an Achilles' heel of vulnerability. The better known a brand name is, the more vulnerable it is. The consumer movement is just beginning to use Internet technology to exchange information around the world – about everything from product recalls to safety complaints"

RALPH NADER

When the French farmer and anti-globalization activist, José Bové, was put on trial in 2000 for ramming his tractor into a McDonald's the general response was largely one of humour and ambivalence. While the case was difficult for the hamburger company, it managed the situation relatively well. However, McDonald's suffered a public relations disaster in the 1990s when it took a couple of penniless British vegetarians to court in its McLibel case. Campaigners from several hundred NGOs launched an international day of action against Exxon in July 2001 to highlight the oil company's stance on issues ranging from climate change to human rights. Protesters targeted offices and petrol stations around the world and placed advertisements in national newspapers featuring a photograph of US president George W Bush with the headline 'Esso ate my brain'.

The backlash against globalization and the rise of NGOs are now facts of life for business. The Exxon campaign was one in a long series of clashes between NGOs and business. Activists have confronted companies on issues ranging from Nestlé's marketing of baby milk in developing countries in the 1970s to Monsanto's championing of genetically modified food, ABB's and Balfour Beatty's controversial dam construction project in Turkey, and Nike's poor labour conditions in overseas factories in the late 1990s.

Companies have to face the fact that activist groups have moved on from banner-waving at annual general meetings to putting their institutional shareholders in the critical frame. As a basic minimum, businesses need to be better prepared to deal with NGO and consumer campaigning. The argument about whether Shell, as the largest oil company operating in Nigeria, could have prevented the country's government from executing Ken Saro-Wiwa, an environmentalist and poet, is a complicated one. What is difficult to challenge is whether it should have tried harder to save him. But I believe reactive preparation isn't enough. The relationship is now much more complex than the acrimonious protests imply and we are seeing the emergence of strategic alliances between business and NGOs. The reasons behind this are that:

- Consumers are more sophisticated, opinionated and hungry for information about the companies behind the brands. Importantly, consumers in affluent societies are recognizing they have a potential power base around which they can make their opinions, expectations and aspirations heard. They are becoming increasingly street-wise in the use of tactics that can be amplified by the media and reacted to – all too quickly – by policymakers and regulators.

- NGOs are increasingly professional in their operations – the woolly headed, bean-eating, sandal-wearing activist of the 1960s and 1970s has been replaced by the articulate, well-presented and well-qualified fund raiser and campaign manager. Larger projects need bigger budgets so project and financial management skills are essential.

- The new face of 'citizen activism' empowers anyone to launch a campaign. New technologies enable small groups of protesters to make their message heard through the use of simple, accessible tools such as the news story, the e-mail, the legal claim and the stunt. Protests against road-building, the World Trade Organization and high taxes on fuel in Europe have been the work of informal groups.

- Technology, in the shape of the Internet and mobile telecommunications, not only helps organize, it also helps to inform. As part of its 'Stop Torture' campaign, the human rights NGO, Amnesty International, provides notices of urgent cases to subscribers' mobile phones using SMS text messages.

- There is a desire to move beyond mere protest and problem identification towards solution-focused advocacy, influenced by a gradual recognition that government can no longer be the main provider of solutions, and that business is becoming the power base of the future.

- Companies are recognizing that environmental and social issues can provide commercial benefits, ranging from differentiating products to cutting costs. Environmental performance is increasingly seen as a competitive and strategic issue for companies. Furthermore, relationships with NGOs contribute to a company's radar system through early warning of potentially damaging risk issues.

- In Europe, NGOs are regarded by the public as far more trustworthy than business on environmental health and social issues. Effective working relationships between NGOs and businesses can support credibility and bolster reputation. There is a health warning here, however, because short-term tactical approaches to offset an imminent risk can back-fire and create accusations of 'greenwashing'.

This chapter examines the rise of consumerism and direct action, the influence of the Internet in information dissemination and developments in campaigning. Businesses have a choice in response: to anticipate the potential for campaign platforms, head them off by communicating openly and accountably and, where appropriate, working with NGOs to find solutions; or fight against them and face the consequences of huge costs and damage to reputation. I'll examine:

- The rise in consumerism and NGO activism
- The heritage of environmentalism and the new social agenda
- The Internet as a key facilitator for direct action
- Campaign tactics and the shift towards engagement and partnering
- How to plan for and manage single-issue campaigns

Affluence, angst and action – the rise of the socially conscious consumer

As business is becoming the main target for evidence of 'responsible behaviour', through greater transparency, open governance *and* leadership in sustainable development, consumers are becoming the most vocal task-masters. Now, the active consumer:

- Demands and exercises personal choice
- Responds to single issue politics
- Is more likely to question the value of new developments, and
- Regards environmental issues as important

The active consumer is also uneasy about corporate power. In a *Business Week* survey, nearly three-quarters of Americans felt business has gained too much power in recent years (*Business Week*, 14 September 2000) and that figure may well have risen further. Because with the failures of Enron and WorldCom in the first half of 2002, it isn't just investor confidence in corporate America that is collapsing. A growing sense of corporate wrong-doing in the world's largest economy is illustrated by opinion polling that shows popular resentment at the fact that millions of Americans have seen their savings shrink, as the hype propagated by corporations and Wall Street has given way to financial reality. Similar research reports that 60 per cent of voters sampled thought 'the administration always seems to do what the big corporations want' (*Financial Times*, 1 May 2002).

Few issues excite the Americans more than environmental causes, who pour as much as $3 bn into them every year, particularly through contributions to mainstream groups such as the Environmental Defense Fund, Greenpeace USA, the National Wildlife Federation, the Nature Conservancy and the Sierra Club. The active consumer not only has greater affluence, access to mountains of information and with increased longevity, thinks longer-term, but also – certainly in Europe – looks to NGOs to drive the CSR agenda and places more trust in the legitimacy of what they say than in business, government or the media.

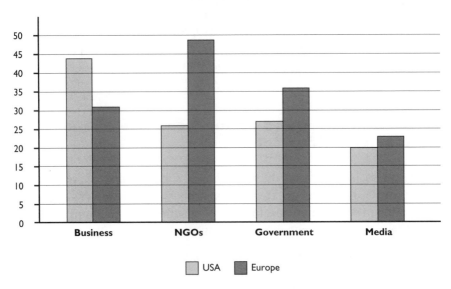

Figure 4.1 *Who do the public trust to do the right thing?*
Source: Edelman PR, 2000

In comparison with equivalent data from the United States, where consumer activism started much earlier than in Europe and where business is reluctantly seen to dominate the economic and social agenda, NGOs in Europe are masterminding increasingly sophisticated campaigns. Their own research reinforces the view that social as well as environmental responsibility is a key issue for the public.

According to Peter Melchett, former Executive Director of Greenpeace UK, "The vast majority of people are not anti-science, nor are they Luddite. But people are increasingly aware, and mistrustful, of the combination of big science and big business." He continued, "people scorn patronizing assumptions based on the premise that they don't know what is good for them. On the contrary, people insist that it is their society and their world, and they will decide what is acceptable, and what is not."

Table 4.1 Some of the issues that concern active consumers

Marketplace	Workplace
• Impact on society of core products and services • Issues around buying and selling • Supply chain management • Vulnerable customers • Cause-related marketing	• Workforce diversity • Work-life balance • Health and safety • Human rights • Training and lifelong learning
Environment	Community
• Emissions to air, land and water • Use of natural resources • Environmental risk • Transport impacts • Impact on environment of core products and services	• Impact on local operations on the community • Business investment in the community

Source: *Impact Indicators*, Business in the Community, 2000

Effective consumer campaigns have contributed to a rise in popular sensitivity to a range of environmental and social issues and a plea for restraint in corporate activities. This has been accelerated by the Internet which, says management guru Gary Hamel, has "spawned a Cambrian explosion of new competitive life forms" generating a pace of change which will mean that "every company that was 'built to last' must now be 'rebuilt to change'". New technologies like the telegraph, railroad, the telephone, the car, the airplane and now the Internet "allow ideas to circulate, combine, and recombine in ways never before possible" (Hamel, 2000). This 'recombination' process is being articulated through consumer and environmental groups, demands for alternative or 'sustainable' production and practices. Global companies are the main targets of these demands because of their visibility and their perceived ability to shape economies and politics for their own ends.

In our newly transparent, Internet-driven world, businesses have no place to hide, no time to think and no second chances!

The new non-governmental order

Charities, consumer groups and other NGOs are building enormous influence.

Direct action campaigns clearly pose threats to reputation risk. Protestors at the WTO and G8 meetings in Seattle, Washington DC, The Hague, Prague, Genoa and Barcelona, expressed concern about growth of big corporations, environmental degradation and the widening global gap between the 'haves' and 'have-nots'. They also criticized the IMF, the World Bank and WTO as three undemocratic institutions whose policies deprive people of food and water, and thus start wars.

NGOs with operations in more than one country are estimated by the Yearbook of International Organizations to number over 26,000, up from 6000 in 1990. The bi-monthly magazine of the World Watch Institute suggested that the USA has about 2 m NGOs, 70 per cent of which are less than 30 years old. India has about 1 m grass-roots groups, while another estimate suggests that more than 100,000 groups emerged in Eastern Europe between 1988 and 1995. The environmental groups continue to lead in membership growth. The World Wide Fund for Nature (WWF) has around 5 m members, up from 570,000 in 1985, generating an income of $32 m, while The Sierra Club has over 570,000 members, up from 180,000 in 1980 and generating an income of $50 m. Greenpeace has about 2.5 m contributors, generating an income of $130 m. Amnesty International, which campaigns to support fair treatment of political prisoners, has over 1 m members and subscribers in over 140 countries, and an annual budget of around $30 m. Some of the biggest NGOs are primarily aid providers, such as CARE and Médecins Sans Frontières. Oxfam is both an aid provider and effective campaigner as its involvement demonstrated in the failed legal action brought by pharmaceutical companies in South Africa in 2001 to protect pricing structures for AIDS drugs.

Post September 11, the global economic justice agenda championed by these groups is once again gaining momentum. Companies are seeking their advice on strategies for environmental, social and supply chain management. WWF, for example, has worked with industry to establish the Forest Stewardship Council and Marine Stewardship Council.

Even Greenpeace, amongst the most aggressive of campaigners, is collaborating more with business. It cultivates industry outsiders that could be potential allies, encourages them to adopt environmentally friendly technology, and then targets its members to place orders. This approach led to the launch of chlorine-free paper and Greenfreeze, a CFC-free refrigerant. The group also developed smILE, a fuel-efficient prototype car based on a Renault Twingo and designed to demonstrate that a 50 per cent reduction in carbon dioxide emissions from cars is feasible. Greenpeace has established a unit to find technical solutions to environmental problems and believes that it can bring technology to the market which would not otherwise happen. Marketing pressure is a key driver for the organization's campaigns, together with a streamlining of tactics based on research, the use of the media and the law, and targeted lobbying.

While environmentalism has been alive and well since the 1960s, the watershed was the Earth Summit in Rio de Janeiro in 1992, when NGOs generated sufficient public pressure to push through agreements on controlling greenhouse gases. In 1994, protesters dominated the World Bank's anniversary meeting with a 'Fifty Years is Enough' campaign and forced a rethink of the Bank's goals and methods. More recently, the Bank's boss, James Wolfensohn, made 'dialogue' with NGOs a central component of the institution's work.

In 1998, a loose coalition of nearly 600 consumer groups and environmentalists saw off the Multilateral Agreement on Investment (MAI), which aimed to establish a liberalized framework for international investment under the auspices of the OECD. Incidentally, the collapse of these talks was attributed to the groups' use of the Internet to publicize their belief that the agreement would undermine national environmental regulations. These criticisms and responses to the negotiations were constantly updated and sent around the world at the touch of a button. Since 2000, another global coalition, Jubilee 2000, used the Internet and the media to push successfully for a dramatic reduction in the debts of the poorest countries.

So the early environmental agenda has shifted to include a range of new economic and social issues. Banning landmines has been one of the most successful campaigns of the last ten years, spear-headed by several hundred NGOs and the Canadian government. Curbing bribery and corruption are seen by many corporate observers to be new benchmarks for responsible business across international markets, spear-headed by NGO, Transparency International, headquartered in Berlin.

NGOs or citizen's groups as they are also called, have become

IKEA partnering with Greenpeace

IKEA is the largest furniture retailer in the world, with 143 stores in 22 countries and an annual turnover of $8 bn. IKEA is a good example of a company that has worked to partner with NGOs as an integral part of its business strategy, seizing competitive advantage in the furniture retail market. IKEA adopted a systematic approach to environmental issues in 1991, following criticism of practices which included:

- In the mid 1980s, being sued by the Danish government for violating a law regulating the maximum emissions of formaldehyde
- Being the target of NGOs in Germany who protested against the use of chlorine in the bleaching of the pulp for the IKEA catalogue and objected to the number of trees felled to make the catalogue
- Being a recipient of Greenpeace's vocal campaign against furniture retailers and loggers who use wood from ancient forests

In an attempt to remedy the environmental issues it faced, IKEA contacted Greenpeace to develop a partnership approach to improving its environmental performance. As a result:

- IKEA has an international group network of environmental co-ordinators
- The IKEA catalogue is printed on Totally Chlorine Free (TCF) paper
- PVC is being phased out of all products
- The use of formaldehyde and aromatic solvents in laquers is banned
- Approximately 75 per cent of an average store's waste is re-used, recycled or used for energy production
- All purchases of furniture are made using wood from intact natural forests, or wood certified by the Forest Stewardship Council (FSC)

IKEA has received international praise for its practices. When the company announced the introduction of stricter regulations in the use of tropical wood in November 1999, Greenpeace forests campaigner, Christoph Thies, said:

"IKEA is joining the movement of responsible corporate consumers concerned about ancient forests, and Greenpeace looks forward to working with IKEA around the world to implement the new policy and to identify good forestry operations that IKEA suppliers can purchase from."

As revenues have grown steadily and more than 168 m people visit IKEA stores every year, the company believes its approach to environmental management has contributed to customer loyalty.

WWF and Lafarge

The French construction company Lafarge became a conservation partner of WWF in 2000. WWF is helping Lafarge to develop a strategy for biodiversity to integrate into its international quarry rehabilitation programme. In turn, Lafarge is providing financial support to WWF's 'Forests Reborn' project which aims to increase forest cover around the world, and is also helping the construction industry to become aware of the importance of protecting biodiversity.

Conservation International and Aveda

A partnership between Conservation International and the beauty products manufacturer, Aveda, led to the company using a by-product of the Brazil nut, Morikue, in six of its hair products. This strengthened existing local Brazil nut businesses in Peru by providing added value to nut processing. Aveda also supports training activities for Brazil nut collectors in the area and in the spring of 2001, part financed and participated in CI's Enterprise Development Workshop programme.

---

increasingly sophisticated and powerful in targeting government and business at local, national and international level. Under greater scrutiny and with expectations of more open governance and accountability, businesses are being pressured from many different quarters to respond to a culture of growing individuality and assertiveness, where every opinion is perceived to matter.

Campaign tactics are varied, often well managed and increasingly co-ordinated through Internet and mobile communication technologies. The boycott is one of the oldest and most effective – a threat that can haunt any company today that fails to consider the ethical as well as environmental consequences of its commercial activities. These have ranged from student boycotts of Barclays Bank in the apartheid South Africa of the 1980s, through boycotting Exxon products over the Valdez spill in Alaska in 1989 and Shell gas stations over Brent Spar and its interests in Ongoliland in 1995; PepsiCo in Myanmar through the mid 1990s, and clothing manufacturers such as Levi Strauss, Nike, Gap and Marks & Spencer over employment practices in developing countries.

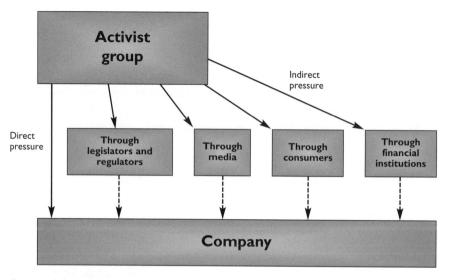

Figure 4.2 *Pressure points*
Source: Adapted from Winter and Steger, 1998

One of the longest running boycotts has been against Nestlé. Baby Milk Action has been waging a record 25-year long war against the company over the way it has marketed infant formula products, which it claims contravene the World Health Organization's (WHO) code. In the 1970s, when the company was accused of selling infant formula in developing countries at prices that could not be afforded and where clean water was virtually non-existent, the company decided to ignore allegations of irresponsible behaviour and greed. Baby Milk Action became a powerful, critical force against Nestlé, generating negative media coverage and succeeding in targeting the company where it hurt – for example, through campaigning for boycotts of its market-leading Nescafé coffee brand. Nestlé suffered significant reputational and commercial damage by refusing to debate the issues in public. By the time the company woke up to the need to build bridges with campaigners and other stakeholders, disaster had well and truly struck. No amount of resource or attempts to align with the WHO through the development of a health code for infant feeding and nutrition made a difference. Furthermore, the student leaders and activists of the 1970s have become the media and social commentators and business people of today, consolidating the polarization of opinion.

One of the most successful boycotts of all time targeted the tuna fishing industry in Central and North America. When the public was informed in the early 1990s that more than 50,000 dolphins were

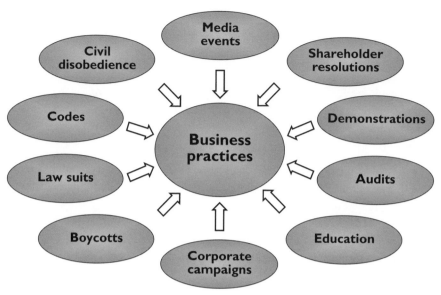

Figure 4.3 *NGO tactics*
Source: Regester Larkin

accidently killed each year in tuna nets, public outrage in the United States was immediate. Animal welfare groups used advertisements in America with headlines like: 'Kill a dolphin today – all you need is a tuna can and a can opener'. US teenagers took up the campaign and soon their parents were responding in the supermarkets. Any canned tuna that was not clearly labelled as being caught with 'dolphin friendly' nets was boycotted. Star-Kist, the subsidiary of Heinz, and other major tuna marketers switched to 'dolphin-free' fishing methods and market share rose dramatically. This became one of the most popular labelling programmes ever, but it resulted in the loss of 30,000 jobs in the Mexican fishing industry and a financial hit to the Mexican economy of well over $500 m. More recently, the drinks company, Bacardi, has become a boycott target. Bacardi was once manufactured in Cuba but the company relocated to the Bahamas when Fidel Castro came to power. Rock Around the Blockade campaigners argue that Bacardi has played a major role with the US administration in maintaining the island's isolation through restricting inward investment.

Boycotts in Action lists companies around the world being boycotted, identifies who is boycotting them, and why. Some examples are shown in Table 4.2 on page 136.

Boise Cascade – out of step confrontation on logging

Boise Cascade is the fourth largest logging company in the United States. The environmental NGO, Rainforest Action Network (RAN), has waged a lengthy campaign against Boise Cascade, calling the company the 'dinosaur of the logging industry' for continuing to cut trees in old-growth forests while its competitors adopt a more environmentally friendly approach. RAN is calling on Boise Cascade to:

- Phase out logging and selling of all wood products from old growth forests
- Terminate all logging and selling of wood products from public lands in the United States
- Commit to no further conversion of native forests to plantations
- Cease development and planting of genetically modified trees
- Adopt logging standards that meet or exceed those of the Forest Stewardship Council

The campaign has been supported by Greenpeace USA, Alliance for Democracy, the Center for Environmental Health and the Chicago Religious Leadership Center, and has generated a lot of publicity. This is partly due to Boise Cascade's poor response to the campaign, and partly due to RAN's tactics. One tactic that RAN has used throughout the campaign is media savvy publicity stunts; when the campaign was launched in October 2000, RAN floated a 120-foot hot air balloon shaped as a dinosaur and bearing a sign reading 'Boise Cascade: I love logging old-growth' over the company's headquarters. RAN has also used the Internet to put pressure on Boise Cascade. The organization encourages Boise Cascade's customers to express their opposition to destructive logging, and the RAN website enables them to send e-mails direct to the company.

Instead of meeting with RAN to try and establish a way forward on the logging issue, Boise Cascade adopted a more confrontational approach. In July 2001, the company aligned RAN with terrorist groups by holding a forum on 'Eco-Terrorism and Extremism' in Washington DC. Boise Cascade also attacked the 501(3) non-profit status of organizations that participate in non-violent civil disobedience in an attempt to silence RAN. Boise Cascade tried to get the Internal Revenue Service (IRS) to cancel RAN's tax exempt status and pressured its funders to cut off the group's money. In the past, the IRS has drawn the line at tax exempt nonprofits engaging in legislative activity, but RAN was not trying to change laws – only corporate behaviour – so the action by Boise Cascade was unsuccessful. However, Boise Cascade's backlash was treated critically by the US media and the company's popularity continued to wane while protests increased. For example, on 20 December 2001, students and environmentalists from across Illinois joined Santa Claus at Boise Cascade Office Products' Itasca headquarters to deliver thousands of letters from children begging the logging company to 'Stop Destroying Old Growth Forests'.

The reputation of the company took another knock when it was the lead plaintiff in a successful lawsuit to prevent the implementation of the US Roadless Area Conservation policy. The initiative would have prevented commercial logging and road building in 58.5 m acres of undeveloped wilderness. The roadless policy was the most popular federal policymaking decision in US history – more than 1.5 m Americans submitted comments expressing support for the measure. It was alleged that after this incident Boise Cascade lost a contract with Kinko's, the world's largest copy centre chain, because their position on old-growth forests did not comply with Kinko's environmental position. In March 2002, Boise Cascade agreed to phase out its practice of logging US old growth forests over the next two years although CEO George Harad denied that the decision to phase out old-growth logging was due to pressure from environmentalists. While RAN welcomed the move, the campaign against Boise Cascade has not ended as the organization believes the company continues to log endangered forests in Indonesia, Chile, Canada and Southeast Asia.

The big question is whether these groups are becoming the driver for a new international civil society or representative of a worrying shift in power to the unelected and unaccountable.

"Luddites, extremists and the leftover left; unaccountable interest groups that undermine the authority of elected officials; armchair radicals from the rich world who have no right to speak for the developing-world poor ... it would be wrong for NGOs to dismiss these claims as ill-informed and self-serving. NGOs must build their legitimacy by pushing through much needed reforms in their own community"

Source: Michael Edwardes, Ford Foundation

Legitimacy must be at the centre of effective NGO campaigning; without it NGOs are left stranded without a course to steer. Citizens' groups have the right to a voice but, in my view, they need to demonstrate

Table 4.2 Boycotts

The company being boycotted	The organization leading the boycott	Alleged reason for the boycott
Adidas – shoes	International Wildlife Coalition	Uses skins of threatened Australian kangaroos for shoe leather
American Home Products	Action for Corporate Responsibility	Unethical marketing practices to sell infant formula in developing countries
China – any products	International Campaign for Tibet and Tibetan Rights Campaign	Boycotting all products from China to protest ongoing human rights abuses
Wal-Mart	Save a Country – Boycott Wal-Mart	Engagement in unfair labour practices, exploitation of third-world labour, environmental destruction and destruction of local economies
Texaco	Rainforest Action Network	Environmental destruction after ending operations in Ecuador
Phillip Morris/ RJR Nabisco	INFACT	Through their advertising campaigns, they encourage under-age smoking
Procter & Gamble	In Defense of Animals	Conducts unnecessary animal testing
Shell	FoE/Rainforest Action Network	Involvement in Nigeria contributes to repressive political situation and environmental destruction
Levi-Strauss	Fuerza Unida	Inadequate worker compensation following relocation to Costa Rica

greater transparency and accountability themselves, and more commitment to the facts as opposed to fashion and sensation.

Some activist groups are increasingly anxious to play an active role in shaping legislation, regulation and international treaties. They recognize the power of the law and use judicial review and tort law as a weapon. However, much of the influence of pressure groups depends on their ability to argue convincingly. Quality of information and an ability to persuade audiences of the justice of their arguments is crucial. Greenpeace's overestimation of the amount of oil and other pollutants on the Brent Spar in 1995, for example, has led to repeated attacks on its scientific accuracy. The importance of credibility to NGOs is illustrated in the Amnesty International Campaigning Manual, which highlights key principles for good campaigning.

Amnesty International Campaigning Manual (extracts)

Principles of good campaigning:

Focus
- Objectives must be specific
- Resources and energy must be concentrated
- Research and analysis are needed to decide focus

Clarity
- Objectives and strategy need to be communicated clearly
- All action needs to be clearly related to the objectives
- Communications must be clear, internally and externally

Credibility
- In communications, the messenger can be as important as the message
- AI's motivation and information must be trusted and reliable

Relevance
- AI's campaigning has to connect with the people whom it wants to involve
- AI's campaigning has to offer a solution relevant to the problem

Timing
- The same situation will have different effects at different times

Commitment
- The campaigning will not stop until the violations end
- Different strategies and techniques will be tried to discover the most effective

---

Source: Amnesty International Campaigning Manual

Interestingly, some leading NGOs are experiencing self-doubt, questioning whether they have had any real success in influencing companies. They suggest that their expectations about future impact and their capability to influence continues to be directed at government, the media and the public. They claim that there are fewer demands for accountability from the private sector than from their members and non-business audiences. Clearly, the media has a big impact on public and political thinking about corporate social responsibility and sustainable development. Journalists and media organizations are less accountable and are accused of overlooking broader trends in favour of immediate, sensational stories. There are no excuses. If NGOs are to be influential, but also effective, they must apply the same approaches to risk radar planning, assessment and management that I am advocating for corporate reputation risk management strategies. They must accept the need for accountability themselves, utilizing research and marketing techniques as well as their own reporting standards. The benefits of adopting this approach include more opportunities to generate resource and funds. Few would deny that campaigning is good for society. What constitutes good campaigning requires greater scrutiny.

Support for environmentalism is steady, levelling out after a sharp rise in the early 1990s. But competition between campaigning groups is growing with numbers quadrupling over the past 25 years. Issues like climate change are scientifically complex; their impact lies in the future so campaigning is difficult. Dealing with changing demographics and a

---

Greenpeace profile:
- 25 national offices and presence in 39 countries worldwide
- 2.6 million active financial supporters in 101 countries
- 100,000 'cyberactivists' (members who are dedicated to using the Internet as an activist platform)
- Independent (does not accept funding from governments, corporations or political parties)

Campaign strategies are based on:
- *Creativity:* creative direct action ensures the campaigns attract publicity and are covered by the media
- *Exposure:* revealing hidden environmental abuses
- *Acting as a catalyst:* Greenpeace plays a role in galvanizing environmental movements through coalition building, lobbying, Internet activism and environmental teaching programmes at schools and colleges
- *Scientific enquiries:* Greenpeace has its own science unit and research laboratories

Greenpeace aims in targeting the corporate sector:
- Change the activities of selected companies in the energy and chemicals industries so they contribute to sustainable development through radical changes to their activities, for example, the Stop Esso campaign
- Gain the attention of institutional decision-makers on the importance of sustainable development
- Make companies responsible for the environmental impact of their businesses

new generation that has grown up with protest require new approaches. For example, young people in North America and Europe are highly environmentally conscious but they are reluctant to take action outside their immediate, personal sphere of influence. Opinion polling suggests that young people have less faith than their parents in the effectiveness of campaigning over complicated issues like global warming. Environmentalists have also come under fire for ignoring jobs and local communities in their quest for environmental protection. So, a number of the largest campaign groups have agreed to chop up the agenda between them as a mechanism to maintain their individual distinctiveness.

When business gets it wrong – protecting drug prices in South Africa

Protection of patents and prices has been a constant challenge for the pharmaceutical industry, particularly concerning the costs of essential drugs, such as HIV/AIDS medication. The issue came to the fore in October 1997, when the South African government introduced the Medicines Control Act to make all medicines more affordable. The government was concerned that over 4.5 m people in South Africa were infected with the HIV virus, and the vast majority of those infected did not have access to effective treatment.

In February 1998, 39 pharmaceutical companies, co-ordinated by the Pharmaceutical Manufacturers Association of South Africa (PMA), responded to the Medicines Control Act by bringing a lawsuit against the South African government to prevent the implementation of the Act. The argument was that patents, and therefore drug prices, must be protected for research and development purposes. The United States government and European Community were sympathetic to the pharmaceutical industry's position.

From September 1998, the case was suspended while the pharmaceutical companies negotiated with the South African government to stop the Act. These negotiations were unsuccessful, however, and the case was resumed in March 2001. However by this time, the political, public and media reaction was very different – the pharmaceutical industry had failed to anticipate how the issue was to develop.

That year, the South African AIDS advocacy group, Treatment Action Campaign (TAC), was formed and began to mobilize global support against the pharmaceutical companies. TAC worked within South Africa to politicize the AIDS problem as a poverty issue, and used the established networks of European and US AIDS support groups to raise the profile of the campaign. The international NGOs Oxfam and Médécins Sans Frontières (MSF) also latched on to the drug pricing issue, helping to make the case more visible and international. MSF and Oxfam both have influential political and campaign networks; they actively use their websites to convey the latest information. The NGOs publicly condemned the 'profiteering' practices of the industry while emphasizing the terrible consequences of AIDS. Emotive news reports in Europe and the United States showed African children dying from AIDS inflicted from birth.

The public profile of the AIDS pandemic in the developing world rose dramatically during this period, coinciding with a series of new initiatives in poorer countries. By the time the court case was resumed in March 2001, the AIDS pandemic topped the agenda of the United Nations, World Health Organization and the G8 countries.

The trial became a subject of industry, government and media debate in Europe and the United States. The pharmaceutical companies continued with the case in spite of rising pressure, intensifying protests (GlaxoSmithKline was nicknamed 'Global Serial Killers') and boycotts. MSF and Oxfam posted a 'Drop the Case' petition on their websites and in the six-week period after the court case was resumed, over 250,000 people from 130 countries signed it, including members of governments and celebrities.

The issue escalated to such an extent that in April 2001, two of the largest pharmaceutical companies, GlaxoSmithKline and Merck, asked Kofi Annan, the UN Secretary General, to help negotiate a settlement. A joint working party to govern the Act was established and the court case was dropped. The settlement allowed the South African government to implement the Medicines Control Act if it agreed to abide by the World Trade Organization's Trade-Related Intellectual Property Rights Agreement (TRIPS). This was widely reported as a climb-down by the industry and a reputational disaster. Campaigners say it was a victory against pharmaceutical industry profiteering.

The pharmaceutical industry clearly took far too long to acknowledge public concern. The issue has now ignited a discussion in Europe and the United States about the cost of drugs in the developed and developing world – for example, the pricing policies of Bayer were called into question after the 11 September terrorist attacks increased international demand for the smallpox vaccine, Cipro.

The industry also made the mistake of dealing with the issue of drug pricing in South Africa from a strictly business point of view. Dealing with such emotive issues demands demonstrable sympathy and concern. The industry should have assessed the significance of the issue as it developed. The terrible consequences of AIDS were sensationally promoted by NGOs and the media as the case developed, removing any initial support for the industry that the international community may initially have had.

Regardless of the extraordinary innovations that it creates in advancing health care and the strict regulatory environment in which it operates, the global pharmaceutical industry is perceived to be secretive, arrogant and greedy. If it is to avoid further claims of drawing large profits from affluent societies with little regard for the poor, it may well hit the same iceberg that sunk the oil companies in the 1970s, causing the rise of the new environmental movement.

Activism on the net

> "Corporate spin is dead ('hyperjuju'). The cause of death is the Internet. The explosion in information means that consumers, employees and journalists now can find out more about organizations than company PR departments ever wanted to reveal"
>
> MICHAEL SKAPINKER, MANAGEMENT EDITOR, *Financial Times*

The trend in consumer activism has been strongly supported by the Internet, facilitating information sharing and planning through the use of well structured e-mail databases, enabling groups with diverse ideological interests to maintain contact and plan direct action. As the battle over GM trials in the UK hotted up in the late 1990s, a number of e-mail lists also sprang up. Anyone with an interest could join one or more of these lists to receive any mail generated by anyone else on the list, enabling discussion of the latest scientific research, background information, lobbying techniques, campaign tactics or plans for direct action. A group called Genetix Snowball produced a Handbook for Action on its web site. At the site you could download your own biohazard signs and receive advice on what protective clothing to wear, how to identify GM plants, how to pull them up safely and what to do if you get arrested. The handbook has links to other sites including 'An Activist Guide to Exploiting the Media' in which the writer and campaigner, George Monbiot, advises protestors on how to steal a march on news reporters.

In early 2000, a lone Filipino hacker rocked the forces of global capitalism by hiding a vicious computer virus in what looked like a love letter. Computer

Radio = 38 years Television = 13 years Cable = 10 years Internet = less than 5 years	Internet user universe = 350 million 500 new web sites launched each day Over 8 billion sites by 2002/3 More phones connected to the Internet than computers

Figure 4.4 *Growth of the Internet*

systems went crashing all over the world – in government departments and big business – at considerable cost and to great embarrassment. There was hardly a major corporation which wasn't affected. The 'I Love You' virus exposed the terrifying vulnerability of our high-tech computerised world to a hacker with or without an agenda. We now live in an era of Hacktivism, Infowar, Cyberterrorism and Electronic Attack (Easton, 2000).

A number of major US sports good and apparel brands have faced continued attack over 'sweat shop' employment conditions in factories in developing countries. Nike is just one of the companies that has been pushed into the vanguard of brands targeted by anti-globalization and consumer groups.

One infamous e-mail exchange between a member of the public and Nike highlights the perceived corporate arrogance that activists so despise. Jonah Peretti e-mailed an order in response to a promotion to have his Nike trainers personalized, with the word 'sweatshop'. Nike declined the order under a set of *pro forma* headings indicating a trademark or intellectual property breach, a failure on the customer to submit a personal 'i.d.', or the use of a personal id containing a 'profanity or inappropriate slang'. Peretti e-mailed back saying that 'sweatshop' fitted none of the categories and would Nike progress the order. Nike responded saying that 'sweatshop' equated to inappropriate slang. After further exchange, Peretti e-mailed Nike as follows:

> *Dear NIKE id,*
> *Thank you for the time and energy you have spent on my request. I have decided to order the shoes with a different id, but I would like to make one small request. Could you please send me a color snapshop of the ten-year-old Vietnamese girl who makes my shoes?*
> *Thanks,*
> *Jonah Peretti*

Peretti received no further response from Nike, but the e-mail exchange has been widely publicized as an example of the company's perceived poor ethical performance.

Stop Esso

In May 2001, a coalition of environmental groups, under the banner of 'Stop Esso' launched a successful boycott campaign against ExxonMobil in the UK. The campaign is now spreading across the world to Germany, Norway, New Zealand, the United States and Japan. The campaign is run by an alliance of three NGOs – Greenpeace, Friends of the Earth, and student group People and Planets – and is supported by many more NGOs including the Sierra Club, WWF, the Royal Society for the Protection of Birds (RSPB) and the National Resources Defense Council (NRDC).

Environmentalists complain that Exxon was the biggest corporate opponent of the Kyoto treaty on climate change and, as a major contributor to the George W Bush presidential campaign, was a big influence on the United States' decision to pull out of the Kyoto treaty. Campaigners allege that unlike other oil companies, such as Shell and BP, Exxon has made no investment in renewable forms of energy and continues to lobby against the general scientific consensus that burning oil and gas is the main cause of global warming.

The campaign has used innovative tactics to raise awareness. The Internet has been used to powerful effect and Stop Esso is the largest online campaign to date. From the campaign website, activists can: download campaign materials including stickers and leaflets bearing the Stop Esso logo; forward movies attacking Bush and Exxon to others *via* e-mail; buy merchandise; get the latest campaign news; sign up to a monthly update; sign a pledge promising to boycott Exxon/Esso garages; and lobby Exxon's Chairman and companies that use Exxon products via e-mail.

Stop Esso has also made strong use of advertising – for an international day of action in July 2001 protestors placed advertisements in national newspapers featuring a photograph of George Bush with the headline 'Esso ate my brain'. Celebrity support from Bianca Jagger, Sting and Anita Roddick has further raised the campaign's profile.

As a result of 'Stop Esso', economists estimate that Exxon-Mobil sales in the UK alone could be reduced by more than $1 bn a year (*The Guardian*, 6 May 2001). Greenpeace commissioned two public opinion polls on British motorists' attitudes to Exxon: the August 2001 poll found 500,000 motorists who said they would no longer use Esso forecourts, while the January 2002 poll found that figure had doubled. Greenpeace campaigner Rob Gueterbock concluded that "business as usual isn't an option for Exxon".

Source: *PR Week*, 31 May 2002

The emerging phenomenon of disparate NGOs linking on-line to effect direct action has been dubbed an 'NGO swarm' by US think-tank, RAND, who say that a swarm is impossible to target because "it lacks any central leadership or command structure; it is multi-headed and impossible to decapitate". So-called 'technical' groups specialize in supplying very sophisticated analysis and are essential to the working of some international treaties.

For example, the verification for the Chemicals Weapons Treaty in 1997 was devised by the world's chemical-manufacturing associations and some NGOs have specialized in the detail of debt reduction models and contributed to related policy development.

A good example of a swarm effect occurred in 1998, when a new e-mail was passed around by a growing community of net activists. The Action Proposal for 18 June 1999 changed the nature of modern protest and became a precursor for the larger scale anti-globalization demonstrations in the United States and Europe. Thousands of people converged on the City of London, tens of thousands more were involved in linked protests in over 40 countries. The City protest attracted supporters from all kinds of groups. Friends of the Earth, Class War, The Campaign Against Arms Trade, Church Action on Poverty, Striking Thameside Care Workers, Reclaim the Streets, Corporate Watch, and more. The greens (environmentalists), the reds (socialists) and the blacks (anarchists) were all represented.

Having converged on London's Liverpool Street Station, coloured ribbons were waved dividing the crowd into four groups so that like-minded protestors could co-ordinate their protests. Maps of the city were handed out with the locations of banks, law firms, exchanges and multinational companies. An estimated $3.5 m of damage was caused with offices trashed, cars set alight and shops looted. Particularly worrying for the police and the government was that there were no obvious organizers: no-one to take responsibility, no-one to co-operate with the police and therefore no-one who could be successfully prosecuted. J18 was followed by N30, A16 and MayDay2K – all planned, discussed and organized on the Internet, and all providing useful input into the larger scale demonstrations that were to follow (Easton, 2000).

Although McDonald's has been the subject of direct action through the expanding anti-globalization protests, greater damage has been wreaked through the anti-McDonald's campaign waged on the Internet. The McSpotlight site went on line in February 1996 during the infamous libel trial. Even today, McDonald's has failed to successfully counter the web site which carries the same information used to libel it. The McSpotlight

---

Number of CEOs who ...

- Are concerned about the negative impact of the Internet on their business reputation
  60 per cent

- Have a strategy for managing their company's Internet image
  50 per cent

- Are concerned about unhappy customers on the Internet
  40 per cent

- Evaluate Internet mentions of their company
  11 per cent

Source: Yankelovich, 2000

site contains 20,000 files relating to the McDonald's trial and is run by volunteers in 22 countries with mirror sites in four. Often the web pages are backed up with e-mail campaigns and protestors are adept at raising issues in online discussion groups. The site www.mcspotlight.org can register more than 1.5 m hits per month; the campaign has achieved a global reach that would have been impossible before the Internet.

The academic, the Internet and a bill for $500 m

At Lynchburg College, Virginia, in the United States, mathematics professor Thomas Nicely discovered the Intel Pentium bug. His moment of fame came as he completed a complicated long division early one morning in June 1994. He always liked to check his sums by hand but for some reason this time it simply wasn't working out. According to Nicely, "Intel's tech support desk said they had never heard of it. They said they would speak to an engineering group and return my call later; in fact we did exchange calls for a period of six days or so but they never came up with an explanation or acknowledged that the error actually occurred."

So Professor Nicely did what any self-respecting American mathematician would do and raised the alarm on the Internet; he discovered that he was not alone. Within days he was getting reports of similar errors and there was agreement that the cause was an error in the floating point unit of the innovative and highly powerful Pentium chip. Within a week the e-mail momentum around the issue spilled over into the media. The *Electrical Engineering Times* published a lead article detailing the claims against the chip, in turn bringing the problem to the attention of Internet newsgroups which created increasingly hot debate. Intel was accused of hiding the flaw and inferences were made that other errors in Intel microprocessors could exist. Over five million Pentiums were estimated to have been sold during 1994.

The timing could not have been worse for Intel, which had decided to target the emerging but lucrative home PC market with a massive international advertising campaign based around the 'Intel inside' branding. Intel was becoming a consumer company and its transformation was one of the big technology success stories of the 1990s.

Intel's response was slow and hardly customer friendly. Realizing that most of the negative publicity and associated energy around the debate had come from cyberspace, the company posted a note on the newsgroup sitecomp.sys.intel in November claiming that the error would occur only once every 9 billion random division operations and that the typical spreadsheet user would encounter the problem once every 27,000 years! Intel offered to resolve users' problems "in the most appropriate fashion including, if necessary, replacing their chips with new ones". The newsgroup posting, however, gave further life to the problem. Customers were incensed that even though there was admission of a flaw, they would have to prove it before a chip was replaced. By December 1994, IBM forced Intel's hand by saying the bugs were worse than reported and suspended shipments of all products containing Pentium microprocessors. IBM considered that its reputation as a quality supplier – and one for which customers paid a premium – was at stake. Competitors may have argued this positioning was cynical; but, even then, Intel was reluctant to recall the chips. The company's CEO, Andrew Grove, said: "I don't think it is part of our open and honest culture to make a commitment that we don't believe in (that is, to replace the chips, no questions asked), and that we could not deliver. I think that would be an irresponsible thing to do." Under continued media pressure and the filing of a number of class action lawsuits against the company, it backed off asking customers to qualify for an exchange, replacing chips without condition. On 21 December, the company published an advertisement in the *Wall Street Journal* which stated:

> *"To owners of Pentium processor-based computers and the PC community: we at Intel wish to sincerely apologize for our handling of the recently publicized Pentium processor flaw."*

Following the announcement the issue disappeared from the mainstream national media. The cost to the company of its poor handling of the Pentium bug amounted to almost $500 m. Early acknowledgement of failure is crucial in managing the crisis response. What made this particular story escalate with such damaging consequences was the speed and access to information over the Internet.

Campaigning on the Internet

Corporate opponents have proved themselves adept at utilizing online communications resources. With limited resources to provide access to traditional media, the Internet has become the perfect vehicle for co-ordinated protest. This early experience means that even now many NGOs are infinitely more sophisticated in their use of online resources than many large corporations.

The effect of these developments has been to shift the power of 'voice' in the formation of corporate reputations away from companies themselves and towards their stakeholders. As new opinion leaders

---

Free Burma: PepsiCo

In January 1997, PepsiCo ended a five-year boycott – initiated on human rights grounds – by severing remaining commercial ties with Myanmar. The Internet was regarded as a potent weapon in PepsiCo's capitulation. Protestors had posted a flyer to many Internet newsgroups explaining the linkage between the company's investments in Myanmar and support for the SLORC dictatorship's human rights abuses. In 1995, the Free Burma Coalition (FBC) developed the Free Burma website and co-ordinated a variety of actions designed to raise awareness of human rights abuses and encourage boycotts of products manufactured in, or supplied to, Burma. A key factor related to the use of the Internet in raising awareness of the issue among affluent American consumers. PepsiCo started to lose contracts in other countries, creating concern among institutional investors and negative coverage in the mainstream US national media. The FBC coalition generated a share of voice well beyond its actual size, reaching the media, government agencies, customers of PepsiCo, shareholders and other activists with ease and considerable impact. Eventually, the FBC's influence on PepsiCo's own stakeholder network contributed significantly to the company's retreat from Myanmar.

Climate change campaigning

Greenpeace

The home page keeps visitors informed of the latest developments on the Kyoto treaty, through daily logs of events, extensive background information about the key players in Bonn, and details of ongoing protests against President Bush and Exxon. Greenpeace has an online arm, or 'cyberactivist' community which was created just over a year ago. It aims to co-ordinate grassroots action across the world *via* e-mail, newsgroups, discussion boards and other online forums. Over the period of the Bonn talks, the Cybercentre saw a substantial increase in membership to approximately 30,000 from over 170 countries. The initiative is an example of an increasing realization of the Internet's potential for co-ordinating action on an international scale. It is likely to become a key hub of online environmental activism.

Friends of the Earth

Friends of the Earth has previous experience of successful online campaigns. In March 2002, the group launched an international e-mail campaign in protest against President Bush's decision to reject the Kyoto treaty, aiming to 'flood the White House'. Calls to join the protest quickly spread across the Internet. The response was immense, with a reported 10,000 e-mails per day being sent during the first week of the campaign. Progress was covered by the online media, with some hailing its potential to become the largest online protest to date.

Source: Infonic, 2000

emerge *via* the Internet, reducing the share of voice of corporations, reputation risk management is becoming defined increasingly by external stakeholder perceptions than by what a company says and does.

It isn't just the established activist groups that exploit technology so well. Individual consumers can secure share of voice quickly and powerfully.

Flaming Fords

April 1996 marked the largest single automobile and truck recall in history. Over 8.7 m Ford Motor Company vehicles were recalled to replace ignition switches that could be a fire hazard. While Ford had fought a long battle for years against a total recall, becoming the subject of Federal investigations along the way, the final capitulations was largely driven by the Internet and resulted in recall costs of up to $300 m.

The protagonists were a couple living in Georgia, whose 1985 Ford Ranger suddenly burst into flames in their driveway. They created the Association of Flaming Fords web site which contained comprehensive information about the ignition problem, a database of affected cars and trucks, photographs of burned vehicles and a national media archive. The web site itself generated a large volume of negative media coverage. The *New York Times* commented: "Ford came under extra pressure to recall the vehicles when Debra and Edward Goldgehn ... set up a page on the Internet ...", and CNN noted that "... the last nudge may have come from the Association of Flaming Ford Home Page". The couple's challenge had legitimacy because of consumer expectation of safe products and there was documented evidence of a possible safety flaw. The Internet was used successfully to build greater awareness of and consumer pressure to contact local Ford dealers about the problem, creating a new level and source of pressure for Ford and its stakeholders.

Source: Adapted from Coombs, 1998

Some online services have emerged with the explicit goal of allowing Internet users to share their views on others' sites, products and services. Third Voice (www.thirdvoice.com), epinions (www.epinions.com), The Complaint Station (www.thecomplaintstation.com) and Norbert's Bookmarks for a Better World (www.betterworldlinks.org) in their different ways all undermine corporate control of brands by enabling consumers to swap experiences and opinions directly, and on a global scale.

For companies at the centre of Internet targeting, responding to critics' concerns, but also recognizing their right to an alternative point of view and providing space for them to articulate this view, is an effective way of engaging and reducing opposition.

Shell

Shell has used the Internet to engage with activists. The company has recognized its critics' right to an alternative point of view and provides space for them to articulate this view on their site. Shell established a network of discussion boards on its website (www.shell.com). The discussion boards provide uncensored commentary on the company; highly critical comments are left online for all to see. Shell staff participate on the boards to respond to the specific issues raised.

Dunkin' Donuts

In 1997, a disgruntled individual set up an anti-Dunkin' Donuts (dunkindonuts.org) site as he claimed to have had difficulties obtaining a 'quality' cup of coffee at the Dunkin' Donut franchises in his local area. The site grew over time as other disgruntled customers accessed it and began to e-mail their complaints to the author.

Attempts by Dunkin' Donuts to close the website down in July 1998, on the basis of copyright infringement, were unsuccessful. Following this, Dunkin' Donuts changed its approach. The company sponsored the site and recognized it as a valuable source of customer feedback; employees started to post responses to customers' complaints and a potentially difficult situation was averted.

Companies should recognize online forums and resources as a source of business intelligence and work with them rather than against them.

Pioneer

In March 1999, Pioneer used online forums as a tool to quickly and quietly solve a problem with one of their products. Pioneer discovered substantial numbers of complaints on Internet newsgroups about synchronization problems with its DVD players and scanned postings for complainants' contact details. They approached individuals *via* e-mail and offered to fix their DVD players for free, regardless of warranty status. By adopting a low-key approach, Pioneer successfully reduced the amount of negative publicity their players were receiving online without 'officially' amending their warranty policy.

On its own, the corporate voice is not enough in the electronic world.

Procter & Gamble

Procter & Gamble faced a potentially difficult situation when a story emerged that its fabric conditioner, Febreze, allegedly killed pets. The rumour began to escalate out of control and acquired the status of an urban myth. Procter & Gamble developed a 'Household Safety' web page, but also sought third-party confirmation from well-respected sources such as the American Society for the Protection of Cruelty to Animals, who refuted the story prominently on its own site.

Third-party endorsement is crucial in helping to refute or diffuse allegations.

Unilever

Unilever has developed a section of its corporate web site, entitled Web Watch, given over to third-party and media coverage of the company and its industry. It allows the company to present news of interest to both internal and external stakeholders with the credibility of an independent perspective (Infonic, 2000).

Companies can use the Internet to build bridges with their stakeholders in a way that is difficult logistically and expensive offline. There are new opportunities to reach online, and not just for commercial relationships. One of the most important aspects of effective reputation risk management is the ability to spot emerging risk issues. Another is the importance of engaging with stakeholders to share information, demonstrate accountability and transparency and build relationships. Larger corporations are gradually making greater use of Internet resources for corporate and financial reporting, to present themselves as socially responsible citizens and to advance their own policy positions. There is less evidence, however, that companies are actively using their web sites to monitor stakeholder opinion on issues or advocate policy positions. One way or another, the Internet provides a vital means by which any organization – regardless of size or resources – can sustain its messages over time and reach different audiences, virtually anywhere, any time and any place.

A checklist for action

Activists deal with problems; companies tend to deal with issues, and there is a difference. A problem has a wide context – pollution, bad employment practices, poverty, human rights abuse, hunger, racial discrimination. An issue tends to be more specific and involves con-sidering potential solutions – regulation to curb emissions, codes of practice to improve workers' rights or reduce bad behaviour, financial or regulatory penalties for failing to meet required standards. Some activist groups today are shifting their campaigning towards winning issues and seeking solutions, rather than merely creating awareness of problems. This provides opportunities for constructive partnering between business and NGOs but the navigation work remains complex.

A key guideline for avoiding a collision course with activists in icy waters is for companies to switch on and monitor the radar. The objective is to scan stakeholder attitudes in relation to emerging, current or linkage issues that may have the potential to impact on commercial or reputational objectives and become familiar with the profile, personalities and working practices of activist groups.

In the same way that an NGO will develop its campaign agenda, a company facing potential direct action from an NGO must *analyse the problem and decide what kind of solution to work towards*. It requires answers to:

- What impact will dealing with this issue have on the organization?
- What are the risks (and opportunities) if we ignore the issue?
- How are our key stakeholders likely to react?
- How confident are we that we can influence the issue in the way we want?
- What potential resources will be required?
- What's the simplest solution and what's the most far-reaching?
- What are the potential benefits from actively seeking a solution?

Meanwhile, the activist's checklist for developing a campaign strategy around an issue is likely to consider whether it will:

- Result in a real improvement for people
- Give people a sense of their own power
- Be worthwhile and winnable
- Be felt in an emotional way
- Be easy to understand
- Have a clear target and timeframe
- Build leadership
- Have a financially beneficial angle
- Enhance profile to support subsequent campaigns
- Raise money and membership
- Fit with objectives and values

Source: Adapted from *Organizing for Social Change*, Midwest Academy, 2000

As a counterpoint to this, the reputation risk manager's checklist for considering whether the company may be a potential NGO target and how to respond, will need to address the following questions:

- **Can a credible argument be made against the company's position?** This plays to two of our recurring themes – first, the importance of focusing on the values and beliefs of stakeholders who may be engaged in the issue, not just on proving a case through scientific or technical fact – and second, recognizing that trust in business tends to be low.

Being open with information and securing the support of credible third-parties, who are willing to support your viewpoint, is therefore essential.

- **Does the issue evoke emotion?**
  In Chapter 3, we explored the emotional dynamics of risk perception – the drivers that inform our judgements about risk issues; if they are sensational, scary, the subject of conflicting opinions, visual, out of our direct control and subject to embedded bias and subjectivity, we are likely to feel strong emotions that are easily manipulated by NGOs and the media.

- **Is the issue media and Internet friendly?**
  Mass media and the Internet are the primary channels for disseminating a risk issue across geographic and social boundaries. As Shell defines its stakeholder environment today, it is a 'show-me world' rather than the 'trust-me world' of the pre-Brent Spar era.

- **Are there linkages to other issues?**
  If the issue can be linked through the media to previous failures or comparable situations that have been badly handled by policymakers or business, the resonance of the issue becomes stronger with accusations of further problems to come. Once the issue is spotted on the radar, it's rather like seeing a succession of icebergs blocking the projected course. Nestlé not only continues to suffer the ravages of a long-standing campaign against it over infant formula, it is an easy target when related environmental health scares emerge, as in the case of genetically engineered soya.

- **How strong are the key activists?**
  I have already highlighted some of the most sophisticated NGOs and their approach to campaigning. The Internet has democratized the campaigning process on an enormous scale. Even at a local level, for example, I have been involved with parent and local community groups campaigning against the siting of mobile phone base stations in their communities, the construction of waste management facilities and other localized land legacy issues, and they can have a disproportionate impact on disrupting operational activities with real financial consequences. Thorough research and monitoring of activists is, therefore, vital.

- **How strong is the company's support base on the issue?**
  Activists prefer to pick on large sophisticated brands which have most to lose through damage to reputation, customer and institutional loyalty. Extreme, intimidatory tactics on the part of animal rights activists have inflicted considerable damage on the financial viability of Europe's largest animal research laboratory, Huntingdon Life Sciences. Working for both biotechnology and pharmaceutical companies, I believe support was mute for fear of reprisal. At the height of the Brent Spar campaign, few people were aware that it was part of a 50-50 joint venture with Exxon, which failed to make a single public statement on the issue.

- **How far have the dynamics of the issue lifecycle developed?**
  In Chapter 2, we explored the stages and escalation triggers for the risk issue lifecycle. Getting a handle on the dynamics of the issue and the potential for further icebergs is a top priority for reputation risk managers. This will not only help to predict the triggers for further escalation but will also second-guess likely activist tactics and potential response strategies that can be employed.

- **How can a worthwhile solution be achieved?**
  Most stakeholders don't want to see the demise of a company or the recall of a popular product unless there is no alternative on environmental health or ethical grounds – real or perceived. Similarly, regulators don't want to impose impossible actions on targeted companies or industries. Solutions can be achieved by replacing withdrawn products with alternatives that are deemed to be safer. Solutions to social issues require demonstrable changes in attitudes and behaviours (Texaco and Coca-Cola racial discrimination cases; Arthur Andersen fall-out from Enron collapse).

  As no size fits all in determining what constitutes a worthwhile solution, my benchmark is for the reputation risk management team to abide by the maxims of accountability and transparency, work out what constitutes the right behaviour as a responsible business and either put the required changes into place, or defend existing practices with conviction!

Source: Adapted from Winter and Steger, 1998

Once again, accountability and transparency are the watchwords for a corporate response to NGO attack. The view of one senior reputation risk practitioner is that, "public opinion demands accountability and transparency from business today and it will expect performance delivery on social and environmental issues pretty soon after!" However, no company should feel bullied into automatic capitulation over NGO demands if the tactics employed involve unfounded allegations or misinformation. These should be rebutted in a clear, credible and consistent manner. Many companies by their nature are involved in complex manufacturing and supply chain issues where accidents can happen or trade-offs need to be made.

Tim Sharp of Balfour Beatty, says: "Construction is both complex and controversial. Our reputation is built on actively seeking out and demonstrating that we can successfully manage both; but creating huge public infrastructure projects won't please everyone and we are frequently targeted by activists. So our job is, first and foremost, to rigorously assess and manage risks, including reputation risks, and put in place mitigation and avoidance measures where appropriate. We then make those processes transparent and accountable to all our stakeholders. Our next task is to deliver key performance indicators for environmental risk management, ethical business practices and human rights that can provide appropriate benchmarks for the future. If we are attacked, we believe we can (and do) make a credible case for our actions, which is crucial to keeping our key stakeholders onside, maintaining our licence to operate and managing our reputation. It may not be perfect, but it is crucial to making constructive progress."

Appendix

NGO Database

American Forests
General
• US NGO • Founded in 1875 • Budget: $4.5 m, 1999/2000 • Founding member of Earth Share, a federation of US environmental and conservation charities
Agenda
• Encourages communities and companies to plant trees • Tries to improve understanding of the relationship between trees and greenhouse gases • Protects wildlife living in American forests
Tactics
• Corporate sponsorship (for example, Crystal Geyser) • Corporate partnerships (for example, Mobil) • Education programme (for example, Global ReLeaf) • Quarterly magazine

Amnesty International (AI)
General
• International NGO, headquartered in London • Launched in 1961 • Over 1 m members worldwide • Supporters in more than 140 countries and territories • Budget: £19.5 m, 2000/2001 • Website receives over 6 m hits a month
Agenda
• Promotes human rights enshrined in the Universal Declaration of Human Rights • Key themes: torture, arms control, death penalty and women's human rights
Tactics
• Public demonstrations • Letter writing • Human rights education • Celebrity endorsement • Fundraising concerts • Detailed reports • Publicizes concerns in leaflets, posters, advertisements, newsletters and on the Internet

Conservation International

General

- US based international NGO
- 300,000 members
- Budget: $40m, 2000/2001
- Member of Earth Share, a federation of US environmental and conservation charities

Agenda

- Environmental conservation

Tactics

- Research and science
- Environmental partnerships with companies (such as Aveda, Intel and Starbucks)
- Education

CorpWatch

General

- San Francisco-based NGO
- Founded in 1998
- Internet-based umbrella organization that provides an up-to-date resource base for other campaign groups

Agenda

- Campaigns against environmental and human rights abuses by large corporations, and corporate-led globalization

Tactics

- Comprehensive website
- Supplies monthly e-mails to members
- Encourages members to send faxes and e-mails to CEOs of offending companies
- CorpWatch gives out bimonthly Greenwash awards to corporations that put more money, time and energy into slick PR campaigns aimed at promoting their eco-friendly images, than they do to actually protecting the environment

Environmental Defense

General

- International NGO based in America
- Founded in 1967
- 750,000 members internationally; 300,000 members in the US
- Budget: $42.8m, 2000/2001

Agenda

- Four main goals: stabilizing the earth's climate; safeguarding the world's oceans; protecting human health; and defending and restoring biodiversity
- Targets policymakers, businesses, journalists and consumers

Tactics

- Advocacy
- Publishes reports on programme activities
- Prints and e-mails newsletters
- Fact sheets and educational material on 'green' behaviour and business practices
- Has developed an e-mail 'Action Network' which has enrolled thousands of activists who contact legislators and other policymakers on fast-moving issues

Friends of the Earth

General

- International NGO headquartered in Holland
- 1m activists worldwide
- International network in 58 countries
- Network of 240 activist groups

Agenda

- Promotes sustainable development in companies, industries and governments
- Safeguarding the earth and resisting economic globalization
- Campaign focuses on waste management, biotechnology, GMO pollution, WTO and globalization, safer chemicals, human rights, food safety (Real Food campaign), nuclear power, mining and climate change (Kyoto)

Tactics

- Leverage – look for weaknesses in opponents and key moment at which to exploit them
- Acts as a catalyst to form mass movements – through coalition building, large-scale demonstrations, e-mail targeting, and so on
- Transparency – strong interest in free and open debate, role as public interest lobbyists
- Engages with private sector audiences to persuade them to adopt environmental principles in their business strategies
- Commissions research
- Lobbying
- Publishes its own quarterly magazine, *Link*, which contains campaign news, global action alerts, book and publication reviews and interviews with leading environmentalists
- Use of the Internet: Extensive information and educational materials on the website. The site provides assistance and encouragement for activists and potential activists developing their own campaigns, for example, campaign guides and briefings (such as the Incineration Campaign Guide) are available. Sample letters (lobbying public officials) and press releases can be obtained as well as leaflets and posters to recruit volunteers. The site provides details of other websites that might prove useful, for example, in sourcing scientific information to support campaigns

Grassroots International

General

- International NGO based in the US
- Budget: $2.4 m, 1999/2000

Agenda

- Human rights and development campaign group
- Provides cash grants and material aid to partners in Africa, the Middle East, Latin America and the Caribbean
- Anti-corporate globalization

Tactics

- Advocacy
- Public education
- Online magazine

Greenpeace

General

- International NGO
- Established in 1971
- 2.65 million active financial supporters from 101 different countries; 250,000 members in the USA
- 25 national offices and a presence in 39 countries worldwide
- 100,000 'cyberactivists'
- Budget: 143,646,000 Euros in 2000; $8.9 m in the USA in 1999

Agenda

- Promotes sustainable development and the concept that companies should take responsibility for their environmental impact
- Key themes internationally are forest protection (Amazon), climate change (Kyoto), toxic chemicals (POPs), nuclear power (campaign for a nuclear free future), oceans (marine pollution, whaling, overfishing), genetic engineering (no to GM) and anti-globalization
- Key themes in the USA are anti-whaling, climate change, nuclear testing, anti-PVC, stop GM, off-shore drilling and protecting the Amazon

Tactics

- Creativity – creative direct action ensures the campaigns are covered by the media
- Coalition building
- Lobbying
- Internet activism
- Environmental teaching programmes at schools and colleges
- Scientific enquiries – Greenpeace has its own scientific unit and research laboratories
- Confrontational tactics if they think they have been 'stonewalled' by a company or government

National Resources Defense Council

General

- US NGO based in New York
- 500,000 members
- Budget: $34 m, 1999/2000

Agenda

- The group has air/energy, health, land, nuclear, urban, water and coastal programmes

Tactics

- Advocacy
- Quarterly magazine
- Education
- Supporters can join the Earth Activist Network where they are sent bi-weekly e-mail alerts

National Wildlife Federation

General

- US NGO
- Founded in 1936
- 4.2 million members, including those who subscribe to magazine
- Budget: $11 m, in 2000

Agenda

- Protects wildlife, wild places, and the environment

Tactics

- The primary focus is education – books, magazines and nature programmes

People for the Ethical Treatment of Animals (PETA)

General

- International NGO based in Virginia, USA
- Founded in 1980
- 700,000 members; largest animal rights organization in the world
- Budget: $14 m, 2001

Agenda

- Educates policymakers and the public about animal abuse and promotes an understanding of the right of all animals to be treated with respect
- Encourages veganism; is anti-fur and leather; is against animals being used for entertainment purposes; and is against animal testing

Tactics

- Lobbies companies and governments
- Product boycotts
- Organizes demonstrations
- Releases videos depicting cruelty to animals
- Celebrity support, for instance, Christy Turlington, Tyra Banks, Marcus Schenkenberg, Kim Basinger and others have posed for its 'I'd Rather Go Naked Than Wear Fur' campaign
- Corporate sponsorship, for example, Pangea, Liberty Management Group Inc., Gourmet Italian and Candle Cafe

Public Citizen

General

- US NGO
- Founded in 1971 to represent consumer interests in Congress in terms of health, safety and democracy
- Budget $3.4 m, 2000

Agenda

- Fights for openness and democratic accountability in government; for the right of consumers to seek redress in the courts; for clean, safe and sustainable energy sources; for social and economic justice in trade policies; for strong health, safety and environmental protection; and for safe, effective and affordable prescription drugs and health care
- Six national divisions:
  - Auto safety – improve vehicle safety and more sensible regulation of the trucking industry
  - Congress watch – monitors Congress and fights for consumers' interests before US Congress. Lobbies to strengthen health, safety and environmental protection; end corporate subsidies; and preserve citizens' rights in the courts
  - Critical mass energy and environment programme – protects citizens and the environment from the dangers posed by nuclear power and seeks policies that lead to safe, affordable and environmentally sustainable energy
  - Global trade watch – created in 1993 to promote government and corporate accountability; educates the American public about impact of international trade and economic globalization
  - Health research group – promotes changes in care policy and works to ban or re-label unsuitable or ineffective drugs and medical devices
  - Litigation group – public interest law firm (founded in 1972) that specializes in federal health and safety regulation, consumer litigation, open government, union democracy, separation of powers and the First Amendment.

Tactics

- Advocacy
- Lobbying
- Education
- Sends e-mails to activists

Rainforest Action Network (RAN)

General

- International NGO founded in 1985
- 25,000 members
- Budget: $3 m, 1999/2000

Agenda

- To protect tropical rainforests and the human rights of those living in and around them

Tactics

- Product boycotts
- Publicity stunts
- Corporate partnerships (for example, Mitsubishi)

Sierra Club

General

- US NGO
- Founded in 1892
- 700,000 members
- Budget: $50 m, 2000

Agenda

- Encouraging sustainable energy, protecting wild lands, preventing global warming, promoting responsible trade, preventing commercial logging, protecting and restoring the quality of water and encouraging stable population growth

Tactics

- Magazine
- Petitioning
- Lobbying
- Education

Sweatshop Watch

General

- International NGO
- Established in California in 1995
- 10,000 members in US
- A coalition of labour and community organizations; civil rights groups; womens' organizations; and attorneys and advocates that support causes

Agenda

- Aims to eliminate sweatshops in the garment industry and raise awareness of sweatshops across the world and the companies that use them

Tactics

- Coalition building
- Website as an information resource – uses hotlinks to member groups
- Public education – offers material for use in schools/universities including videos, literature and speaker visits
- Quarterly newsletter to members

Transparency International (TI)

General

- International NGO that aims to combat corruption
- Launched in May 1993
- Headquartered in Berlin
- Budget: $3.7m, 2000

Agenda

- Raises awareness about the damaging effects of corruption at a global level
- Advocates policy reform
- Works towards the implementation of multilateral conventions
- Monitors compliance by governments, corporations and banks
- Works to ensure that the agendas of international organizations give high priority to curbing corruption
- The TI national chapters (active in more than 80 countries) work to build coalitions to strengthen integrity systems in their countries

Tactics

- A Corruption Fighters toolkit is available on the website, which documents the range of chapter programmes, best practices, and lessons learnt
- TI's annual Corruption Perceptions Index (CPI) ranks countries by perceived levels of corruption among public officials
- The Global Corruption Report (GCR) brings together news and analysis on corruption, addressing international and regional trends, highlighting noteworthy cases, and providing empirical evidence of corruption
- An annual Integrity Awards programme honours individuals and organizations that make a distinct difference in curbing corruption
- The bulk of TI's income comes from government development agency budgets and foundations. Other sources of income include project funds from international organizations, donations from private sector companies and income from honoraria and publications
- Builds coalitions of concerned stakeholders from the private sector, the public sector, NGOs and international institutions
- TI has a Corruption Online Research and Information System (CORIS) on its website – a database on corruption and governance.

World Wide Fund for Nature (WWF)
General
• International NGO   • Founded in 1961   • 5 million members worldwide; 1.2m members in the US   • WWF is the largest privately supported international conservation organization in the world   • Budget: $360m worldwide in 2001; $119.9m in the US
Agenda
• Protects wildlife and wetlands
Tactics
• Tries to influence global environmental policies   • Corporate partnerships (Lafarge, Canon, Ogilvy)   • Lobbies politicians by launching fax and e-mail actions on the website   • Education: focus upon children

Resource list

Websites

American Forests	www.americanforests.org
Amnesty International	www.amnesty.org
Baby Milk Action	www.babymilkaction.org
Bookmarks for a Better World	www.betterworldlinks.org
Boycotts in Action	members.primary.net/ ~gmarshal/boycotts.htm
Business in the Community (Impact Indicators)	www.bitc.org.uk
Columbia Journalism Review	www.cjr.org
Conservation International	www.conservation.org
CorpWatch	www.corpwatch.org
Edelman PR	www.edelman.com
Environmental Defense	www.environmentaldefense.org
Friends of the Earth	www.foei.org
Grassroots International	www.grassrootsonline.org
Greenpeace	www.greenpeace.org
Infonic	www.infonic.com
McSpotlight	www.mcspotlight.org
National Resources Defense Council	www.nrdc.org
National Wildlife Federation	www.nwf.org
People for the Ethical Treatment of Animals (PETA)	www.peta-online.org
Public Citizen	www.citizen.org
Rainforest Action Network	www.ran.org
Sierra Club	www.sierraclub.org
Stop Esso	www.stopesso.com
Sweatshop Watch	www.sweatshopwatch.org
Tell Shell	www.euapps.shell.com/TellShell
The Complaint Station	www.thecomplaintstation.com
Third Voice	www.thirdvoice.com

Transparency International   www.transparency.org
WWF   www.panda.org
Yankelovich   www.yankelovich.com

Articles and reports

Bunting, M. and Lipski, R., *Infonic Internet Intelligence*, 2000

Coombs, W.T., 'The Internet as a Potential Equalizer: New Leverage for Confronting Social Irresponsibility', *Public Relations Review* 24 (3), 1998

Easton, M., Reputation Management Conference, *PR Week*, 2000

Hemel, G., 'Revamping the Corporation from Inside Out', *Business2.com*, September 2000

Midwest Academy Manual for Activists, *Organizing for Social Change*, Seven Locks Press, 2000

Books

Winter, M. and Steger, U., *Managing Outside Pressure: Strategies for Preventing Corporate Disaster*, Wiley, Chichester, 1998

Expanding liabilities, science and the precautionary principle – the greatest risk of all?

"The policy of being too cautious is the greatest risk of all"

NEHRU

One hundred years ago, science had little impact on people's daily lives. Scientists might have been trusted experts but this was of minor consequence for most people who rarely brushed with science, either in the laboratory or in the field. During the twentieth century, modern warfare probably brought about the biggest change to the speed of scientific innovation and discovery. The development of the atomic bomb, jet propulsion, radar, satellites and space flight, microelectronics and biological weapons have all produced technologies that have transformed our lives. Together with medical experimentation on humans these developments began to create the view that science could no longer remain independent from social and ethical issues. Science today is very much centre-stage and represents some 2–3 per cent of GDP in major industrialized economies. Both the benefits and the risks associated with scientific innovation are becoming more and more visible and, in our fast flowing world, scientists have a crucial role to play in assessing new hazards – both real and perceived.

So why is there a perceived decline of public trust in scientists as impartial experts? How intrusive will precautionary policy approaches become in protecting our health, environmental and consumer interests? Can the ethical consequences of technological progress be taken into account without restricting the future of commercial research and development? What will be the financial and reputational consequences for business? How should we manage risks emerging from scientific and technological innovation?

Public fear of the unknown consequences of new developments has the potential to seriously constrain commercial innovation. In an attempt to allay this anxiety, policymakers have introduced more and more complex and costly regulation designed to protect us even from hypothetical hazards that have yet to be documented and defined. The emergence of the precautionary principle, initially in US environmental regulation in the 1970s, and more recently in a host of existing and planned European legislation, is indicative of these changes. Businesses need to recognize the potential impact of precautionary policy approaches on commercial progress and the powerful opportunities that the principle provides for anti-business campaigning. Together with the growing burden of regulation, litigation and a developing culture of compensation in Western economies, companies face some deceptively large icebergs on the voyage to assuring their licence to operate. Active management of reputation risk can signific-antly offset these costly and constraining barriers.

In this chapter, I shall examine how, at a European level, the perceived decline of trust in experts and in the scientific community's reputation is bringing about policy changes that risk institutionalizing a loss of public confidence in the benefits of innovation to the material detriment of business. I will consider the impact of precautionary regulation and, with it, some of the developments that are pushing ordinary people to seek mind-boggling financial redress through the courts. Examples of the commercial impact of precautionary regulation are provided together with decision-making guidelines for anticipating and responding to these changes. I also provide some navigation tools designed to avoid the icebergs and chart a successful course towards stakeholder acceptance and commercial progress.

What's got to science?

The philosopher David Burns called reason "the slave of the passions". Possessing rational capacity does not mean that we always think and argue rationally; instead, we often make profoundly irrational assumptions, then argue rationally to reach the conclusions we want! For example, some of us believe that organic vegetables are more 'natural' and free of chemicals so they must be safer to eat and more nutritious. The evidence base as reported by a number of European public health agencies is actually the opposite. Organic farming can involve the use of over 30 chemicals, it poses a potentially greater risk of e-coli infection and is no more nutritious or better tasting than conventionally produced vegetables.

For over 50 years, management scientists have been concerned about how to make 'rational' decisions in the face of scientific uncertainties about the world. More recently, public officials have been wrestling with the challenge of how to communicate uncertainty to the public and still keep their votes. Much of our discussion has centred on the argument that scientific and technological advances often generate public concern about potential, emotionally driven risks to our health, safety, security, privacy and to the environment, compounded by the fact that:

- We now question all authority, including scientific authority
- There remains in most parts of Europe a culture of government and institutional secrecy which encourages cynicism and suspicion
- In an environment of greater individuality, we falsely believe that all thoughts, opinions and values are of equal merit
- The emergence of a victim culture encourages risk aversion and a greedy compensation culture
- Scientists working either for government or industry are perceived to be corrupt
- There are a host of different social, ethical and multi-cultural influences that affect our values and beliefs, and which shape our attitudes to innovation and progress, and also to new risks

Confusion over who to trust, and scepticism over the role of science in policymaking, have probably been the most significant outcomes from the BSE crisis and discussion over issues like BSE, GM crops, food safety or anything nuclear is now so immediately public that the voice of rational, evidence-based scientific inquiry is drowned out.

An article in *The Economist* entitled 'Genetically Modified Government' stated that after, BSE, simply quoting scientific authority is no answer to the question of public trust. 'What impresses the public in these matters is transparent and impartial decision-making based on wide consultation'.

Source: The Economist, 1999

British blood products were banned in Europe and the United States because of fears – rather than epidemiological evidence – that they may transmit vCJD. The introduction of GM food and crops was slowed despite the lack of hard data on deleterious effects. Computer models of global climate informed environmental policy despite our imperfect understanding of the Earth's complex weather systems. Although the science was speculative, it was at least plausible, whether based on experiments on pollen distribution or our ability to model past climate change. Now, however, there are calls for policymakers to go beyond established science and examine unanticipated consequences or 'unknown unknowns'.

So, on the one hand, expectations of science and technology are increasing rapidly. Science today is exciting and full of commercial opportunities for improving our health, lifestyles and working environments. There are few problems facing society where science and technology are not expected to provide a solution. On the other, advances in knowledge are greeted with growing suspicion, even hostility.

These negative responses are expressed as lack of trust and have major implications for businesses wishing to successfully commercialize innovation in Europe.

But public perception of science has also been influenced by other factors, for example:

- Academic science has been matched by 'corporate' science. Business has a vested interest in the results of innovation as a means to develop new products and processes. On occasion it is accused of skewing or suppressing evidence of harmful effects, casting a shadow over definitions of what constitutes reasonable doubt and, therefore, 'acceptable' levels of risk (for example, accusations against the tobacco industry of withholding evidence of adverse health effects)

- Private sector funding of science in universities and research institutes has blurred the distinction between objective science and science designed to support promotional claims

- The search for funding has encouraged academics and research organizations to publicize findings which have not been the subject of formal peer review. Poorly designed or statistically insignificant studies promoted through the media have created a view of science as speculative or superficial (such as the link between the third generation contraceptive pill and deep vein thrombosis, the adverse health effects of radio frequency emissions from mobile phones, controversy over the safety of the MMR (measles, mumps and rubella) vaccine, the 'discovery' of cold fusion)

- Scientists working for government have to contend with a public perspective of low trust and disregard of expert opinion

- Scientists working for NGOs are often regarded to be more trustworthy than those working for government or business (for example, Shell and Brent Spar; the banning of phthalates in soft toys; anti-nuclear campaigning)

A Eurobarometer survey published in 2000 asked people across Europe about their trust in information originating from different sources concerning modern biotechnology. They were asked to identify the source they trusted most, and to indicate whether they trusted other types of organizations (see Table 5.1).

Table 5.1 *European survey of trust*

Group	First	Others	Total	Class
Consumer organizations	26	29	55	1
Environmental organizations	14	31	45	3
Animal welfare organizations	4	21	25	5
Medical profession	24	29	53	2
Farmers' associations	3	12	15	9
Religious organizations	2	7	9	11
Public authorities	3	12	15	9
International institutions	4	13	17	8
A specific industry	0	3	3	12
Universities	7	19	26	4
Political parties	0	3	3	12
Television and newspapers	4	16	20	6
None of these	6	5	11	10
Don't know	6	12	18	7

Source: Eurobarometer, 2000

Consumer organizations and the medical profession emerge as trustworthy, with environmental organizations lagging third. Universities and the media are low as first choice but, together with animal welfare organizations, are trustworthy second sources. It comes as no surprise that industry and politicians are right down at the bottom of the trust list.

Exploring this further, consumers were asked in a separate survey which two or three scientific developments they would regard as beneficial for society and which two or three have not been beneficial (see Table 5.2).

Americans do not appear to share the apparent decline in confidence reported by the media in Europe and are generally more positive about the overall effects of innovation. However, levels of trust in the media's ability to report on these developments in a balanced way is questioned. The US National Science Foundation asked people about their confidence in those running various types of institutions. While the data

Table 5.2 Beneficial developments

Development	Beneficial %	Not beneficial %	Net %
Medicines, new drugs, Penicillin, Antibiotics, Vaccines	57	I	+56
Transplants, such as heart, liver, kidney	51	I	+50
Cures for or eradication of illnesses	43	I	+42
New operations, surgery	31	–	+31
Computers, the Internet, e-mail	28	4	+24
Genetic testing or disease screening	24	2	+22
Discovering global warming, climate change, disruption to weather patterns	19	6	+13
New and alternative sources of energy	17	4	+13
New telecommunications (fax, mobile phone, TV)	14	5	+9
Test tube babies, IV fertilisation	11	9	+2
Faster, cheaper travel	6	16	–10
Robots in industry and medicine	3	18	–15
Splitting the atom	4	20	–16
Space research, people to the moon	2	25	–23
Genetic modification/engineering of animals and plants	I	28	–27
Genetically modified food	I	45	–44
Cloning, Dolly the sheep	2	57	–55

Source: MORI/OST, 13 March to 14 April 1999: base 1109 British adults

show a slight decline in trust in medicine, confidence in scientific institutions remains the same as 25 years ago, but there is a marked decrease in confidence in the media (see Figure 5.1).

Twenty or thirty years ago, public response to environmental health scares was characterized by a general expectation that a combination of existing regulation and the advice of scientific and technical experts, would provide an adequate safety net.

Levels of trust in government to protect, and in experts to supply the evidence base to reassure, was much higher – symptoms of a traditional respect for authority, the assumed integrity of experts and a basic belief that scientific and technological innovation was generally a good thing. For example, childhood vaccination programmes were generally seen to be

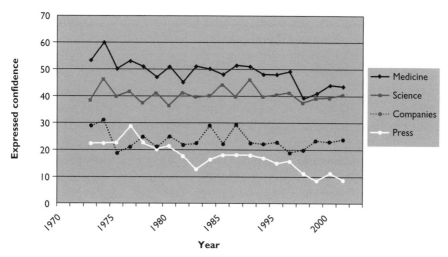

Figure 5.1 *Public confidence in people running various institutions in USA*

Source: National Science Foundation, 2000; average sample size 1500

highly beneficial in reducing risk from whooping cough, measles and tuberculosis. Risk from side-effects was not considered to be a matter of contention, let alone public debate. A very different picture has emerged over the last two or three years in the case of the combination MMR vaccine.

At a time which is dominated by the new religion of consumerism, a much stronger sense of individualism and lack of trust in government institutions and industry, the policy consequences of managing new or changing risks are very different. Now, when a new hazard, however poorly characterized, is identified public officials have to decide whether protective actions should be taken quickly, or whether they should be delayed until scientific uncertainties about the hazard are reduced or resolved. But in our 24/7 media environment, delay through uncertainty carries zero credibility. This dilemma is increasingly widespread, with newspapers and news programmes reporting on controversies about electric power lines, wireless communication devices, synthetic chemicals, genetically engineered foods and medical products, food production and distribution practices, and sources of energy to fuel motor vehicles, utilities and industry.

So why and how has science failed us? According to a document prepared by the European Commission on the subject of 'Science, society and the citizen in Europe' (Commission Working Document, November 2000), openness and dialogue are the keys to better public acceptance of science. Hardly contentious stuff today! The report states that in the past science developed on the basis of an unspoken contract between research institutes, universities, industry and government. Little or no reference was made to members of the public.

In our new knowledge economy, 'the consequences of science and research on economic growth, competitiveness, jobs and creating a balanced and just society require a much more dynamic approach to inform and build relationships with and between researchers, industries, policymakers, interest groups and the public as a whole'. The report highlights the importance of sustainable development in relation to the environment but also to the economy and society, and calls for a debate and suggestions for action to create dialogue and improve public understanding and acceptance of science. The underlying theme advocates much greater openness, and where scientific advice is uncertain, this should be admitted from the start. At least the Food Standards Agency in the UK picked up on this point in June 2001 when it issued a statement (generating considerable media interest, of course), saying that there may be a possibility that sheep can be infected with Mad Cow (BSE) disease as a result of eating feed produced from rendered cattle carcasses, and that studies were well underway to establish if this could be the case. Unfortunately, not long after, the UK government was forced to own up to the fact that three years' worth of research had to be discarded because cattle brains had been used instead of sheep brains!

Another EU Communication entitled 'Innovation in a knowledge-driven economy' (EU, 2000) acknowledges that 'the creation of a planned European Research Area as a central plank of Europe's knowledge-based economy and society will only be achieved by an economy geared to innovation and a society fully committed to it'. The Communication also highlights the need for consistency in approach across Europe '... as the recent food crises showed, the problems arising in this area or requiring action in scientific terms very often occur simultaneously throughout Europe'. So as the UK government admitted it got it wrong and was 'unduly precautionary' over the outbreak of Foot and Mouth Disease in 2001, there is recognition in political circles that all is not well. Reason enough for a radical harmonisation of European food law with particular reference to safety and greater transparency throughout the food chain.

Against a backdrop of uncertainty, something that is certain is that sources of information are crucial to the way in which we perceive and respond to risk. Public opinion polling after the Brent Spar incident in 1995 showed that members of the public trusted scientists working for environmental groups much more than those working for industry or government (MORI, 1995). Successful risk communications and risk management – the outcomes of which strongly influence stakeholder trust and beliefs – depends on providing the right kind of information, often through trusted third parties. In other words, having the right navigation chart with the right information on it provides the basis for a company and its stakeholders to negotiate a compatible passage.

Research in Europe certainly suggests that consumers are totally confused about who to trust on food safety issues. The furore over GMOs, especially when they were perceived to be creeping quietly on to our supermarket shelves, was a risk communication disaster and engendered further suspicion of science and of the companies at the heart of commercializing the results.

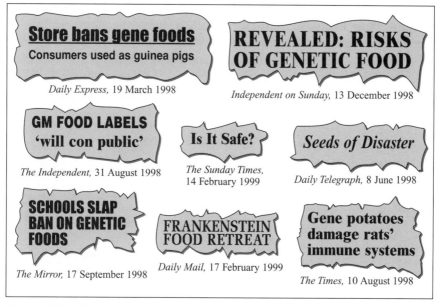

Figure 5.2 *Why should business worry?*

Monsanto's plans to introduce genetically modified crops in the mid to late 1990s, initially in the UK and more widely in Europe, met with a strong backlash from consumers, environmentalists, regulators and retailers. The company had achieved significant success from the application of biotechnology to food production in the United States and obtained EU approval in 1996 for imports of GM foods and the development of research and supply sites. In spite of growing concerns about inadequate testing of genetically modified organisms (GMOs) in a market environment already prone to low trust over food safety, it was not until 1998, when the company introduced a national advertising campaign, that it rapidly became the focus of a national media debate. Reassurances from government and industry scientists about health risk claims simply fuelled front page headlines in UK national newspapers and quickly spilled over into continental European media. An unpublished study by a scientist, Dr Arpad Pusztai, implied that immune damage was possible as a result of feeding GM potato to rats. Although senior colleagues refuted his claims, the controversy escalated, with consumer groups accusing Monsanto of 'bio-colonialism' and criticizing it for suggesting that agricultural biotechnology could resolve food shortages in developing countries. Greenpeace pursued high profile direct action, with senior representatives uprooting GM crops and being arrested for their trouble. Politicians, keen to see the development of a healthy biotechnology industry, singularly failed to stem the tide of negative scrutiny and growing public concern. Retailers rushed to remove GM products from their shelves and started to use 'GM free' labelling as a competitive ploy. Monsanto's share price continued to fall and became a major factor in its forced merger with Pharmacia Upjohn in

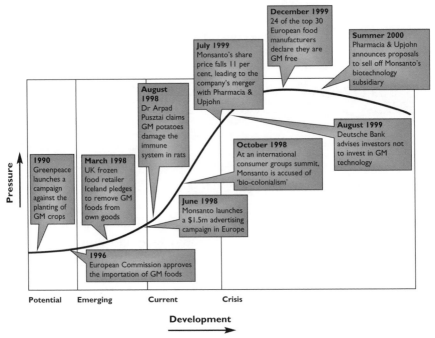

Figure 5.3 Risk issue lifecycle: Monsanto

Source: Regester Larkin

the summer of 1999. Deutsche Bank subsequently advised institutional investors to drop investments in companies involved in GM technology, noting European consumer concerns over food safety and stating that "hearing from unsophisticated Americans that their fears are unfounded may not be the best way of proceeding"!

In the summer of 2000, Pharmacia Upjohn announced proposals to sell off Monsanto's biotechnology subsidiary, precipitating a major restructuring across the international agrochemicals sector. The Monsanto brand has never recovered. At a Greenpeace conference late in 1999, Monsanto's Chairman, Bob Shapiro, admitted by video conference from the US that "because we thought it was our job to persuade, too often we have forgotten to listen". High levels of public concern about the safety of and need for GM food, magnified by negative media coverage and NGO campaigning, forced retreat at national government level and brought about a three year freeze on GM crop and food production in the EU.

The lessons from this sorry mess? Firstly, risk issue icebergs *must* be anticipated and planned for – and there was plenty of warning in this case! Secondly, companies at the centre of controversy must acknowledge public concerns – real or perceived – and respond very quickly.

Anticipate:
- Be sensitive to cultural differences between markets
- Research existing consumer and NGO campaign issues
- Build stakeholder relationships and trusted third party support
- Think outside the box by anticipating people's attitudes
- Build benefits separately

Respond:
- Acknowledge concerns
- Take responsibility for 'owning' issues
- Listen and tailor information to the sensitivities and needs of different groups
- Understand supply chain concerns
- Regularly assess relevance/success of response and adapt

No wonder then, that a poll commissioned by pharmaceuticals and agrochemical giant Novartis (July 1999) showed widespread opposition to such technology. Among 991 respondents, 62 per cent opposed the genetic modification of plants for crops, and opposition was even more widespread to the cloning of animals (74 per cent) and to the genetic modification of animals for medical research (71 per cent). However, when people were presented with the hypothesis that without these practices, a cure for Alzheimer's would not be possible, 15 per cent changed their minds on the genetic modification of crops. Bill Fullagar, President of Novartis UK, sees this as a worrying breakdown of communication between scientists and the public:

> "Very little about the potential benefits of scientific research has been discussed in the press. Instead, with GM crops, we are riding on a tide of emotion and fear.
>
> But once you relate technology to the benefits, then in intelligent people you get a shift of opinion. If you say you are testing GM crops, people think only of the risk. But if you say 'I'm trying to produce a plant that has a minor genetic variation and can be grown using fewer pesticides so there is less contamination of ground-water', they get interested."
>
> *Source: The Times*, 8 September 1999

The poll also highlighted greater risk aversion – in the case of governments, politicians and regulatory authorities being scared away from funding or approving controversial studies because of the threat of a public outcry.

> "Personally speaking, I think aversion to risk is a serious threat to science", Fullager adds. "People want zero risk but that means society stagnates instead of progressing. What happens if you don't get permission for scientific studies here? You go to North America where they do give permission. So scientists leave and this translates into a loss of wealth."
>
> *Source: The Times*, 8 September, 1999

Failure to acknowledge public concern over the uncertainties associated with scientific and technological innovation can have devastating consequences for corporate reputation and business continuity with traumatic consequences for an entire industry, as Monsanto's actions demonstrated. It is the biggest iceberg of all and really can crush asset value. The emergence of precautionary approaches to policy development, largely in response to public aversion to risk, adds a new and complex dimension to reputation risk management.

Business also has to worry about the litigation and compensation penalties associated with low trust and resulting precautionary regulation and legislation. The explosion in litigation that took root in the United States twenty-odd years ago is now creating stormy conditions in parts of Europe – most noticeably, in the UK, France and Germany. A culture of compensation has taken litigation into previously immune areas.

People now claim for tripping over paving stones and damaging their cars in pot-holes; former school pupils sue their old schools alleging that they were let down by the system; soldiers, policemen and fire-fighters seek redress from trauma, Gulf War syndrome and the events of 11 September – and in some cases receive more money than the victims they were trained to protect. Some of the craziest cases include a Canadian woman who was awarded $300,000 after alleging her employer did not do enough to stop her driving home drunk after an office party; a New Zealand prisoner who was awarded $20,000 after breaking his leg while attempting to scale a prison wall; and the verdict of a US jury to award $4.9 bn against General Motors when a Chevrolet stopped at traffic lights exploded when a car rammed into its back at speed – they argued that the gas tank could have been better protected!

According to the American Insurance Association, over 21,000 insurance claims have been filed in New York State since the terrorist attacks and the international insurance industry is expecting claims totalling up to $50 bn.

Importantly for companies, employees threaten legal action over harassment, discrimination, stress and other occupational health effects in the workplace, while patients and consumers use the legal system to extract money over the most minor of alleged side effects, psychiatric distress and product defects. I have a friend who has made a lucrative hobby out of complaint to the extent that the threat of media exposure or legal action has brought him many free holidays, replacement cars and other consumer goods! Turnover in legal business in the United States and the UK is estimated to equate to 2 per cent of GDP.

In the UK, regarded as the second most litigious country after the US, one in seven members of the public seek dispute resolution through the courts; compensation and legal fees are estimated to total around £10 bn a year and rising.

The main justification for tort law is that it holds individuals and organizations to account for the damage or injury that their negligent action has inflicted on others. Unfortunately, greed and blame have overtaken this function of allocating responsibility, and so the link between the demand for compensation and actual responsibility has become negotiable. And it is little comfort to note a decline in the number of cases reaching courts under the tort system, because most litigation now takes place in court-linked arbitration and mediation schemes, and out-of-court settlements. Personal injury lawyers know all too well that companies do not want damaging publicity. And there are plenty of publicity-seeking lawyers establishing long-term strategies for expert testimony to support causation in plaintiff-friendly jurisdictions between, say, electromagnetic frequency from mobile phones and brain tumours, or Gulf War Syndrome and debilitating ill health. In addition, nervousness about litigation means that insurance companies are increasing premiums to businesses for public, professional and product liability. American-style contingency fee systems, access to class action litigation and relaxation in European regulations which facilitate 'ambulance chasing' advertising makes the spectre of a pay-out as accessible as seeking financial, medical or property advice. This kind of action brought Dow Corning to its knees in the mid 1990s over the health effects of silicone breast implants, will continue to sap the financial and reputational energy of Firestone and Ford Motor Company over the tyre recall associated with Ford's SUV through 2000 to 2002, and will take years to unravel with untold and far-reaching international commercial consequences following the failures of Enron and WorldCom in 2002.

Multi-party action is becoming institutionalized in Europe and widely supported by activists who argue that it represents a redistribution of power from public institutions and big business to the individual.

The point I want to make about these developments goes beyond the fact that the financial consequences are clearly significant. The root cause is a mood of scepticism and a lack of trust, and the use of litigation by anyone including companies, reinforces the erosion of trust and can result in hugely damaging reputational disasters. Remember the failed legal action by 39 pharmaceutical companies in South Africa in early 2001 designed to protect patents and therefore prices for AIDS drugs? The action collapsed as a result of effective direct action and damaging international media censure. It was widely agreed that recourse to legal action was an international public relations disaster and has already placed the global pharmaceutical industry – quite rightly – in the spotlight over lack of transparency on pricing policies and the social and ethical consequences of access to medicines in developing countries. As a result, the industry has lost the moral high ground and will, doubtless, have a rougher ride with regulators regarding pricing approvals for new drugs.

Policy wonks and the new precautionary language

A new policy framework is emerging based on ambiguous definitions and guidelines under the guise of the precautionary principle, which is fast becoming a mantra for responding to all sorts of uncertainties in everyday living. The principle has emerged as one of the most influential regulatory tools for EU environmental health and consumer protection policy. It has also increased in popularity beyond Europe, underpinning international agreements such as the Convention on Biodiversity. We now talk about taking precautionary measures for anything from using a cough remedy to ward off the onset of a routine cold, to stocking up the wine supply on the offchance of a spontaneous party, to wearing a raincoat in anticipation of clouds accumulating overhead. So, although it feels as though the principle has been around a long time, it is becoming much more visible and pervasive in public and policy language.

The underlying implications for business are that while it is deeply confusing, poorly defined and highly subjective in interpretation, the principle provides a formidable new weapon for NGOs with an anti-technology or anti-business agenda to define public policy by forcing tougher regulation in the broad areas of public health, consumer and environmental protection.

The main aim of the principle is – quite sensibly – to call for prompt protective action rather than delay under the guise of scientific uncertainty. And it does have a sound basis in decision theory, particularly in situations where the potential hazards are serious and the costs of protective actions are tolerable. However, there is no universal approach and one recent study reported 19 different definitions! (Sand, 1999).

The Rio (1992) version of the principle captures its essence: '… where there are threats of serious or irreversible damage, lack of scientific certainty shall not be used as a reason for postponing cost-effective measures to prevent environmental degradation'. In other words, it's a 'better safe than sorry' stance toward concerns about technological danger. The principle has been called 'the most important new policy approach in international environmental co-operation' (Freestone, 1991) and it has not taken long for it to become integral to policy formulation in areas such as public health, food, consumer goods generally, information access and any form of innovation.

For example, European reforms designed to minimize risk from chemical hazards require the precautionary principle to be 'a basis' for bringing new and existing substances under one regime, but the process is as clear as mud! The objective is to collect information on key risks on a public 'right to know' basis, classify substances according to their potential environmental health risk and suspend use of substances and products posing unacceptable hazards. Critics of the chemicals industry say that companies have been less than forthcoming either about self regulation or information disclosure associated with risk management, so it is high time that tougher regulations are introduced.

Justifiably then, the burden of information gathering and disclosure rests with industry, but it does pose complex questions about how and where to prioritize this work across the manufacturing and supply chain. Furthermore, these new measures also raise questions about the cost and bureaucracy associated with authorizing every use of every single substance. The view that dangerous substances should be substituted by safer chemicals is fine in theory but difficult to apply in practice. Although none of this is a formal legal requirement – yet – and industry is responding – environmental groups now have a very large iceberg with which to block industry at any stage in the process.

Few policies for risk management have created as much debate as the precautionary principle, both because of the extreme variability in interpretation and the fact that in spite of an increase in case law, the legal community remains divided about its meaning and applicability. At one extreme, application may mean stopping a particular activity in its entirety, at the other it can mean limiting or mitigating it. In addition, critics have interpreted 'precautionary' decisions as veiled forms of trade protectionism. Examples include 'precautionary' decisions at a European level to ban American and Canadian beef reared on growth hormones, the use of a natural hormone, BST, designed to boost milk yields in cows, to ban aflatoxins in ground nuts, and to delay approving genetically engineered crops for sale in European markets. Needless to say, the US has responded with retaliatory tariffs on EU exports to North America.

Evolution and gestation – the principle's coming of age

The precautionary principle evolved from environmental law and public policy. It first emerged in Germany in the 1960s as a founding principle for environmental policy (although there is evidence that precautionary approaches were used in the US in the 1950s against fluoride and radiation). Described as 'foresight-planning', it called for a distinction to be made between human actions that cause 'dangers' – which government should prevent by all means, and those that merely cause 'risks' – which require government to carry out risk analyses which may necessitate preventative action. Social scientists in the 1970s argued that where there is a possibility of catastrophic risk from the use of a technology, potential problems created by that technology (such as disposal of nuclear waste) should be solved *before* proceeding with its use or else it should not be used at all. An early application of this open-ended approach came in 1985 when the European Commission banned hormones used for animal growth promotion on the basis that 'their safety has not been conclusively proven'. So even then the burden of proof was shifting.

The principle gained international recognition in the late 1980s and at the UN Conference on Environment and Development in Rio de Janeiro in 1992, where a ministerial declaration argued that where there are threats of serious environmental damage, lack of full scientific certainty should not be used as a reason for postponing cost-effective measures to prevent it. It was subsequently incorporated into the EU Treaty of Rome with the statement, 'The Community policy on the environment shall be based on the precautionary principle'. Other countries have adopted a similar approach for environmental policy and there is now wide acceptance through the courts that the principle should not be limited to environmental damage, and can be applied to situations involving public health. The European Court of Justice applied what equated to the principle to justify the bans on British beef at the height of the BSE scare in 1996 and 1998.

In early 1999, and in response to a number of public health scares, the European Council of Ministers urged the Commission to 'be even more guided by the precautionary principle' in the preparation of proposals for legislation and consumer related activities. An EU Communication in February 2000 on how to apply the principle stated that it would be activated 'when scientific evidence is not conclusive enough to determine a level of protection and when there is a need (public concern) to take measures for the purposes of protecting public health, safety and the environment'.

The February 2002 EU Communication stated that the principle should be considered within a structured approach to the analysis of risk based on three elements – **risk assessment**, **risk management** and **risk communication**. 'Recourse to the principle presupposes that potentially dangerous effects derived from a phenomenon, product or process have been identified and that scientific evaluation does not allow the risk to be determined with sufficient certainty'.

In addition, 'decision-makers need to be aware of the degree of uncertainty attached to the results of the evaluation and that judging what is an 'acceptable' level of risk for society is an eminently *political* responsibility. Decision-makers faced with an unacceptable risk, scientific uncertainty and

▶

public concerns have a duty to find answers. Therefore, all these factors have to be taken into consideration'... 'and procedure should be transparent and should involve as early as possible and to the extent reasonably possible all interested parties'. Finally, 'where action is deemed necessary, measures based on the precautionary principle should be, *inter alia*:

- *Proportional* to the chosen level of protection (that is, tailoring measures to the chosen level of protection)
- *Non-discriminatory* in their application (that is, comparable situations should not be treated differently)
- *Consistent* with similar measures already taken (that is, of comparable scope and nature to those already taken in equivalent areas)
- *Based on an examination of the potential benefits and costs* of action or lack of action, including, where appropriate and feasible, an economic cost/benefit analysis (that is, comparing the overall cost to the community of action and lack of action, in both the short and long term)
- *Subject to review*, in the light of new scientific data (that is, measures should be periodically reviewed through scientific progress and amended as necessary)
- *Capable of assigning responsibility for producing the scientific evidence* necessary for a more comprehensive risk assessment (that is, in the same way that countries that impose a prior approval (marketing authorization) requirement on products that they deem dangerous *a priori* reverse the burden of proving injury).'

Most of the leading environmental groups refer to the principle in their campaign agendas seeking, for example, bans on toxic substances called POPs (Persistent Organic Pollutants), phase-out and improved waste management of plastics and heavy metals. Any one of them choosing to target a product or industrial process simply needs to produce some evidence of ambiguity for the precautionary principle process to unfold, calling for:

- **Reversal of the burden of proof:** Businesses and scientific bodies have to show harm will not be done, rather than others showing that it will
- **Duty to take action to prevent harm:** A duty enforceable through the tort system, in the same way that we have a duty not to drive in a way that injures other drivers

- **No 'safe dose' for carcinogenic substances:** A particularly ambiguous claim and a dilemma for business response because any possible association with cancer has significant potential for generating public outrage; however, many carcinogenic substances are naturally occurring and many everyday products are carcinogens in large doses
- **No technology admitted until proven harmless**
- **Examination of the full range of alternatives:** The problem here is that examining alternatives could be infinite and many alternatives are not known until a technology is introduced and improvements identified
- **The merest possibility of harm should justify preventative action/ postponement:** This doesn't take into account the fact that many risks associated with new products or processes are lower than existing ones

The onus to demonstrate absolute safety is now much more demanding on business. Switching on the radar to help predict the potential for precautionary attack and being prepared to communicate swiftly is vital in establishing share of voice and legitimacy for the product or process under review. The alternative is to be regulated out of the marketplace. Take a look at the case of phthalates and it is not difficult to see how NGO campaigning in the name of environmental health precautionary policies can push an industry straight into a field of icebergs.

Phthalates in toys – who dictates safety?

Phthalates have been used in a wide range of products for almost 50 years, because of their ability to turn rigid polyvinyl chloride (PVC) into a flexible product. In the mid 1990s the safety of phthalates, particularly in childrens' toys, was called into question amid claims that they could cause cancers, liver damage and hormonal disruption. Environmental NGOs in Europe and the United States launched a concerted campaign to ban phthalates in childrens' toys and, despite a lack of clear scientific evidence that phthalates could pose a health risk, the EU eventually banned phthalates at the end of 1999 in teething rings and toys that could be sucked by children under the age of three. Similar measures were subsequently introduced in the United States.

Greenpeace was the most influential campaigner against phthalates in toys, and for many years had highlighted environmental health risks from

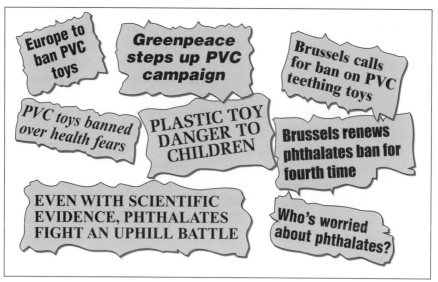

Figure 5.4 *Media headlines*

chlorine and associated plastics manufacture. In 1996, it began contacting leading toy manufacturers requesting meetings to discuss concerns about PVC toys, and began targeting the European Commission.

By April 1997, the Danish Environmental Protection Agency (EPA) stated that the level of phthalates in teething rings was 'unacceptable' and Danish importers voluntarily withdrew teethers from the market pending further research. The European Commission referred the concerns regarding phthalates to the newly appointed Scientific Committee on Toxicity, Ecotoxicity and Environment (CTSEE) for investigation.

In September 1997, Greenpeace launched its 'Play Safe' campaign in New York and London, 100 days before Christmas. The campaign increased direct action against manufacturers and retailers – a list of PVC and non-PVC infant toys was made available to parents in an attempt to target manufacturers such as Mattel and retailers such as Toys 'R' Us. Greenpeace's claims continued to be widely and sensationally reported by the media. The following month saw requests from the Austrian Consumer Affairs Minister and Belgian Public Health Minister for the voluntary withdrawal of PVC toys on the basis of precautionary consumer protection. A domino effect followed across Europe with similar restrictions being introduced in Italy, Germany and Spain. Retailers in these countries began to withdraw branded PVC products from sale. In December 1997, a German toy retailer association responded by calling for a total withdrawal of PVC toys.

Although scientific evidence indicated no adverse human health effects, under growing media and NGO pressure the European Commission requested that the CTSEE set up a working group to investigate the impact of phthalates on children's health, and to suggest appropriate limits and test methods. The Commission removed all PVC toys from its childcare facilities as 'a precautionary measure' in February 1998.

Throughout 1998, there was considerable scientific debate on phthalates, but not much in the way of a united response from industry. The World Health Organisation (WHO) denied phthalates had carcinogenic properties but, under concerted NGO and media pressure, the European Commission still agreed a non-binding recommendation to withdraw teething rings from use. Member states were invited to adopt appropriate safety measures while Community legislation for permanent protection was prepared. Between 1998 and 1999, eight EU countries introduced their own restrictions on the production and sale of phthalates. The government bans gave Greenpeace considerable ammunition to advance its crusade against the plastics industry.

In July 1999, the European CSTEE reported that scientific research showed there was no immediate health risk. However, in December 1999, the EC went ahead with a three-month renewable ban on PVC toys and teething products intended to be put in the mouths of children under three, pending future legislation. The ban has been continuously renewed since then. On 6 July 2000, the European Parliament voted on a draft council Directive on phthalates in toys, requiring the banning of all phthalates in plastic toys for children under three years of age. This was followed by a demand by the European Parliament for a policy to replace soft PVC.

In the United States, industry capitulation was also swift. Government agencies, toy manufacturers and toy retailers came under pressure to remove phthalates from their products following the regulatory action in EU countries. Greenpeace accelerated its campaign in the United States during this period; at the opening of the International Toy Fair in New York in autumn 1998, activists abseiled down the side of a building to unfurl a banner that said 'Play Safe, Buy PVC Free'. Relentless pressure from Greenpeace and the US environmental NGO Environmental Defense (ED) led some larger US manufacturers to remove phthalates from their products and Mattel announced voluntary action to remove phthalates from soft toys in 1998.

In December 1998, the US Consumer Product Safety Commission (CPSC) asked industry, as a precautionary measure, to remove one particular phthalate (DINP) from soft rattles and teethers in spite of a CPSC study demonstrating that 'the amount ingested does not even come close to a harmful level'. The plastics industry was requested to remove phthalates from soft toys and teethers to "alleviate the mood of fear and as a precaution while more scientific work is being done".

Environmental Defense maintained the pressure. In October 2000, it wrote to 100 US toy manufacturers requesting voluntary disclosure of the chemical constituents of their products "either targeted for young children or that in use involves mouthing or extensive skin contact by children including older children". The Juvenile Product Manufacturers Association (JPMA) and the Toy Manufacturers Association (TMA) responded by saying that they did not think this was necessary, enabling Environmental Defense to claim that "they would say that wouldn't they" through ongoing media articles and advertising campaigns.

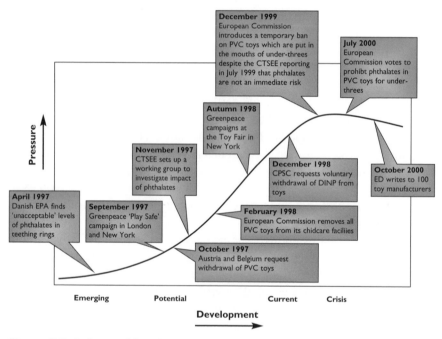

Figure 5.5 *Risk issue lifecycle: phthalates*
Source: Regester Larkin

European and American regulatory reaction towards the phthalates campaign ultimately forced the plastics industry to withdraw its products. Companies producing, selling and using phthalates took a wholly unnecessary hit to their reputation and to their financial performance. Why? Because of a failure to understand the dynamics of the issue lifecycle curve, the triggers that can escalate a risk issue out of control and an inability to communicate early on and in any concerted way to offset public perception of an exaggerated health risk.

If you see national regulatory agencies calling for voluntary restrictions on products, recognize that you are already forfeiting any chance of navigating your way round the risk perception icebergs!

A referee's nightmare

In its strongest form, the precautionary principle can be interpreted as calling for absolute proof of safety before allowing new technologies to be adopted. Other formulations advocate cost-benefit analysis and discretionary judgement.

Some versions of the principle are designed to address complications that arise from real-world problems. If a precautionary action is likely to be costly, a preference for 'cost-effective' actions might be expressed (as in the Rio statement). To avoid getting bogged down with less important risks, the principle can be applied only to serious and/or irreversible hazards, or it might be stated that the stringency of the protective action should be linked to the gravity of the potential hazard (the principle of proportionality). These sorts of variations help to complement the principle's intuitive appeal by addressing factors that arise in practical decision-making.

Lofstedt quotes work by Wiener and Rogers which argues that there are three different formulations of the principle:

Version 1: *Uncertainty does not justify inaction. In its most basic form, the precautionary principle is a principle that permits regulation in the absence of complete evidence about the particular risk scenario.*

Version 2: *Uncertainty justifies action.*

Version 3: *Uncertainty requires shifting the burden and standard of proof. This means that uncertain risk requires forbidding the potentially risky activity until the proponent of the activity demonstrates that it poses no (or acceptable) risk.*

Different versions are used by different European countries in relation to individual risk scenarios, for example, with Sweden likely to adopt Version 3, while Germany, France or the UK may choose to adopt the softer Version 1.

Source: Lofstedt, 2002

However, there is plenty of room for ambiguity here. For example, some experts are citing complications caused by *beneficial* (as well as adverse) health and ecological effects arising from exposure to hazards – there is now a compelling body of evidence that moderate alcohol intake reduces rates of chronic disease. The revival of thalidomide's reputation as an anti-tumour agent is a striking example.

Another factor relates to the creation of unintended potential hazards from precautionary actions. In the 1970s and 1980s, the potential hazards of nuclear energy stimulated calls for precaution, contributing to the demise of nuclear power as a major source of electricity in the USA.

Yet the price of precaution, measured in health and environmental damage, has been high as more fossil fuels have been burned to generate the electricity required – a major cause of soot and smog in the air as well as greenhouse gas emissions implicated in global climate change. Now there are calls in the USA for a precautionary approach to fossil fuels! Experts also point out that the prohibition of hazardous waste incineration at sea is likely to increase incineration on land, which could release dangerous pollutants into ecosystems that are actually more vulnerable. The banning of DDT has forced farmers to use other, more toxic pesticides and has resulted in a rapid re-emergence of malaria in developing countries (Graham, 2000).

There are opportunities for companies, however, to make targeted scientific investments using decision analysis and cost-benefit analysis. If planned and managed appropriately as a precautionary strategy it is possible to reduce or resolve uncertainty and thereby facilitate sensible long-term decision-making, as the following case study illustrates.

Do mobile phones cook your brains?

In April 1996, *The Sunday Times* newspaper in the UK printed a story with the headline 'Danger – mobile phones cook your brains', which set off a long-running media and NGO campaign regarding alleged health effects from mobile phone electromagnetic frequency (EMF) emissions. The health effects from EMFs have been studied since the second world war and have been the subject of international media, NGO and scientific scrutiny in relation to links between leukaemia and emissions from electricity transmission pylons. Concerns over risk of brain tumours and other health effects from mobile phones began in America and then Australia in the early 1990s, following litigation alleging that a woman's fatal cancer was the result of prolonged exposure to a mobile phone.

Electromagnetic fields are emitted by all sorts of electrical equipment from television masts and radio networks to hairdryers and ovens, and they are also naturally occurring. The science relating to EMF health effects is complex; it has been comprehensively reviewed by expert panels and government appointed inquiries and has formed the basis for national and international exposure guidelines. None has definitively concluded that EMF exposure within international guidelines causes adverse health effects; however, some recent data examining both thermal and non-thermal effects have proved controversial – suggesting a range of unpleasant health conditions.

In line with public inquiries in different countries and international scientific reviews, the majority of experts have called for further research and the adoption of precautionary policy approaches, for example, recommending avoidance of prolonged use of mobile phone by children. Scientific complexity coupled with uncertainty and risk aversion have provided impetus for continued media coverage, mobilization of public opinion against mobile base station sitings and on-going attempts to demonstrate causation between EMFs and brain cancers through the courts. Some of the key triggers that have projected the issue through a roller-coaster ride in recent years are highlighted in the life cycle diagram (Figure 5.6).

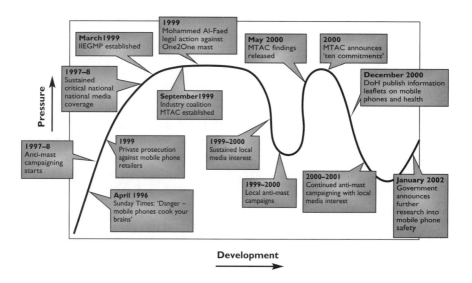

Figure 5.6 *Risk issue lifecycle: mobile phones and health*

Source: Regester Larkin

Using the risk perception wheel model, it is not difficult to see how concern levels can rise.

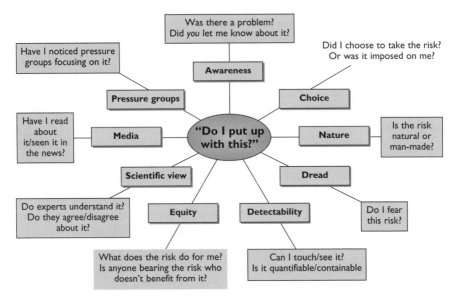

Figure 5.7 *Risk perception wheel – mobile phones and health*

Source: Regester Larkin

The highlighted text indicates an active trigger for raising public concern. In the case of choice and equity, while we can choose whether or not we want to use a mobile phone, it is difficult to object to the siting of base stations close to our backyards. Residents who don't use mobiles but do live close to base stations are in a less equitable position regarding the risk benefit equation. Moving house may not be a realistic option!

When I first got involved with this issue five years ago, Cable & Wireless was the first mobile company in the UK to recognize its potential for public concern and impact on the reputation and commercial health of the mobile phone industry – and not just in the UK. Mobile telecommunications is, by definition, an international business and companies like C&W, Vodafone, Deutsche Telecom, BT, France Telecom and Hutchison have invested enormous sums in creating global capabilities and global brands. Although there wasn't a shred of evidence that worry over health effects was affecting consumer purchasing or usage patterns, C&W called on other mobile operators to work together to establish a consistent and responsible industry voice on health issues. Quite naturally, some operators were sceptical of the need to do anything.

After all, 40,000 mobile phones were being sold a month, the companies were making huge sums of money in a demand-led market and it was crystal clear that consumers were becoming increasing dependent on mobile phones for business and leisure use.

C&W's senior director responsible for the issue, Ann Sullivan, commissioned my consultancy to undertake a risk assessment, present the findings to senior management and work to establish a risk issue management function within the corporate centre. The aim was to support local operating companies around the world to handle consumer, media, NGO and regulatory inquiries and requests for information on health issues. In particular, operating companies in Australia and Hong Kong were some years ahead of the emerging issue in Europe, so sharing experience and good practice in consumer communication, and liaison with regulators and public officials proved to be highly beneficial in briefing management teams around the world and in developing clear and consistent communication tools. Figure 5.8 describes the responsibilities of the issue working group within C&W.

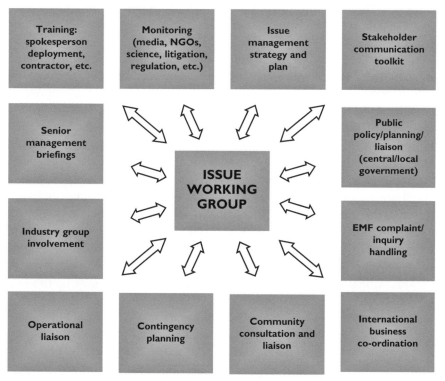

Figure 5.8 *Issue management approach*
Source: Regester Larkin

The health issue began to escalate in the UK in 1998 through 1999 with an increase in tabloid media reports highlighting the results of poorly designed studies connecting mobile phone usage with memory loss, headaches, increased blood pressure and fatigue. At the same time, an application for judicial review was made by Mohammed Al Fayed, the high profile owner of London's Harrods store, against the siting of a base station near his son Dodi's mausoleum on the multi-millionaire's Surrey estate. Calls for tougher regulation against operators were emerging in Australia, further litigation was being attempted in the United States and the World Health Organization established a working group to review international science on the subject with a five year timeframe for reporting. It was time for mobile phone operators in the UK to consider their position.

We helped to facilitate an informal group of senior managers from C&W, Vodafone, BT, One 2 One (now T-Mobile) and Orange to consider options for establishing a co-ordinated strategy in response to public interest in mobile phone health effects. Participants trawled company experience in international markets, participated in international scientific and risk communication fora and tapped into equivalent global operational, regulatory, litigation and public consultation experience within the electricity industry over EMF issues.

It didn't take long for the group to determine that organizing a single issue industry forum was the only realistic and credible route to go. What was needed was an executive director with appropriate experience, a decision as to whether the forum should be established as an entirely new entity or affiliated to an existing industry group and a decent budget. Group contacts, international networking and executive search identified an experienced corporate lawyer and risk communicator (Michael Dolan) with direct experience over many years of the electricity industry situation. A forum was set up to co-ordinate policies around the issue through the Federation of Electronic Industries in London – a well established group with expertise and links to equivalent groups around the world. Following a series of 'get to know' meetings and assessments of resourcing and policy requirements, the UK Mobile Telecommunications Advisory Committee (MTAC) was established towards the end of 1999. Over the next two years the Group developed a risk issue management framework along similar lines to the C&W model, designed to:

- Acknowledge and respond to public concern

- Develop and disseminate information to anticipate and respond to public interest in the issue, directly and through the media and NGOs

- Prepare industry spokespeople for media management and inquiry handling and participate in international industry, scientific and risk communication events

- Create tools for liaison with local government officials in relation to base station planning applications

- Develop expertise in participating in public meetings

- Establish and support independent scientific assessment of, and research into, EMF health effects

- Liaise with public policy officials to achieve a balance between commercial, regulatory and public interests

- Implement regular consumer and other stakeholder opinion polling as a means to gauge opinion and potential attitudes towards industry responses

- Provide for contingency planning requirements

Practical experience and learning also encouraged operators to establish their own EMF units designed to communicate around company-specific network management requirements. Our work in this area was based on creating a risk management case to justify additional resourcing for an EMF unit against a background of:

- Reducing increased cost of capital and loss of revenue through delays in network commissioning as a result of direct action, by swifter and improved information quality

- Managing the 'opportunity costs' associated with significant additional handling of public and customer inquiries about health related issues; a key measurement criterion was based on an inquiry response procedure with in-built escalation to process responses appropriately and within defined time periods

- Offsetting the potential for costly litigation or additional insurance liability through structured dialogue with public officials, local planning officers, regulators, technical and scientific experts and the media

At the time of writing, attempts in US jurisdictions to win judicial approval for litigation on mobile phone health effects has not succeeded; however, high profile plaintiff-friendly lawyers are determined to pursue legal action in this field and it is possible that in the next few years, scientific data and expert opinion may make this strategy stick, with major liability consequences for industry. In addition, international scientific review programmes have yet to report their findings. While essential use of mobile phones continues to dominate and transcend global economies and cultures, public concern over mobile phone safety isn't denting customer usage patterns. Public opinion polling in Europe is, however, suggesting more precautionary attitudes to the use of, or exposure to, mobile phone emissions in the case of children. It is also indicating that people are confused about the science and quality of information in making decisions; one clear indicator is that they are not inclined to trust the mobile phone companies in helping them to make decisions!

Who knows how this issue will roll on and roll out? Industry has done some excellent work in the area of acknowledging and responding to the emotions and vagaries of public risk perception associated with mobile phone health effects. A great deal of good practice has been pursued and implemented. What is worrying in 2002 is that against this positive reputation risk management background but declining financial performance, there is a real risk that the companies will quickly lose sight of the benefits achieved so far and strip out the associated costs on short-term performance grounds. According to Ann Sullivan, "applying the reputation risk radar now is even more important than ever before".

Untangling controversy

Controversy over interpretation and application of the precautionary principle as a basis for global risk management continues, sometimes explosively so, as the collapse of negotiations for a biosafety protocol at the Cartegena meeting in February 1999 demonstrated. Disagreement on precautionary draft provisions was a contributing factor and even after compromise was reached in Montreal in January 2000, the new protocol is very confusing to interpret. The dilution of the 1999 Kyoto agreement on curbing carbon emissions, and disarray at the 2002 Earth Summit, are other cases in point. One of the first significant policy decisions of the Bush administration and criticized by the international community as a pay-back to the industries that helped put it in power, the precautionary parameters of the agreement were, nevertheless, considered by many to be unworkable.

Confusion arises in particular around three questions summarized in the panel opposite.

1. **How rigorously should the 'precautionary' component be applied?**

   The definition of 'precaution' could, for example, be applied by placing the onus on ensuring consumers are well informed to make their own choices based on their individual attitudes to risk, rather than food and consumer protection agencies imposing extensive regulatory restrictions on behalf of all consumers.

2. **What range of principle(s) should be taken into consideration?**

   It could include environmental protection, sustainable development, ethical, social, health, safety and welfare, of both humans and animals, and range from the short term to the long term. The final scope of the principle may well be those enshrined in the new EU Charter of Fundamental Rights. However, the focus at European level of single issue campaigns, often including direct action by NGOs (such as the fuel tax protests in Europe during summer 2000) undermines the efforts of European and national policymakers to develop a 'balance of risk' approach to interpretation of the principle, and often increases in the public a tendency towards zero tolerance.

3. **What are the roles of EU authorities in the application and enforcement of the principle?**

   For example, the organization of EU policymaking bodies regarding biotechnology issues cuts across a number of sectors and so involves Directorates dealing with Agriculture, Competition, Employment and Social Affairs, Enterprise, Environment, Health and Consumer Protection, Internal Market, Research, and External Relations. However, each Directorate represents a different client base, is embedded in different policy networks, has a different institutional mandate and different standard operating procedures, and is, therefore, concerned with slightly different product or problem areas related to the use of biotechnology. These Directorates also have widely differing beliefs and perceptions of biotechnology and the extent to which biotechnology products and processes require regulation. The process by which these different subcultures merge (or not) is critical to understanding the development of EU biotechnology policy and its potential impact on managing reputation risk within the biotechnology sector.

While the EU and its member states have yet to decide how in general they will interpret the principle, from a management perspective there seem to be two main alternative labels which have very different implications for successful innovation, business continuity and reputation risk management:

- One label says *'Danger! Proceed with Extreme Care'*. It's like being given a yellow card on a soccer pitch or a technical foul in basketball. It places a stronger duty on the developer and the supply chain generally. The clear implications of this approach are a more defensive as opposed to innovative approach to research and development.

- Another label says *'This is a Formal Caution'* in the legal sense of a formal warning prior to prosecution. This version is more like a being given a red card in a soccer game, a fighting foul in basketball or being put in a 'sin bin' in ice hockey, and so the presumption would be against the developer. The implication is that there is a need to police the commercial application of scientific innovation with a view to banning certain developments, rather than stringently controlling them.

These two interpretations represent significant differences in public and political attitudes towards innovation. The former reflects a greater degree of scepticism but effectively gives a green light to future developments. The latter version reflects outright distrust and aims to delay, halt or even ban future developments.

There is also a big difference between the use of *precautionary* and *preventative/cautionary* approaches.

- *Precautionary* means a 'conservative regulatory approach in which regulation anticipates environmental hazards which have not already been documented but which could conceivably occur' – predicting 'unknown unknowns'!

- *Preventative or cautionary* means 'a less conservative regulatory approach which attempts to minimize harm only after existence of harm has been scientifically proven'.

'Precautionary' and 'preventative/cautionary' are often used interchangeably by different arms of a single agency, producing considerable policy confusion, notably for the biotechnology sector as the following box illustrates.

Regulating biotechnology

Looking at EU biotechnology regulation again as an example, the Environment Directorate embraces a policy network of ecologists and environmental interest groups, and views GMOs as unique. It tends to take the view that biotechnology regulation should be product-based, vertical and preventative. The Research Directorate, however, works within a policy network largely composed of scientific specialists, including biologists and microbiologists. It tends to believe that biotechnology regulation should be process-based, horizontal and precautionary. The Internal Market and Employment and Social Affairs Directorates have long histories of regulating and interacting with producers in specific sectors. Biotechnology is viewed by them as just another technology for producing products and so the products, not the technology, are important. They argue it is not necessary to produce new regulations for the protection of people and the environment since existing regulations are quite adequate to cope with biotechnology products and could be easily adapted as necessary. As a result, these Directorates tend to favour a preventative approach.

All new technology innovations, whether communications, biotechnology or commercial application of the new map of the human genome, will involve ongoing debate on what type of precautionary or cautionary interpretation applies. As the GM crops debate illustrated, the key stakeholder groups involved – developers, investors, opponents and politicians – are unlikely to agree. Managing this diversity of perspectives is a key reputation risk management challenge for scientists and developers – a challenge that so far has benefited neither group but *has* provided reputational and, therefore, commercial benefit to major food retailers and the organic farming sector. The GM crop debate also indicates that the precautionary principle will be applied differently in different markets, resulting in a case-by-case basis for conflict resolution.

A formal risk assessment of a potential hazard should always be the first step to be taken in considering use of precautionary or preventative approaches. Clarification of how the principle will be applied in the EU continues on an issue-by-issue basis, often separately, in the development of a wide range of policies, including environment policy, public health policy, food safety policy, consumer (protection) policy and biotechnology policy. Companies need to recognize the uncertainty of this fragmented approach and plan accordingly.

For example, consider the technologies in Table 5.3. The table lists some older technologies and some newer ones. Would the older ones be acceptable if they were introduced today? Would they encourage a preventative or a precautionary approach to regulation? And will the newer ones survive the hoops described in the EU Communication and Treaty of Nice requirements? In today's environment how would you feel about the 'old technologies' *versus* the 'new ones' in the right hand box?

Table 5.3 Potentially risky technologies

Old issues	New issues
Nuclear power	Genetically modified food
Waste incineration	Xenotransplantation
Chlorinated chemicals	Endocrine-disrupting chemicals
Electric power pines	Mobile phones
Pesticides	Airbags
Diesel engines	Cloning

Some predictions

Effective reputation risk management will require companies to acknowledge and work to reconcile differences between markets and within markets and to anticipate and negotiate which application is appropriate for specific innovations in different markets.

Some risk issues that I forecast as a result of EU interpretation of the precautionary principle will include:

- Public attitudes to *nutraceuticals: functional foods and drinks*.
  Will the principle with its onus on the health of animals, inspire legal action to end all use of *animal testing*?

- Heightened public concern about the social/psychological as well as physical health implications of *communication technologies*. For example, what will be the effect on social interaction skills of children spending long hours at computer terminals? What will happen about concerns associated with electromagnetic fields emanating from mobile phone handsets and base stations, and other electrical or radio based products?

- Interpretation of the precautionary principle in the context of the *human genome project*. For example, will DNA information/knowledge itself become a safety hazard with regard to employee and insurance health checks? Who will be responsible for managing the outcome implications for people if or when individual mapping indicates serious physical or psychological conditions?

- Balancing *privacy* and *data access* requirements. For example, is it feasible to establish responsible guidelines in relation to changes to data protection legislation in the aftermath of 11 September that were designed to make telephone companies and Internet service providers retain customer data for longer in order to improve law enforcement agency targeting of terrorism? What are the implications of protecting individual privacy in the context of data access and freedom of expression and information under human rights legislation?

For all industries, there is likely to be increasing emphasis on securing safety in the long term with regard to the health and environment of people, plants and animals. As a result, and in order to establish a legal and reputational defence, companies may increasingly be required to invest in technologies that will enable them to simulate potential outcomes. All consumer products are implicated, but especially those designed for children. In general, I predict that there could be an increasing trend towards more intensive prelaunch product safety reviews for non-medical products.

A brake on the future?

Is the precautionary principle a brake on scientific development? The EU Commission's adoption of the principle in cases of scientific uncertainty regarding potential harm to the health of humans, animals and the environment has been seized upon by consumer and environmental groups as a licence to block commercial developments.

Whether it is a long-familiar product such as PVC, or new applications associated with genetics, companies are coming under increasing pressure not simply to 'take all reasonable precautions' but to effectively guarantee that their products are safe – and not just today, but in the long term.

I believe that the application of the principle is yet another symptom of political expediency – a knee-jerk response to adverse public opinion rather than structured policymaking. After all, extensive and robust regulation already exists with the specific objective of safeguarding public health and the environment. The costs associated with introducing further protective measures enshrined in layers of complex bureaucracy is a sure-fire route to slowing down innovation and, with it, the array of life-saving and quality-of-life benefits that scientific and technological advancement brings.

In due course, hopefully, European policymakers will cotton on to the realization that their US counterparts had some 20 years ago – that the principle is far too costly, complicated and burdensome for industry and that creativity and innovation will be lost in the process. In the meantime, and for some years to come, the precautionary principle is here to stay because consumers have a deep interest in health, safety and environmental protection – and it's a big iceberg. The historical failures to take sensible precautionary action are now well known and include the epidemics of disease caused by tobacco, asbestos in the workplace and lead in the environment. The trouble is that waiting for scientific certainty of harm prior to taking protective action is a prescription for new disasters as well as continued decline in public trust – and with it reputational damage – in government, industry and technology.

This lack of public trust in science and scepticism over the ability of regulatory agencies and business to protect environmental health has been a key driver for the principle, particularly in a Europe still wondering what the long-term impact of the BSE crisis will actually be. This sets European countries apart from public attitudes towards innovation in the United States where a much stronger belief in innovation and in the ability of agencies and business to provide and protect exists.

So organizations that may have operations vulnerable to precautionary policy approaches wait on the sidelines at their peril. Ignoring or adopting a 'wait and see' approach as to whether or not the principle may be invoked in a particular area is like anchoring in front of an advancing ice flow.

So what can you do?

Businesses need to anticipate and assess the risks, engage early with the appropriate agencies and lead the consultation and negotiation process that will define the criteria for market and public acceptance.

The red card model must be avoided at all costs to protect and enhance capacity for innovation, as well as to maintain a licence to operate. Typically, a collision course results when organizations adopt a stance of denial in the face of change, particularly when it is shaped by adverse

Denial
- Relies on negative science
- Ignores risk perception
- Polarizes positions
- Hinders government responses

Preventative
- Neutral to science
- Information sharing/active communication
- Stakeholder partnering
- Mitigation strategies

Precautionary
- Recognizes there is a risk
- Quantifies risk
- Duty to warn
- Prudent avoidance

Figure 5.9 *The precautionary principle and response options*
Source: Michael Dolan, 1999

risk perception and a public policy environment that is inclined to respond to public outrage. The characteristics of denial are those identified in the left hand column in Figure 5.9. The minimal acceptable stance is to adopt a 'middle ground' or preventative approach and accept that a yellow card is inevitable. This requires active support for further research, engaging in stakeholder dialogue and information sharing, and volunteering or at least negotiating appropriate cautionary or mitigation strategies. Finally, if the political and public climate is seriously precautionary, there is no choice but to recognize that there is a risk – real or perceived, acknowledge a duty to warn and an obligation to quantify the risk. In addition, the regulatory environment will demand that certain product modifications are made which are likely to be commercially restrictive. This may be a cost burden too far, so think ahead of the risk issue lifecycle curve, implement a thorough risk assessment, factor in the risk perception wheel and plot a dead reckoning for the middle ground.

Understanding the power of public perception and what angers people is an integral part of risk management and risk communication strategies. Ensuring the organization's 'risk radar screen' is finely tuned to monitoring and assessing different stakeholder attitudes, beliefs and expectations, with particular reference to scanning NGO activity through Internet and other sources, is an essential pre-planning activity in determining the likely acceptance of, or barriers to, a new development. Review of scientific literature, technical and academic databases will be important for identifying possible triggers for debate or controversy that could become linked to planned innovation.

And routine, formal risk assessment can determine important changes in opinion, influence or regulatory potential, whether directly or indirectly related to developments under review.

The need for and value of using precautionary-based policy approaches is controversial simply because:

- They are viewed as subjective and biased against using the best available scientific or technological information, and
- They lack boundaries to their costs

However, they do facilitate greater transparency and, therefore, access to individuals and organizations prior to formal regulatory actions, and they do provide a sensible response both to scientific uncertainty and public concern. Precautionary approaches provide an opportunity for business to take incremental steps to improve the appeal of scientific and technological innovation in relation to emerging risk issues. Coupled with the inclusive process I have described, they can help to address people's concerns and minimize the potential for public outrage which can quickly result in polarized perspectives, the regulated suppression of innovation, and competitive and reputational damage.

In my view, precaution-based policies can actually *increase* the support for and use of formal science-based standards and guidelines through information, dialogue and public participation in risk assessment and risk management processes. These activities empower people to take advantage of decision-making processes and to be more receptive to industry viewpoints. Without this, there is a real risk that policy will be developed solely in the domain of public perception, substituting the politics of technological fear for scientific reasoning. In turn, this undermines informed and rational decision-making.

By keeping the reputation risk radar tuned and treating stakeholders intelligently, business and society can work together to harness the benefits (and minimize associated hazards) of future innovation.

Resource list

Websites

Eurobarometer	europa.eu.int/comm/public_opinion
MORI	www.mori.com
MTAG	www.mobilemastinfo.com

Articles and reports

European Commission, *Innovation in a Knowledge-driven Economy*, Commission communication, 20 September 2000

European Commission, *Science, Society and the Citizen in Europe*, Commission working document, 14 November 1999

Food Standards Agency, press release: *Agency Takes Further Precautionary Measures on Risk of BSE in Sheep*, 24 June 2002

Freestone, D., 'The Precautionary Principle', in Churchill, R. and Freestone, D. (eds), *International Law and Global Climate Change*, Graham & Trotman, London, 1991

Graham, J.D., 'Decision-Analytic Refinements of the Precautionary Principle', *Journal of Risk Research*, 2000

Lofstedt, R., *The Precautionary Principle: Risk, Regulation and Politics*, Merton College, Oxford, 2002

Sand, P., *Dimensions of the Precautionary Principle, Human and Ecological Risk Assessment* 5 (5), 1999

Books

Baker, R., *Fragile Science: The Reality Behind the Headlines*, Macmillan, London, 2001

Bate, R. (ed.), *What Risk?*, Butterworth-Heinemann, Oxford, 1997

Morris, J. (ed.), *Rethinking Risk and the Precautionary Principle*, Butterworth-Heinemann, Oxford, 2000

Park, R.L., *Voodoo Science: The Road from Foolishness to Fraud*, Oxford University Press, Oxford, 2000

CHAPTER 6

Corporate social responsibility – the new moral code for doing business?

"The apparent unstoppable momentum of globalization has generated anxiety among the public in rich and poor countries alike, as globalization of opportunity seems nowhere to be accompanied by globalization of responsibility"

FRIENDS OF THE EARTH

Corporate social responsibility – how important is it to reputation risk management?

Is achieving a balance between meeting financial objectives, delivering environmental quality and social justice just another anti-business fad foisted on unsuspecting business leaders by ever inventive NGOs, or does corporate social responsibility punch in the heavyweight league of reputation risk management? The business jargon generators have been working overtime. CSR (corporate social responsibility), CC (corporate citizenship), TBL (triple bottom line), BSC (balanced score card), BE (business ethics), SEE (social, ethical and environmental), EQ (environmental quality), SJ (social justice), SRI (socially responsible investment), HR (human rights) are just some of the acronyms in use to capture today's view of responsible business.

CSR is an emerging, as yet poorly defined process, used by some as a fashion statement through glossy reports and web sites, and by others as a potential framework for demonstrating a more open approach to doing business. But there are mushrooming numbers of disparate accreditation schemes and international guidelines being promoted by their owners or sponsors, and it is difficult to point to a single corporation that has adopted a truly integrated approach to CSR right across its businesses and on a consistent basis internationally. In any case, critics of CSR argue that, because of global economic, social and cultural diversity, it would be wrong to attempt to impose policy positions on a 'one size fits all' basis.

Whether or not organizations are enthusiastic about embracing greater social and environmental accountability, there seems to be a growing business imperative to do so. This can be defined in four categories of commercial penalties and incentives:

1. Socially responsible investment (SRI) and shareholder targeting

Socially responsible investment and shareholder targeting are developments that are beginning to receive serious attention from financial analysts and institutional investors. Banks, term assurers and asset managers are screening their shareholdings in favour of companies that demonstrate commitment to social and environmental programmes and against those that engage in activities deemed detrimental to society and the environment. With institutional investors potentially deterred by the 'hassle factor' of picking non-SRI stocks, a company's ability to conform to sustainable development models will, potentially, have share price implications. The growth of ratings agencies is likely to mean that companies will find their financial position rated on CSR issues as well as conventional criteria – whether they like it or not. It is likely that in the future regulators will make companies hold capital against such risks.

2. Regulation, reporting and liability

Regulation (increasingly enforced through financial instruments), reporting and liability not only have a bottom line impact, but take the initiative away from organizations in determining how broad social and environmental goals can be achieved. A greater emphasis on transparency and information access is now expected by stakeholders, and regulators are writing these requirements into the rule books. Meanwhile lawyers worry – for their clients and for their own pocketbooks – about how to minimize liability in the face of greater disclosure, while managers look on anxiously as to the effects these developments are having on strategic and operational issues, such as planning permissions and licensing.

3. Competitive advantage

As demands for environmental and social responsibility in business have developed, they have also become more mature. Concerned consumers look at the corporate face behind the brand and this influences purchasing decisions. At the same time, there is public acceptance that not every company can be the perfect eco-friendly business – society needs products like oil and chemicals. There is consequently an emerging emphasis on CSR best practice and leadership within sectors of industry, opening the way for individual companies to gain competitive advantages.

4. Reputation opportunity costs

The opportunity costs of damage to reputation – loss of existing investment and innovation in marketing; difficulty with recruitment and staff retention; advertising that is undercut by public perception – merits serious consideration. The need to safeguard reputation is already implied in the substantial budgets dedicated to marketing, compliance, recruitment, public affairs and communications. As society becomes less tolerant of companies that do not conform to social and environmental standards, the risks to reputation are much greater. Even more importantly, however, 'doing the right thing', by adopting and integrating a values system into the organization, actually does generate financial value. People want to bring their own values to work, as employees, and to have relationships with companies – as customers, suppliers or investors – that relate to their own behaviour, expectations and methods of working.

This chapter explores the emergence and potential importance of corporate social responsibility and its impact on reputation risk management. The CSR agenda is about responding to and achieving a balance between the hungry needs of the *3 P's – People, Planet* and *Profits* through careful cultivation and harvesting of the *3 S's – Socially Responsible Investment, Stakeholder partnering* and *effective Stewardship*.

Is there a commercial case for CSR? Are socially responsible investment and its junior partner, shareholder targeting, effective tools in helping to value reputation risk management? Is there evidence here that by creating a corporate code of good behaviour and treating stakeholders intelligently, companies can meet their expectations and assure their licence to operate? Will the world's leading businesses become engulfed in an icy wasteland if they cannot adapt to climate change, biodiversity, social equity and human rights in a world of greater transparency, more explicit values and more fragile corporate assets? This is not a world for the faint-hearted. The guiding principles outlined throughout this book hold true in this new era and provide the basis for self-management models designed to secure and enhance corporate life expectancy.

People, Planet and Profits – the evolution of corporate social responsibility

Over the past two decades, the pressure upon business to become accountable and perform a social and environmental role has dramatically increased. Incidents such as the Union Carbide accident in

Bhopal, India, in 1984 and the Chernobyl nuclear power station disaster in the Ukraine in 1986, helped put corporate responsibility for environmental hazards on the international agenda. Western governments responded to such incidents and established legal and regulatory frameworks for corporate accountability. The result has been that even companies in sectors with high levels of environmental risk have introduced ways to reform their businesses by looking and listening.

Globalization has had an extraordinary impact on this trend over the last decade and a half. Throughout the late 1980s and 1990s, the new, knowledge-based economy generated millions of new jobs and a rash of innovative products and services for Western consumers. The offset of this has been to expose a wide range of labour, human rights and environmental abuses – creating disfunction between meeting people's needs, protecting planetary resources and enhancing corporate profits, and a perfect trigger for anti-globalization demonstrations. While globalization has pushed trillions of dollars of finance from rich countries to poor, some 2.4 bn people lack basic sanitation, a billion are without safe water, nearly 800 m are undernourished and 250 m children are used as child labour. And yet the UN points out that the US and Europe spend almost US\$18 bn on pet food, US\$13 bn on perfume and US\$50 bn on cigarettes. This gulf in equality is reflected in some of the trends and statistics in the following display panel.

Growth Trends
Population
The earth's population has quadrupled over the last century. From 1950 to 2000, the population grew 150 per cent from 3.6 bn to 6.1 bn. This is due to rise to 8.9 bn by 2050, 98 per cent of which will be in the developing world, according to the UN. The 20:80 nature of today's world, with 20 per cent of the world population consuming 80 per cent of its resources, is unlikely to be socially and politically sustainable in a world of 8–10 bn people.
Environment
The global economy is causing environmental problems including ozone depletion, climate change, deforestation, species loss, the collapse of major fisheries and global warming. If CO_2 levels double during the 21st century, forecasters warn that temperatures could rise by at least 1 °C and perhaps as much as 4 °C.

▶

▶

Finance
In transactional terms, there is over $1.2 trillion a day in turnover of currency exchange. This is 50 times the level of world trade. International bank lending grew from $265 bn in 1975 to $4.2 trillion in 1994.
Business
Foreign investment expanded 20 times in 25 years from $21.5 bn in 1972, to $400 bn in 1997. In 1970, there were 7,000 corporations operating internationally. Today, there are more than 50,000.
Institutions and law
Global governance is growing rapidly and is highly diverse, spawning multinational treaties on issues such as crime prevention, disarmament, environment, human rights, trade law, law of the sea and refugees. These treaties have involved sponsorship or support from multinational organizations (such as the UN, IMF, World Bank), international associations (such as G8, OECD, Commonwealth, NATO), inter-regional groups (such as APEC, Trans-Atlantic Partnership), regional bodies (such as EU, NAFTA, ASEAN, Nordic Union, OAS, OAU), private governance processes (such as companies, standard-setting institutions like ISO, trade unions, NGOs), national governments (some 230) and subnational governments (for instance US or Australian states, German Lander, Canadian provinces).
Communications/Travel
Between 1980 and 1986, tourism doubled to 590 m travellers a year. Time spent on international phone calls has increased from 33 bn minutes to 70 bn minutes in 6 years, and the Internet took only four years to reach 50 m users.

Source: adapted from British Telecom, 2001

Ethics and values – the basis for good behaviour – are increasingly regarded as the building blocks of sustainable development or corporate social responsibility. The term 'sustainable development' first entered into the consciousness of policymakers and international corporations in 1987, with the World Commission on Environment and Development's report *Our Common Future*. The Commission's definition, now widely adopted, was 'Development which meets the needs of the present without compromising the ability of future generations to meet their own needs'.

As a result, the definition of corporate social responsibility has evolved to embrace eco-efficiency, business ethics, investment strategies, human rights and a wider social agenda.

"Thriving markets and human security go hand in hand; without one, we will not have the other ... In today's globalizing world, economic power and social responsibility cannot be separated."

"People are poor not because of too much globalization but because of too little".

KOFI ANNAN, UN SECRETARY-GENERAL

The early adopters were PR people who saw value in better communication around environmental impact and the environmental engineers, thinking in terms of inputs, outputs and impacts, who started to recognize that by cleaning up emissions and reducing toxic waste streams, a better overall business solution could be achieved. The debate, however, has shifted from public relations to competitive advantage through good business practice and reaches from the factory fence into the boardroom. The impact on earnings from the climate change levy and pressure to disclose material sustainability issues in annual reporting is now affecting financial institutions' assessments of corporate value as is the discovery of unexpected environmental or other liabilities.

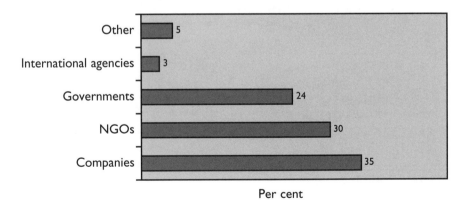

Per cent

Figure 6.1 *Where will sustainable development leadership come from?*
Source: GlobeScan Survey of Sustainability Experts, Environics International, 2001

New voluntary governance and reporting standards such as AA 1000, the Global Reporting Initiative, FTSE4Good and ISO 14001 are adding pressure to the need for greater transparency, better integrated internal risk management controls and a much wider commitment to corporate governance.

Critics of social responsibility argue either that business efficiency will be impaired by the distractions of CSR and that social issues are for governments not business, or that it interferes with the proper working of the market and the efficiency of the corporate sector.

Specialists in the field of CSR claim that the agenda must be managed in the boardroom because it is bigger and more complex than the remit of a single function. As companies like Gap, Nike, Nestlé and McDonald's have found, there are real political and commercial consequences in getting things wrong.

Figure 6.2 Media headlines

More importantly, with the collapse of communism and the relative weakening of governments worldwide, business is increasingly expected to take the lead in delivering sustainable development. While some business leaders welcome this emerging trend, meeting the associated demands will, according to John Elkington, Chairman of environmental consultancy SustainAbility, "require unprecedented public support and government intervention that will be only resolved through new forms of corporate and global governance".

Starbucks

Starbucks is the world's largest coffee retailer, operating more than 4700 coffee shops in 20 countries worldwide. Starbucks has been both praised and vilified for its approach to stakeholder management during a period of rapid expansion and financial growth.

While the company has been taken to task over its failure to protect subsistence coffee farming in Africa, it has done much to focus on reducing environmental impacts from the manufacture and use of disposable coffee cups. Starbucks formed a task force with the Alliance for Environmental Innovation in the United States with the aim of reducing the use of disposable cups and increasing the use of reusable cups. Among initiatives being explored are the testing of over 40 environmentally preferable disposable cups, a $0.10 per cup incentive for customers who bring in their own mug and free fills when customers purchase mugs in-store.

In response to growing public interest in what constitutes acceptable corporate behaviour, the 1999 Millennium Poll, supported by Environics International, The Conference Board and The Prince of Wales Business Leaders Forum, polled 25,000 people in 23 countries to gather information about society's expectations. Some of the key findings included:

- People in 13 out of 23 countries think their country should focus more on social and environmental goals than on economic goals in the first decade of the new century

- In forming impressions of companies, people around the world focus on corporate behaviour and social responsibility ahead of either brand reputation or financial factors

- Two in three people polled wanted companies to go beyond their historical role of making a profit. In addition to paying taxes, employing people and obeying the law, they want companies to contribute to broader societal goals

- Actively contributing to charities and community projects doesn't satisfy people's expectations of corporate social responsibility

- Half the population in the countries surveyed are paying attention to the social behaviour of companies

- Over one in five consumers report either rewarding or punishing companies in the past year based on their perceived social performance, and almost as many again considered doing so

- Opinion leader analysis indicates that public pressures on companies to play broader roles in society will likely increase significantly over the next few years.

Source: Environics International, The Conference Board and the Prince of Wales Business Leaders' Forum, 1999

Reporting, regulation and liability

Three regulatory instruments have traditionally acted as a break on limiting harmful activities: regulations (including financial penalties), taxation (for example, the US Superfund structures and the EC's Treaty in respect of environmental management), and liability rules (strict liability and negligence). There is now, however, a concerted attempt to extend CSR responsibility in other ways, chiefly *via* companies' annual reporting.

The last ten years or so have seen an astonishing proliferation in corporate codes of conduct, often with linked reporting initiatives. In 2000, the OECD catalogued over 230 codes, ranging in scale from single-company codes to the Global Compact between the UN and some leading multinationals, covering everything from baby-milk to bathwater (OECD, 1999). Others fall into the category of 'greenwash' – PR smokescreens designed to delay or deter regulatory measures. Premier Oil has a human rights policy, but this does not appease activists who advocate boycotting companies operating in Myanmar. Nike has a code of conduct based on the International Labor Organization core conventions, but this counts for little to those who perceive Nike to be paying inadequate wages to workers in their global supply chain. Nike, along with other retailers such as Reebok, Liz Claiborne, Sara Lee and The Gap established the Apparel Industry partnership with a view to developing an agreed code and approach to certifiable external verification, but were seen by critics to be conducting a PR exercise. And the idea of a gambling and leisure group, a cigarette manufacturer, a fast food retailer, an alcohol supplier or an arms dealer producing CSR reports appears completely counter-intuitive to many.

Furthermore, more than a few of these companies have resorted to heavy-handed tactics, typified by the 'SLAPP' suit – 'strategic lawsuit against public participation' – used to deter critics by threatening expensive libel trials. These have probably become less popular since McDonald's lost the PR battle associated with the McLibel trial in the 1990s. However, in between, there is still a large group of companies keeping their heads down, trying not to draw attention to themselves and at best, considering adopting an ISO quality standard, which bears limited relationship to the wider CSR agenda.

Recent research highlights some interesting data from a review of 100 global companies.

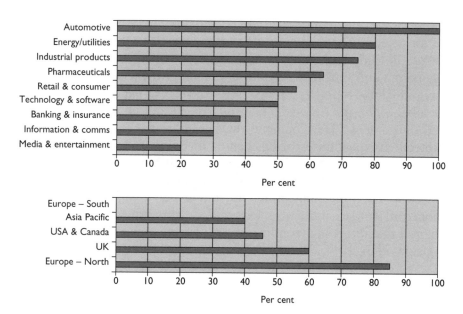

Figure 6.3 *What is being reported?*

Source: Analysis of reports published by top 100 global companies, PriceWaterhouseCoopers, 2000

The research indicates that 'world economy' companies (oil, minerals, automotive, industrial) were the first to embrace CSR reporting, raising a question mark over the extent to which 'new world economy' companies – software, telecoms, financial services – will follow suit. As industrial companies have been subjected to emissions and waste management legislation, so too will knowledge-based companies as pressure mounts for manufacturers and operators to take responsibility for recycling mobile phones, refrigerators, televisions and PCs.

In 1999, the influential US Sierra Club attacked Ford Motor Company's environmental track record by saying, '... the gas-guzzling SUV is a rolling movement to environmental destruction'. Ford included this statement in its 1999 report and in the following year's report stated, 'People buy cars and trucks for a variety of reasons: safety, quality, cost style, dealer service. It is in this context that we must consider our efforts to redefine environmental and social responsibility.' The company has since developed a number of metrics designed to measure and work towards reducing fuel consumption and emissions, and around which it is committed to report progress. In addition to fuel economy measures, the banking sector is now reporting on assets under 'green' management (UBS); the pharmaceutical industry on animals used in research (Novartis) and manufacturing emissions (Roche); and the technology sector on end-life recycling (Fujitsu) and lead-free components (Sony).

And in Europe, the European Commission (Directorate General for Economic and Financial Affairs) is planning to encourage social and environmental reporting using the pressure of financial markets. In October 2000, the European Consultative Forum on the Environment and Sustainable Development reviewed surveys of environmental protection expenditures of businesses in Belgium and Portugal. It is unclear how the EC would exert pressure in this area: for some time its venture and project funding for small and medium enterprises has been linked to environmental initiatives, but larger companies have been more difficult to influence. Recent EC communications appear to suggest that direct intervention through financial instruments is under consideration.

BP in Colombia

The importance of maintaining a licence to operate was illustrated when, prior to its repositioning as Beyond Petroleum in 2000, BP came under international attack from the media, politicians and campaigners over connections with human rights and environmental abuses in Colombia. While the company's other operations insulated it financially, BP was engaged in highly sensitive negotiations with the government in Colombia and elsewhere over drilling rights. Criticism by the British Foreign Office over the accusations threatened the negotiations and also undermined its influence over European regulation.

So, the combination of these statutory requirements, coupled with new investor demands for greater clarity on interrelationships between CSR and shareholder value, highlights the impact of CSR on risk and reputation management. Pioneers of 'triple bottom line' reporting are already actively engaged in setting out reporting standards in an effort to retain the initiative ahead of proposed regulation. Shell has been praised for the comprehensiveness and scope of its recent CSR reports, in which it has not shied away from tackling difficult issues relating to the communities local to its operations. Nevertheless, its 'Tell Shell' website – designed to encourage stakeholder expression, good or bad, of Shell's CSR performance – is not exactly a hive of activity! Moves are now afoot by the Global Reporting Initiative and Accountability 1000 to develop Key Performance Indicators (KPI) at an international level, drawing on best practice. It is worth noting that the emphasis of these organizations is on *global* social and environmental reporting and risk management.

I have already discussed the increasingly litigious environment within North America and Europe. If companies do not act in a socially responsible manner, they are likely to face, and lose, expensive lawsuits. For example, the tobacco and asbestos industries lost class action lawsuits following allegedly inadequate action by the industries to minimize the health risks of their products. Today legal action is targeting the mobile phone and electricity industries, which are facing potentially tougher, precautionary regulation and the threat of lawsuits in the US concerning alleged health effects of electromagnetic frequency emissions from power lines, base stations and handsets.

The regulatory environment is supporting the principle that companies should pay for the environmental and social effects of their business. Since the early 1980s, companies have been subject to increasing regulation on social responsibility, from working conditions to safety, to financial reporting and environmental legislation. In the United States, the Comprehensive Environmental Response, Compensation and Liability Act, CERCLA (1980) provides a Federal 'Superfund' to clean up uncontrolled or abandoned hazardous-waste sites as well as accidents, spills, and other emergency release of pollutants and contaminants into the environment. Through the Act, the Environmental Protection Agency was given power to seek out organizations responsible for any release and assure their co-operation in the cleanup. At a European level, article 174(2) of the EC Treaty adopts a 'polluter pays' principle regarding environmental clean-up, and is enthusiastically embracing the precautionary principle, as Chapter 5 highlights.

The complexity of regulation is growing with the penalties for wrong-doing getting tougher. Directors can go to prison for 'eco-crimes' and, potentially, for any major health, safety or environmental (HSE) failure. The UK Government is taking the lead in this area with its proposal to introduce a new offence of corporate killing. This legislation would make it easier to bring successful prosecutions against organizations whose activities lead to fatalities. Under existing law, deaths resulting from a company's substandard behaviour rarely lead to criminal prosecution because of difficulties in identifying an individual who is the embodiment of the company and who is culpable. The proposed corporate killing legislation includes scenarios where a company representative was aware of the risk that their conduct could cause death or injury, but continued regardless, and also includes the scenario of killing by gross carelessness. The maximum penalties proposed vary between 10 years' imprisonment and life.

Henkel, Chile

Henkel is one of the world's largest chemical companies, operating in over 70 countries and headquartered in Germany. Henkel Chile SA is an affiliated company of the Henkel Group and produces cosmetics, surface technology products and adhesives.

Historically, adhesive products have contained Toluene. This is a popular substance with glue sniffers that can cause neurological and irreversible after-effects if intentionally inhaled.

Because of Toluene's negative social impact, Henkel wanted to stop using the product and develop an alternative that could achieve the same perform-ance, but cause fewer health problems if misused. Research led to the development of a new product; a blend of cyclohexane and acetone that was unattractive to addicts, but satisfied performance considerations.

Henkel took the issue one stage further by encouraging the rest of the adhesive industry to replace Toluene. External partners and independent experts were involved to help take this process forward. The University of Chile provided independent certification of Toluene-free products; the Centro de Informacion Toxicologica (CITUC) agreed to increase research on the improved health aspects of toluene-free adhesives; and the Chemical Industries Association (CIA) formed a committee with Henkel Chile to promote the production and use of Toluene-free adhesives.

As a result, the Chilean Health Ministry introduced a national law to prohibit the production and marketing of adhesives containing Toluene.

Source: Adapted from World Business Council for Sustainable Development, 2001

The response from business

"A way of dealing with the planet as if it is on loan from our children rather than inherited from our parents"

THE NOVO GROUP REPORT, 1999

"Sustainable development builds the platform on which business thrives and society prospers"

SHELL REPORT, 1999

Consumer pressure, fuelling regulatory pressure, helps to explain why we are seeing more companies revisiting or establishing their business principles to create standards and values that integrate and bind an organization together. Business for Social Responsibility suggests that the reasons why organizations are doing this include:

- A wish to create a corporate culture 'touchstone', with business principles creating the glue or moral backbone of the organization

- The provision of a focus for evolving internal conversations, with an initial 'straw man' version drawn from existing policies, codes and principles being used to stimulate internal debate and engagement

- A means to embed values throughout the organization, with the ability to integrate them into strategic planning, decision-making processes, business practices, management systems, employee performance assessment and succession planning.

The Novo Group – the 'Triple Bottom Line' in practice

Sustainable development is a complex concept involving all human activities. For business, it needs to be broken down into manageable parts so as to ensure progress. Therefore, Novo identified six key processes that help the companies develop and implement environmental and social responsibility in practice:
- Actively involve employees at all levels
- Work internationally on environmental, bioethical and social issues
- Educate employees and provide them with the opportunity to investigate and reflect on environmental, bioethical and social conditions
- Define targets, review processes and report on progress
- Integrate environmental, bioethical and social considerations into management decisions to ensure that all decisions contain a balance of financial, environmental, bioethical and social perspectives and consequences

▶

▶
> • Conduct dialogue and partnerships with stakeholders at a global, national and local level in order to promote openness to, and an understanding of, stakeholders' views and expectations

Source: The Novo Group, *Environmental and Social Report*, 2000

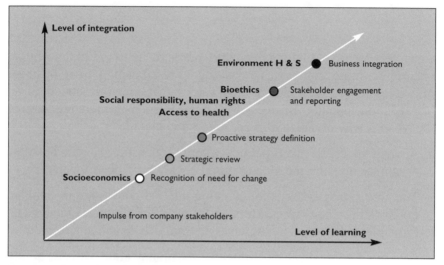

Figure 6.4 *Novo Nordisk learning curve*
Source: The Novo Group, *Environmental and Social Report*, 2001

According to one expert, sustainable business success in this century will depend on the following six values:

> • **Ultra-transparency** – assuming everything is public through to the ethics of privacy
> • **Open governance** – to bridge the gap between global capitalism and global governance systems
> • **Equal opportunity** – between today's generations and tomorrow's
> • **Multiple capitals** – human, social and natural
> • **Real diversity** – as reflected in the immense variety of our present ecosystems
> • **Shared learning** – invention and innovation

Source: John Elkington, 2001

If you compare these values with FoE's three themes for companies seeking to make the CSR transformation – eco-innovation, social accountability and political responsibility – there isn't a huge gulf:

- *Innovate for sustainability:* seek out new practices, new products and services, and new technologies that meet peoples' needs and improve quality of life on minimal material and energy use. This means improving product efficiency and durability, taking responsibility for products over their full life-cycle, and finding ways to replace products with locally delivered services.

- *Prioritize resource productivity:* make 'bottom-line' savings by turning management attention, research and development from labour saving to resource saving through waste avoidance, recycling, reuse and adopting the principles of industrial ecology. Set targets in line with environmental space limits or factor-ten objectives (methods used to quantify the changes in environmental resource use necessary to deliver sustainability; both suggest cuts by up to 90 per cent in economies like the USA and Europe).

- *Spread best practice through supply chains:* ensure that suppliers and sub-contractors adopt the same high environmental and social standards as the company – to help spread good practice to small and medium-sized enterprises.

- *Promote sustainable consumption:* use product development, marketing and advertising strategies to support 'sufficiency' rather than encouraging over-consumption, and the spread of products that replace sustainable practices such as breast-feeding.

- *Invest in people:* adopt high, non-discriminatory labour standards and family-friendly working practices, and invest in the knowledge and skills of the workforce, to enhance their quality of life and their productivity.

- *Account to all stakeholders:* report comprehensively and transparently on environmental and social impacts – with independent verification. Respond accountably to the demands and interests of employees, customers, communities and other stakeholders – not just to investors.

- *Play fair in politics:* use lobbying power and influence transparently, in favour of a high level playing field for fair competition with high environmental and social standards. Support green tax reform and effective regulation for environmental protection and corporate accountability, including legal and criminal liability for defaulting companies and their directors.

Electrolux and CFCs

Greenpeace and other NGOs attacked **Electrolux** in the late 1980s over the damaging effects of CFCs on the ozone layer. The company spent much time protesting innocence, but by the early 1990s, consumer pressure had begun to affect sales as customers turned to alternative CFC-free products. Eventually, the company's environmental manager concluded: "When the stock price depended on our ability to come up with CFC-free refrigerators, of course, managers considered the issue important".

A typical example of how consumer and political action can create a perceived business risk, for example through the potential to reduce sales.

Table 6.1 Shell's view of the business case for sustainable development

Actions			Benefits		
Business principles					Business products
Build sustainable development issues on core values	Embed sustainable development in decision-making	Maximize value of business levers	Enhances reputation as organization of first choice	Attracts resources	Creates wealth
Natural capital	Management framework	Reduce costs	Shareholders	Capital	Shareholder value
Economic prosperity		Create options	Employees	Talents	Wealth for society
		Gain customers	Customers		
Social capital		Reduce risk	Society		
			Business partners		

(Left axis: Business principles. Right axis: Business profits)

Source: Shell International, 2000

So a combination of legal, regulatory and moral pressures is leading to a changed perception of the goals of business and growing acceptance of the idea that responsible business entails social and environmental performance and reporting. Some corporations have found opportunities within this changing landscape to push forward by adopting our three 'S's': to develop reputations as leaders of best practice in product stewardship and environmental reporting, such as The Novo Group; to overcome, as Shell, BP, Ford, Dupont and Toyota are attempting to do, the legacy of damaging reputational crises through improved stakeholder communication and engagement; and like IKEA, the world's largest furniture store, to seize competitive advantage by offering alternatives to questioned practices which is helping to position the company as a credible socially responsible investment. But the jury is likely to be out for some time. Nike's admission in its first 'corporate responsibility report' that it 'blew it' by employing children in Third World countries certainly isn't convincing Oxfam's NikeWatch or the Clean Clothes Campaign!

Figure 6.5 *CSR best practice*
Source: ABI, 2001

Is there a commercial case for CSR?

"Corporate citizenship is an essential feature of the new economy", says Simon Zadek. "Successful companies in the new economy will engage effectively with their stakeholders in the markets for goods and services, finance, labour and political patronage. Corporate citizenship implies a strategy that moves from a focus on short-term transaction to longer-term, values-based relationships with these stakeholders." (Zadek *et al.*, 2000).

Our new world economy relies less and less on physical or tangible assets to create value and more and more on the intangible assets of intellectual property, creativity, know-how, human capital and relationships. In the context of corporate social responsibility accounting, groups have been developing new ways of valuing related risks and establishing new standards to help companies manage aspects of their triple bottom line performance. The World Resources Institute, for example, studied the pulp and paper industry to identify expected financial impacts of environmental risk and found that over half of companies studied expected this would equate to a 5 per cent liability, with some expecting this to rise to 10 per cent and even 20 per cent (World Resources Institute, 2000).

But does value creation fit well with company values? I think there is no question about this. The answer must be a resounding "yes". Corporations are made up of people and relationships, as well as information sharing and learning processes. Successful companies tend to have strong, values-driven cultures, are able to adapt, to build strategic relationships internally and externally, are risk-takers, and willingly embrace transparent performance assessment. Even *The Economist* has argued that it is wrong to assume that capitalism is value-free. It is anything but. 'Capitalism exalts individual freedom and voluntary, rather than obligatory or customary, interaction among the members of society. It is difficult to have capitalism without freedom and almost impossible to have freedom without capitalism. Whether you agree with its values or not, capitalism is a system positively bulging with moral content.' (The Ethics Gap, *The Economist*, 2 December 2000).

Drivers

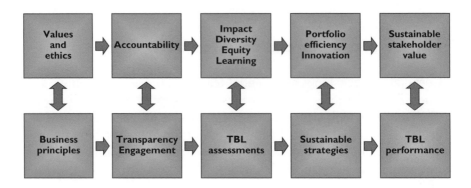

Figure 6.6 *An integrated process*
Source: John Elkington, *The Chrysalis Economy*, 2001

Process

CSR is concerned with many aspects of a company's impact, from sourcing to service delivery or product disposal, and can affect a host of cost-based as well as reputational aspects of a business. The commercial and reputation risk management case for CSR is demonstrated in the risk to shareholder value from poor management of supply chain issues, inadequate environmental management, human rights abuses and poor treatment of employees, suppliers or customers. Human capital has become more important than physical capital, and so the threat to important relationships has become critical. Concerned investors will apply pressure to those that are not managing such risks and reward those that are. Arguably, those companies which do not engage in this process will incur a higher cost of capital. By aligning operational practices with stakeholder expectations and adopting a longer view of the business, CSR offers a route to competitive differentiation. The transit is provided through developing and managing a 3S strategy. Ian Wright, Group Corporate Communications Director of multinational food and drink company Diageo, says, "against a long-term background of community involvement, Diageo formalized its commitment to CSR through a Corporate Citizenship Committee. This committee is chaired by the CEO, includes *all* board directors and manages *all* issues of reputation

Table 6.2 *Investing in social responsibility: risks and opportunities*

Negative impacts	
Aspect of CSR	**Impact on**
Concern with social and economic impacts	Operating efficiency
Human rights	Innovation Operating efficiency
Positive impacts	
Aspect of CSR	**Impact on**
Ethics, value and principles	Risk profile Brand value and reputation
Focus on environmental process	Risk profile Access to capital Operating efficiency Shareholder value
Community action	Brand value and reputation
Workplace conditions	Human and intellectual capital Operating efficiency Revenue

Source: UNEP, 2001

involving our stakeholders and including purchasing, ethical investment, human rights and the environment."

All businesses face risk and CSR risks (and benefits) are no exception. A study for the United Nations Environmental Program (UNEP) published in early 2001 identified the impact of ten aspects of CSR against six financial drivers and four aspects of financial performance. Although the evidence base is not conclusive, the overall conclusions were that CSR has a positive impact on business success, and that this is reflected in conventional financial performance measures and financial drivers.

Research by Ashridge Business School in 2001 explored the views of senior executives from four countries who had developed social responsibility projects, some in partnership with government. More than half said that the impact on business performance was the main reason for their involvement. Other academic studies have found correlations between environmental and financial performance.

More than 80 per cent of European and North American executives questioned in a survey by Arthur D. Little considered that their companies would be able to extract value in moving towards sustainable business strategies, although most felt progress had been limited to date (Arthur D. Little, 1999).

There is now a body of material from environmental and ethical groups, research and policy institutes and media commentators, which makes a business case for CSR, both in terms of benefits to reputation and brand management, and benefits to share price and the bottom line.

The value chain at Sears

A compelling piece of evidence showing that motivated employees help a company increase its profits comes from Sears. Sears has developed a rigorous quantitative model that analyses and predicts the relationships between management quality, employee behaviour and financial performance. Its research reflects the following:

- Improving employee attitudes by 5 points drives a 1.3 point improvement in customer satisfaction, which in turn drives a 0.5 per cent improvement in revenue
- A 0.5 per cent improvement in revenue means additional sales of $65 m per year. At its current after-tax margin and price-earnings ratio, those extra revenues increase the company's market capitalization by nearly $80 m.

Source: Rucci *et al.*, 1998

Several financial commentators have noted, however, that the connection between adopting social and environmental policies and business performance remains an inexact science, and the promised effect on shareholder value is often intangible. While this is true, the fact that the connection is inexact does not mean it is insignificant. Many important business costs, such as marketing, senior management recruitment and broader employee retention, are difficult to break out from financial results or quantify in terms of share price.

CSR, or sustainable development, is generally regarded to be the opposite of short-termism. It is argued that sustainable development looks at the needs of future generations, whereas traditional, unsustainable development focuses on short-term improvements and leaves issues to do with the future up to those who will live in it. The dilemma here is that the use of shareholder value as a discipline in the corporate world has resulted in a strong emphasis on immediate results and a loss of faith in long-term strategic management.

However, issues raised in the CSR discussion have provided a useful starting point for some companies to restate the business case for longer term strategic planning and investment in reputation. The relaunch of BP in 2000, under the banner 'Beyond Petroleum', is an example of utilizing social and environmental issues on the sustainable development agenda to set out forward-looking priorities that situate BP firmly within the sphere of new, cleaner technologies and potential future markets. Vodafone has created a new, global CSR function for identifying and managing reputation risks. Group Corporate Communications Director, Mike Cauldwell says, "we have been fortunate as a relatively new business to be able to create an innovative CSR framework from scratch. We have a dedicated CSR team that reports to Corporate Affairs and Strategy at board level with a global brief, which includes a Group Foundation responsible for charitable giving at international and local levels. An important part of the CSR team's role is to identify and manage reputation risks and opportunities and, as with any other business function, CSR is subject to very specific KPI's." While at international pharmaceutical company, Lilly, the focus is different again. According to Maxine Taylor, Director of Corporate Affairs for the UK subsidiary, "our commitment to CSR is illustrated in a variety of ways. For example, through training and education programmes that are linked to our key therapeutic areas, such as improving awareness of visual impairment caused by diabetes, and reducing stigma associated with mental health."

The accepted prognosis among CSR advocates is that environmental performance is not a sufficient condition for market success in many cases, but it will be increasingly a necessary condition. Consumer pressure, often co-ordinated by environmental campaigners, does contribute to forcing businesses to conform to environmental standards. This is exhibited in product boycotts, the popularity of organic produce, reaction to genetically modified products, demands for clearer product labelling, direct action by campaigners, pension membership campaigns, and it is reflected in opinion polls. The desire to respond to this pressure has led many organizations, particularly retailers, banks and assurance companies, to offer an increasing range of vetted products and guarantees about the environmental impact of all aspects of production and supply.

Examples of these are listed below.

- Cosmetics companies such as Aveda, Chanel, and Almay, that do not use animal testing
- Café Direct coffee that promises 'fair trade' standards
- Collaboration between the Ethical Trading Initiative and major European supermarkets to ensure workers in supplier companies are given fair wages and decent working conditions
- Intel's environmental risk management focus on integrating environmental concepts into product R&D and reducing the time needed to obtain environmental permits, speeding up products to market
- Ecover environmentally friendly detergents
- Ikea's sustainable forestry pledge on Christmas trees
- The Co-operative Bank's refusal to invest in countries with poor human rights records
- Dupont's development of alternative refrigerants in the aftermath of a global ban on CFCs
- Electrolux's focus on energy efficiency in the design of home appliances, which are generating customer approval and higher profit margins

Preferred supplier status is just one way that consumer pressure passes up the business chain. Food retailers, for example, are putting pressure on suppliers to adhere to strict guidelines on environmental considerations, and ultimately withdrawing business from those that do not comply. A range of social as well as environmental issues is now appearing in constraints on suppliers. Gap, Nike and Mattel have all intensified their scrutiny of suppliers' policies following allegations about 'sweat shop' factory conditions in developing countries. Suppliers of chocolate and coffee consumer products – Nestlé and Starbucks, for instance – are also feeling the heat.

These pressures are acknowledged by investors and financial analysts, and consequently have the potential to impact upon share price. As a growing number of institutional investors commit to CSR, a complementary business case is becoming more compelling.

The mining industry and CSR

Mining has had its fair share of reputation risk issues – stakeholder resistance to new mining projects and concerns regarding the environmental health effects of extraction have been widespread.

Since the Earth Summit at Rio de Janeiro in 1992, the mining industry has accepted that, alone, it cannot rewrite its reputation and needs to work with a wide range of non-industry partners, such as governments, international organizations like the World Bank, the media and NGOs. Furthermore, the environmental movement has realized that co-operation and open discussion are essential for real progress towards sustainable development.

The Global Mining Initiative (GMI), a partnership between several of the world's largest mining companies, was established in October 1998 to address a range of issues that have arisen from mining, processing and the use and disposal of mineral products. Issues include: access to land and resources; safety and environmental impacts of exploration; governance of mining projects; stewardship; biodiversity; waste management; and the social and environmental impacts of mine closure. The GMI has provided a framework in which stakeholders, governments, NGOs and community organizations have been able to work together with the industry.

Ten companies are now part of the GMI and all member companies are also members of the World Business Council for Sustainable Development, where an official mining working group has been established.

One initiative commissioned by the mining working group and sponsored by the GMI is Mining, Minerals and Sustainable Development (MMSD). This project aims to "identify how mining and minerals can best contribute to the global transition to sustainable development" and is being co-ordinated by Richard Sandbrook, co-founder of Friends of the Earth, who is undertaking the work with the independent think-tank, the International Institute for Environment and Development (IIED).

One member of the GMI, Anglo American, has taken several steps to try and improve its social and environmental performance. The company has recently

▶

> issued a Global Statement of Business Principles to act as a common set of values and standards for its businesses. This was a difficult process as the company operates in over 40 countries and in economically diverse areas.
>
> A particularly problematic area for Anglo American is the decommissioning of mines. Although it may seem socially responsible to build infrastructure in the community in which a mine is situated, this can prove difficult for the community to sustain in the long term once a mine is decommissioned. Anglo American currently provides education and training for employees to encourage the development of local enterprise independent of mining operations. Socioeconomic impact assessments are becoming the norm for new mines as a means to improve decommissioning practices and encourage sustainable practices in the community.

Socially Responsible Investment – a valuable reputation risk management tool?

"Companies pursuing growth in the triple bottom line tend to display superior stock market performances with favourable risk-return profiles"
JOHN PRESTBO, DOW JONES PRESIDENT

CSR is often held to be all things to all people and, not surprisingly, efforts to formulate business principles based on social responsibility tend to be confusing. While ethical concerns have been slow to engage in the marketplace, new techniques like the Economic Value Added (EVA), Market Value Added (MAV) and Future Growth Value (FGV) tools from management consultancy, Stern Stewart, are drawing interest. EVA represents the difference between profit and cost of capital. MVA represents the difference between a company's current market value (including equity and debt) and monies invested in and retained in the business over time. Future growth value aims to assess the proportion of a company's market value that can be matched to investor expectations of future growth. Amazon.com's announcement in early 2002 that it had finally (and uniquely in its dotcom market segment) made a profit, may encourage investors to justify a higher-than-normal valuation based on a view that the company has cracked the cost structures associated with e-commerce 'customer fulfillment'. Tobacco or chemical companies, on the other hand, which face tougher regulation and declining markets in the developed world, may score lower on the FGV rating.

However, there have been concerted attempts to develop CSR-related business measurement tools. This is most advanced in the area of socially responsible investment (SRI), where companies are screened for evidence of environmental management, policy, products and reporting, as well as packaging reduction and other specifically selected activities. This indicates some advance in the definition of sustainable business, beyond a cruder exclusion on the basis of proscribed activities, such as environmental damage.

Developments in this area are interesting: companies may define their activities as environmentally and socially responsible but the test of this will be whether they can comply with the criteria set by socially responsible investment funds.

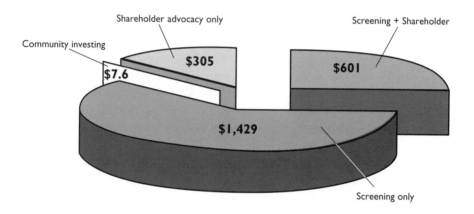

Figure 6.7 Socially responsible investing in the USA ($2.34 trillion in 2001)
Note: Figures shown are $US bn
Source: Social Investment Forum, 2001

SRI is an investment strategy that takes into account a company's ethical, social and environmental performance as well as its financial performance. It has three main mechanisms to assert corporate social responsibility: avoidance, engagement (dialogue) and shareholder activism, which broadly seek to improve corporate behaviour. SRI has supplanted 'ethical investment' as the criteria for judging responsible business and has widened to include environmental and social issues. A range of vetted products, including unit trusts and pensions, are now on offer from most large banks and assurance companies.

> *"Ethical and environmental issues are but a number of non-financial criteria*
> *which can have a profound impact on company performance, and which we*
> *already take into account in our analysis"*
>
> DEUTSCHE ASSET MANAGEMENT

The origins of SRI can be traced back to Quaker and Methodist movements in the nineteenth century. Ethical investment as we know it today developed in the early 1980s through anti-apartheid boycotts. In the UK, for example, The Co-operative Bank defined itself against much larger competitors like Barclays Bank by refusing to invest in South Africa. This policy was then extended to a refusal to invest in any countries with brutal regimes. The strategy was highly successful for The Co-operative Bank, delivering a share of the competitive new personal account market and attracting business away from major retail banks. By the end of the apartheid regime, there were 37 investment funds that did not invest in companies that had their operations in South Africa. In the United States, it was widely predicted on Wall Street that the demise of the racist regime in South Africa would stagnate interest in socially responsible funds but the number of new funds kept rising, growing from 37 at the end of 1990 to 131 at the end of 1996.

Today, SRI is a dynamic and rapidly expanding sector of financial services in North America, parts of Europe and Australia. It is estimated to be worth more than $2 trillion in the US and around £25 bn in the UK, the largest market in Europe. More than one in eight dollars under management in the United States, is influenced to some extent by SRI considerations (Social Investment Forum Survey, 2001). However, these numbers may understate the total amount of money being invested according to social and ethical criteria, as they do not include private and institutional investment portfolios.

The support for SRI has been acknowledged by industry groups as a significant business issue and one which has the potential to positively influence reputation risk management. In the UK, changes to the Pensions Act now require pension funds to declare how far they take social, environmental and ethical considerations into account when choosing stocks for investment, and other European countries are considering introducing similar legislation. US trust law is in agreement with this view and there is also strong and sustained political and regulatory support for this approach.

Term assurers, banks and asset managers are under pressure to extend environmental and social responsibility to mainstream products. Deutsche Asset Management, for example, has asked all companies in which it invests to have a code of conduct describing their standpoint on sustainability issues. Over the past 15 years, these funds have performed at least on a par with their non-ethical equivalents.

> **General Motors** has redesigned its chemicals management processes to better align with supplier and customer objectives. A single supplier works with an in-house team on process innovation, and is paid against plant performance criteria rather than traditional sales volume. The performance criteria include product quality and environmental improvements; this type of approach is welcomed by the company's institutional investors.

The Dow Jones Sustainability Group Index (DGSI) has a listing of over 200 'sustainability-driven' companies, representing 63 industries in 33 countries. This index has consistently outperformed other Dow indices, recording a 163.8 per cent gain over the past seven years, against 111.8 per cent for a regular world index. Actually, the Dow Jones Sustainability Group Index has outperformed the Dow Jones Index by 36 per cent over the past five years.

However, the causal link is not clear: companies that develop ethical policies may also be companies that plan ahead and demonstrate a keen appreciation of market changes. Even if this is the case, CSR may be an indicator of good management – and good management is what investors are looking for.

Financial markets are embracing the potential commercial benefits of social responsibility. SRI funds are indicating positive performance over the long-term. A comparative study of 65 European securities concluded that returns from SRI stocks were '... at least comparable with those for more traditional equity investment' (Bank Sarasin, 2000).

These strands of SRI's development are evident in the screening criteria which cover issues from alcohol and tobacco, through human rights to forestry.

The initial emphasis of SRI funds was on negative screening – specifically excluding companies engaged in particular types of activity. Some of the negative screening criteria are testimony to the origins of ethical investment in religious groups, which screened predominantly against gambling, alcohol, pornography and tobacco. Interestingly, tobacco remains important to some funds because moral objection to the tobacco industry has been

Table 6.2 Screening for sustainable development

Negative screening		
Ethical:	• Animal testing • Intensive farming and meat sale • Pornography and adult films	• Tobacco • Gambling • Alcohol
Social:	• Health and safety breaches • Human rights abuses	• Armaments • Third world concerns
Environmental:	• Greenhouse gases • Ozone depletion • Pollution convictions • Tropical rainforest destruction	• Nuclear power • Pesticides • Roads • Water pollution
Positive screening		
Social:	• Community involvement • Equal opportunities and employee welfare	• Disclosure
Environmental:	• Environmental reporting • Positive products and services, including environmental technology for recycling, safety training and education	• Environmental policy • Environmental management

revitalised by US lawsuits, accusations of smuggling, the European advertising ban and national government health department campaigns.

However, negative screening has partly given way to screening on the basis of companies' positive activities and looking for best practice in what were once seen as controversial industries. Many fund managers now look to invest in companies that make a positive contribution to the economy *and* to society. A survey of the 23 top European ethical and green unit trusts' adoption of criteria revealed that screening under positive measures is rapidly becoming as significant as negative screening:

Table 6.3 Screening criteria

Negative criteria	%	Positive criteria	%
Alcohol	74	Community involvement	70
Animal testing	96	Employee welfare/rights	70
Armaments	100	Environmental management	65
Environmental damage	91	Environmental policy	74
Gambling services	83	Environmental products	65
Nuclear power	96	Environmental reporting	65
Oppressive regimes	74	Packaging reduction	61
Pornography	91	Sustainable forestry	61
Tobacco production	100		

Source: Regester Larkin

Strict screening can exclude whole sectors, such as chemicals, from investment, but some new funds are adopting a 'best of sector' or 'light green' approach and investing in (mostly larger) companies shunned by traditional ethical funds. It is also important to bear in mind that available figures offer limited information about the screening measures for each criterion. Some fund managers will work with profitable companies over a defined time frame to help them achieve inclusion in 'light green' funds. This has enabled companies in the energy, automotive and agrochemicals sectors to warrant inclusion in some funds. For example, car manufacturer Volkswagen, chemicals company BASF and mining company Rio Tinto are included as sector leaders in the Dow Jones Sustainability Index.

Furthermore, a company that employs CSR and is part of an ethical fund should also enjoy a more stable share price. A 1999 study by EIRIS (Ethical Investment Research Service) showed that annualized volatility was 10.4 per cent for ethical funds and 10.9 per cent for non-ethically screened funds. Not a big difference, but an indicator that investors in this type of business may be able to look forward to greater long-term value creation as well as enjoy higher quality earnings overall compared with more volatile stocks.

Shareholder targeting – a new pressure on business and investors?

> *"Minimizing costs and maximizing profits is a priority that has the support of the institutional investors that manage investment and pension funds ... The fate of the global environment is in large part under their control and yours too – because it is your money and you are their client"*
>
> FRIENDS OF THE EARTH BRIEFING: INVESTING IN A BETTER FUTURE –
> YOUR MONEY AND THE GLOBAL ENVIRONMENT, 2000

Shareholder activism, the diminutive partner of socially responsible investing, involves exerting leverage on environmental and social issues, either by dialogue with management or by filing or supporting shareholder resolutions at annual meetings. In the late 1980s, the environmental movement experienced popular expansion in Europe and the United States, leading to far greater support from regulators and governments and a more confident direct action strategy, which sought to punish business commercially for failing to take on environmental issues. This crystallized around the use of SRI, which is now considered by some environmental groups to be a much more significant tool than consumer boycotts. However, while only 2 per cent of the shareholder vote is needed in the US to file a proxy resolution contrary to the Board's wishes, company law in Europe makes such action almost impossible. In France, for example, shareholder resolutions are at management's discretion, while in the UK, 5 per cent of the capital holders and 100 shareholders need to agree on such a resolution.

In 1999, concerned investors in the United States introduced more than 200 resolutions on a wide range of issues relating to environmental health and corporate governance matters. In one case, Home Depot, a large lumber and hardware store, announced it would stop selling forest products from environmentally sensitive areas and would give preference to timber certified as sustainably produced, just three months after 12 per cent of its shareholders asked the company to stop selling wood from old-growth forests. The following year, climate change, executive pay and genetically modified foods topped the list for shareholder activism. Other companies which have been targeted include Shell (environmental and socially responsible management), BP (Alaska exploration and development), Vodafone and Prudential (executive pay) and Nestlé (baby milk). According to some of the largest international insurers, major fund managers are switching from a passive approach to one of active dialogue, engagement and sometimes even confrontation with the management of the companies they invest in.

Whether or not investment analysts agree that environmental policies add value to a business, they are being forced to respond to demands for responsible investment from shareholders and consumers of financial services. An EIRIS survey in 1997 found that 73 per cent of those interviewed wanted their pension scheme assets invested ethically – this figure included 29 per cent who wanted their pension scheme to adopt ethical policies even if this led to reduced returns. Some large companies, such as Ford Motor Company, the Gap and Hewlett-Packard, are now offering their workers a socially responsible option in their retirement plans.

Additionally, a new breed of 'active value', interventionist investors are willing to use ethics as a platform for arbitrage. Even mainstream shareholders are getting involved. At the AGM of mining company, Rio Tinto plc, a large percentage of shareholders voted to implement two resolutions on the improvement of corporate governance policies and greater compliance with international human rights standards in the workplace. Rio Tinto has addressed criticism from shareholders constructively by taking a lead in social and environmental reporting. The company is now cited as establishing best practice for the mining industry

– with tangible potential for reputation management, and is in the vanguard of the international Global Mining Initiative which is attempting to establish industry-wide sustainable protocols.

In a more dramatic development, through the course of 2000–2002, animal rights activists published the addresses of shareholders in Huntingdon Life Sciences (HLS) – Europe's largest animal research laboratory – and threatened to picket individuals' homes if they did not divest themselves of shares by a targeted date. This action, together with the widespread media attention it gained, led institutional investor, Phillips & Drew, to sell its 11 per cent stake in the company. Similar acts of intimidation against senior executives of other advisors resulted in HLS's bankers and market makers bailing out. The company's share price plummeted and a race against the clock followed to secure vital financial backing. This was finally provided by US firm, Stevens Inc; however by Christmas 2001, Stevens' management had also been targeted, Huntingdon decided to call it a day and relisted on the US Stock Market, utilizing the more 'supportive and conducive business and investment environment of the United States'.

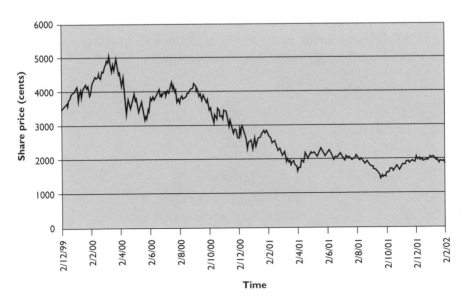

Figure 6.8 *Huntingdon Life Sciences*
Source: Nasdaq

Organizations like Friends of the Earth and Amnesty International are now consulted by fund managers, partly to clarify screening for ethical funds, but also to ensure that future pressures on companies' behaviour are adequately appreciated in financial-led investment decisions. This has developed particularly since the response in Europe to genetically modified products which led to the near collapse of Monsanto and its subsequent acquisition by Pharmacia Upjohn.

Monsanto had previously been strongly commended on Wall Street because of its rapid expansion in the United States. However, NGO pressure in Europe became so intense that it began to affect the US share price. Campaigners targeted all stakeholders, including shareholders. This led Deutsche Asset Management to recommend that institutional investors should sell Monsanto shares quickly. The resulting drop in share price made the company easy prey for takeover at the end of 1999. In spite of being one of the most innovative companies in the agrochemical and biotechnology sectors, the Monsanto brand never recovered from the legacy of this attack.

A four-phase process for CSR policy development and management

From early experience of working with a number of companies across the CSR delivery chain, here are my guidelines for plotting a safe and secure passage to responsible business performance.

Figure 6.9 *A four-phase process for CSR*
Source: Regester Larkin

Phase 1: assessing and planning

Establishing leadership and commitment:

- Identify the business case for and key benefits of a sustainable strategy
- Secure senior management commitment
- Appoint a board-level sponsor(s) (executive or non-executive but allow for an independent audit and assessment function)
- Develop and obtain approval for a framework for management
- Review existing compliance and governance through internal and external auditing
- Review business principles and values

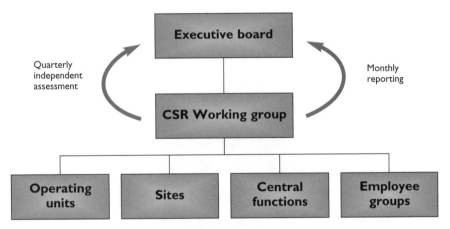

Figure 6.10 *CSR framework for management*
Source: Regester Larkin

Phase 2: policy and target setting

Addressing feedback and policy review:

- Assess feedback; complete a gap/risk analysis associated with policies, procedures, compliance
- Validate or revise business principles and values
- Define/agree policy framework: (a) against compliance; (b) against appropriate accreditation scheme(s) or internal audit procedure
- Agree strategy, priorities and actions required for implementation

Phase 3: implementing policy and training

Consider the most appropriate ways of securing understanding and buy-in across the organization, for instance, by conducting:

- Management workshops to explain purpose, benefits, generate involvement, validate approaches and roll-out (including target setting, KPIs and communication toolkit)
- A 'train the trainers' scheme to facilitate outreach
- A seminar programme and supporting intranet or printed toolkit for middle management/functional teams to outline benefits, policies, targets and programme for internal and external communications implementation
- Identify a 'CSR ambassador network' to promulgate policy rationale, process and solicit employee ideas and initiatives that reflect creativity and innovation in support of business and reputation performance goals

Phase 4: stakeholder engagement

Figure 6.11 *Stakeholder engagement model*

Source: Regester Larkin

- Scope, plan, account and report
- Integrate with compliance and risk management processes
- Prepare and develop for accreditation requirements
- Agree process for external reporting and validation
- Commit to continuous refinement and improvement

Reputation risk and the 3 S's

Corporate social responsibility is about business taking greater account of its social and environmental – as well as financial – footprints. However, it would be an exaggeration to assume that we are seeing the emergence of a moral road to Damascus. "CSR is not about self-gratification – it's about understanding and recognizing wider values", says Roger Hayes of the International Institute of Communications. "Approaches to CSR tend to be fragmented, unstructured and unfocused. There is a big difference between companies that just write a cheque and companies that actively support approaches to better relationships and address societal impacts."

Success in the new economy is about a corporation's ability to build financial performance and product innovation, but creating a sense of shared values with key stakeholders is becoming a necessary imperative. Companies which work to maximize this balance can also maximize premium for their brands and reputation.

CSR does offer a route for creating more flexible and anticipatory reputation risk management processes by sensitizing the business to risks associated with unfamiliar patterns of social change. It is also a means to influence stakeholders which can help to shift the risk burden from one of passive response to one of more active engagement and management.

CSR supports reputation risk management strategies by:
- Managing short-term risk by acquiring quality information through dialogue
- Accessing valuable marketplace and social trends data
- Moving towards consensus and away from conflict through better stakeholder engagement
- Influencing views and behaviour inside and outside the organization with associated performance benefits
- Enhancing value through socially responsible investment

Source: Zadek, 2001

The proliferation of financial and regulatory instruments in support of sustainable development is starting to engineer market forces in some countries to the extent that companies need to take a serious look at it. Failure to do so risks criticism for lagging behind and a detrimental impact on reputation. A perception of moving slowly in response to new societal and consumer trends and demands can now be damaging in financial markets.

Also, with pressure on Western governments to give substance to commitments to CSR improvement, there is a danger that companies or industries that lag behind will become targets, by example, of new regulations. It is worth noting that when Coca Cola failed to institute a product recall in Belgium following health scares, it was forced to do so by a government keen to avoid accusations of inertia. Following a consequent fall in share price, a drop in quarterly profits and the departure of the CEO, Coca Cola spent over $100 m investigating the (groundless) health panic, but the enduring perception was that the company had been forced to do this.

S1: Socially responsible investment

The rise of socially responsible investment, the expansion of regulation and intensified attacks on corporate reputation by NGOs present reputation risk management icebergs for business. However, within these developments there do appear to be some significant opportunities to enhance reputation *and* share value.

The weight of evidence currently available suggests that a combination of fast growing SRI coupled with impending regulation present a viable business case for investing in sustainable development programmes. Most importantly, there is a window of opportunity created by the need for best practice business models – a window which will reduce if the pace is forced by national and regional company law reform.

"Ethical funds are being driven by consumer and investor preferences and concerns", says John Wybrew, Executive Director at multinational utilities group Lattice. "Although ethical funds are small at present, their influence is growing because those companies which are successful in meeting the criteria set can expect to increase their shareholder base and thereby underpin the share price. At Lattice, we aim to make the company attractive to ethical investors. In any case, our business principles and values reflect the fact that the Group's activities impact on the safety and well-being of millions of people on the economy, and on the natural environment."

A coherent CSR strategy can, potentially, help to engage more effectively with the opinions and expectations of stakeholder groups. It can also help to define a clearer course for transitioning from older, costlier and less sustainable business economies, for example industries based on hydrocarbon energy, to new and exciting sustainable hydrogen-based technologies which can generate potential for shareholder value. Indeed, several new venture capital funds have been launched in recent months specifically for new eco-technology companies.

The development and implementation of CSR policies should not simply be viewed as an additional burden on costs. The fact that companies are coming under increased pressure to be acceptable winners in a wider social context creates opportunities for 'early adopters' to demonstrate best practice and achieve competitive advantage. The companies that have already put down CSR navigation markers are being called 'forward looking' and accredited with 'visionary management' by management peer groups and business commentators. "Real CSR is about being able to argue and defend if necessary, business practices against clear business principles", according to Mark Goyder of the Centre for Tomorrow's Company. "If taken seriously, CSR often exposes vulnerabilities and discomfort. For example on the BP Amoco website, CEO John Brown can be tackled on contentious issues such as human rights in Tibet and BP's business links in China, and will provide a response."

The positive impact of enhancing reputation from CSR strategies is probably easiest to identify in terms of opportunity costs – what would happen if the investments were not made? This is already reflected by asset managers in their measurement of companies' environmental policies. They identify a strong reputation for environmental and social responsibility as key to sustaining a licence to operate and developing new commercial opportunities. Reputation risk managers have a positive opportunity to factor in SRI within strategic planning processes.

S2: Stakeholder partnering

Criticism for failing to manage environmental risk or accusations of poor ethical standards are more damaging to reputation in today's climate of increased accountability and transparency. At the same time, other groups – regulators, planners, policymakers, customers, suppliers, investors – recognize the risks to their own reputations of being associated with negative environmental and social impacts. This concern about damage by association appears to be justified. Producers that continued to use Monsanto's genetically modified products found themselves exposed by association to the critical media and NGO campaign against GMOs. The damaging Ford/Firestone tyre recall in 2000/2001 is an example of the commercial 'multiplier' effect that other supply-chain stakeholder groups create, placing even more pressure on global retailers to anticipate and manage any possible adverse event across a product's lifecycle from raw material to finished goods, including promotional claims and warranties.

Deborah Allen, Director of Corporate Social Responsibility at defence company BAE Systems says, "as a defence company there will always be critics who say all armaments are wrong and we recognize their right to a viewpoint. However, there are issues of responsibility and ethics around defence and armaments – our company can work to ensure that it is open and transparent and that it abides by the ethical standards and government regulations related to arms sales. But it must also provide tangible benefits for the business – it is not an exercise in PR spin. CSR is about doing much more than good deeds – it represents good management practice and is to key to controlling risks to the business. In other words it is more than just creating a 'Kodak moment'."

Partnerships have always existed, whether companies combine to drill for oil; NGOs join forces to campaign for the extinction of toxic chemicals; and governments link in the fight against terrorism or hunger. Corporate social responsibility provides an effective vehicle to address social and environmental problems through constructive partnering between industry, government and NGOs. Instead of three being a crowd, tri-partnerships can work to:

- Improve employment opportunities in deprived localities
- Improve labour standards across global supply chains
- Regenerate wasteland for cultivation through agricultural investment, innovation transfer as well as water treatment and management
- Utilize new technologies to deliver effective end-of-life disposal schemes
- Deliver effective skills transfer and learning
- Strengthen community facilities through volunteering

Source: Zadek, 2001

This isn't just a matter of goodwill, however. These groupings embody new governance structures and processes that are evolving over time with the help of public regulatory bodies or through multi-sectoral alliances such as the UN's Global Reporting Initiative, Global Compact and Environmental Programme, where a broad range of expertise is brought together to develop and promote guidelines, and to help align performance against key CSR parameters.

S3: Stewardship

Effective environmental and social stewardship makes business sense. In a rapidly changing world where issues are readily highlighted but solutions are sometimes harder to discern, it is difficult to know where to go and how far to travel. Good stewardship isn't just about adhering to policies. BP considers that it is the outcome of three things: *behaviour*, that is, how the company lives up to its policies; the *impact* of the company's operations and products; and the company's overall *contribution to society*. As part of this process, BP will *consult with, listen to and respond openly with its stakeholders, work with others to raise standards, openly report on performance and recognize those who contribute to improved HSE performance.* Shell highlights the importance of greater *engagement and transparency, exploring new ways to assure performance, focusing on reliability of health, safety and environmental data management systems, and providing a clearer indication of what is verified and how.*

It is easy to be overwhelmed by the proliferation of codes of practice, governance and reporting guidelines emerging at national, regional and supra-national levels. In reviewing existing principles and standards or wondering where and how to start down the route of improved stewardship, consider answers to the ABI's checklist:

- Has your company made any reference to social, environmental and ethical matters? If so, does the board take these regularly into account?
- Has your company identified and assessed significant risks and opportunities affecting its short- and long-term value arising from its handling of CSR matters?
- Does your company state that it has adequate information for identification and assessment?
- Are systems in place to manage the CSR risks?
- Are any remuneration incentives relating to the handling of CSR risks included in risk management systems?
- Does your directors' training include CSR matters?
- Does your company disclose significant short and long term risks and opportunities arising from CSR issues? If so, how many different risks/opportunities are identified?
- Are policies for managing risks to the company's value described?
- Are procedures for managing risk described? If not, are reasons for non-disclosure given?

- Does the company report on the extent of its compliance with its policies and procedures?
- Are verification procedures described?

Source: ABI, 2001.

Frankly, these questions should be integral to any business' risk management processes; if you can't respond positively to at least two-thirds of them, your general risk exposure is likely to be high!

The evidence base is growing and shows that successful companies are those that can operate in relative harmony with the needs, aspirations and, most importantly, values, of their stakeholders. When this works well, it can enhance reputation, performance and shareholder value. However, it isn't simply enough to articulate corporate values in an annual report or code of conduct. Ethics and values must form an integral part of corporate culture and that must apply consistently across all operations, locally and internationally, to become a living and breathing organism. Mark Goyder insists that CSR must be embedded into the 'DNA' of an organization. As Sir Mark Moody-Stewart, former joint Chairman of Shell has said, "It is one thing to produce a set of universal principles, quite another to ensure they are implemented practically and sensitively across different cultures". Nevertheless, he continued "... our commitment to contribute to sustainable development holds the keys to our long-term business success". So values must be considered as an intangible business asset, talked about across the business as a source of competitive advantage, as a basis for good corporate reputation and as a reinforcer of effective risk management. Good business and social responsibility will inevitably move forward hand in hand.

Appendix I

FTSE4GOOD: Selection Criteria

I Environmental sustainability

Companies with the greatest potential to affect the environment are defined as *environmental high impact companies*. Only these companies are reviewed by the FTSE4Good Advisory Committee. Companies who are not deemed high impact are automatically considered to have met the selection criteria for environmental sustainability. The performance of these companies will be assessed against the best practice framework by examining each company's:

- Environmental policies and commitments
- Environmental management systems
- The environmental reports they have produced in the last three years

Each of these areas will be assessed against the indicators shown below

1.1 Environmental policies and commitments

The environmental policies and commitments of high impact companies will be assessed against nine indicators, divided into five core and four desirable as follows:

Core indicators	Desirable indicators
1. Policy refers to all key issues	1. Globally applicable corporate standards
2. Responsibility for policy at board or department level	2. Commitment to stakeholder involvement
3. Commitment to use of targets	3. Policy addresses product or service impact
4. Commitment to monitoring and auditing	4. Strategic moves towards sustainability
5. Commitment to public reporting	

Companies must either meet all five core indicators plus at least one desirable indicator, or four core plus two desirable indicators.

1.2 Environmental management systems

The environmental management systems of high impact companies will be assessed against six indicators:

(continued on page 250)

FTSE4GOOD: Selection criteria

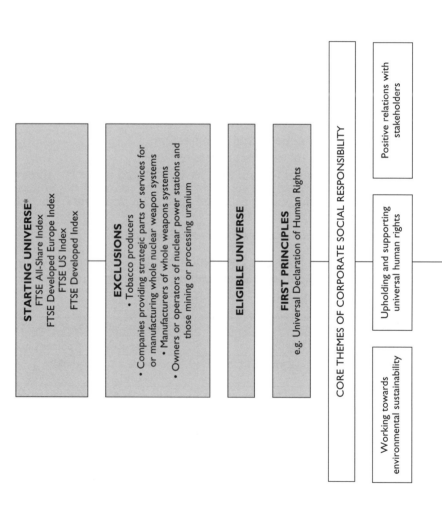

STARTING UNIVERSE*
FTSE All-Share Index
FTSE Developed Europe Index
FTSE US Index
FTSE Developed Index

EXCLUSIONS
• Tobacco producers
• Companies providing strategic parts or services for or manufacturing whole nuclear weapon systems
• Manufacturers of whole weapons systems
• Owners or operators of nuclear power stations and those mining or processing uranium

ELIGIBLE UNIVERSE

FIRST PRINCIPLES
e.g. Universal Declaration of Human Rights

CORE THEMES OF CORPORATE SOCIAL RESPONSIBILITY

Working towards environmental sustainability

Upholding and supporting universal human rights

Positive relations with stakeholders

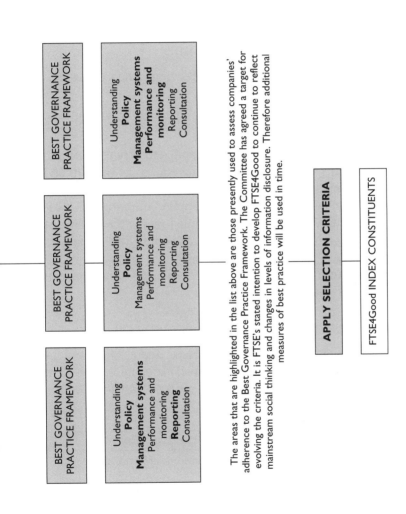

BEST GOVERNANCE PRACTICE FRAMEWORK

Understanding
Policy
Management systems
Performance and monitoring
Reporting
Consultation

BEST GOVERNANCE PRACTICE FRAMEWORK

Understanding
Policy
Management systems
Performance and monitoring
Reporting
Consultation

BEST GOVERNANCE PRACTICE FRAMEWORK

Understanding
Policy
Management systems
Performance and monitoring
Reporting
Consultation

The areas that are highlighted in the list above are those presently used to assess companies' adherence to the Best Governance Practice Framework. The Committee has agreed a target for evolving the criteria. It is FTSE's stated intention to develop FTSE4Good to continue to reflect mainstream social thinking and changes in levels of information disclosure. Therefore additional measures of best practice will be used in time.

APPLY SELECTION CRITERIA

FTSE4Good INDEX CONSTITUENTS

Source: FTSE4Good Index Series Overview, 2001

(continued from page 247)

- Presence of environmental policy
- Identification of significant impacts
- Documented objectives and targets in key areas
- Outline of processes and responsibilities, manuals, action plans, procedures
- Internal audits against the requirements of the system (not limited to legal compliance)
- Internal reporting and management review

To qualify for inclusion in FTSE4Good, the following standards must be met:

- More than one-third of company activities must be covered by the system
- If environmental management systems are applied to between one and two-thirds of company activities, all six indicators must be met, and targets must be quantified
- If environmental management systems are applied to more than two-thirds of company activities, the company must meet at least five of the indicators, one of which must be documented objectives and targets in all key areas
- ISO certification and EMAS registrations are considered to meet all six indicators and are assessed on that basis

1.3 Environmental reports

Environmental reports produced will be assessed against ten content indicators, divided into four core and six desirable. Companies must have reported within the last three years, and must meet at least three of the four core indicators as below:

Core content	Desirable content
Text of environmental policy	Outline of environmental management system
Description of main impacts	Non-compliance, prosecutions, fines, accidents
Quantitative data	Financial data
Peformance measured against targets	Independent verification
	Stakeholder dialogue
	Coverage of sustainability issues

2 Social issues and stakeholder relations

Companies are assessed on the extent to which their annual reports, web-sites or the information provided in response to the EIRIS questionnaire demonstrates a concern about their relations with stakeholders and influence on society at large.

The assessment will be based on the best practice framework and performance and will cover each company's:

- Policies
- Management systems
- Practice/performance on this issue.

To qualify for inclusion in the index, companies must disclose information that meets at least two of the requirements below in any category either globally or in their home operating country. Detail on how this is measured is below.

2.1 Policies on social issues and stakeholders

(i) Adopting a Code of Ethics or Business Principles

(ii) Adopting an equal opportunities policy and/or including a commitment to equal opportunities or diversity in their annual report or web-site

2.2 Management systems

(iii) Providing evidence of equal opportunities systems including one or more of:

- Monitoring of the policy and workforce composition
- Flexible working arrangements and family benefits (meaning at least three of flexible working time, child care support, job sharing, career breaks, or maternity or paternity pay beyond the legal requirements)
- More than 10 per cent of managers being women or the proportion of managers who are women or from ethnic minorities exceeding two fifths of their representation in the workforce concerned
- Or assigning responsibility for equal opportunities policy to a senior manager.

(iv)   Providing evidence of health and safety systems including one or
       more of:

   • Awards
   • Details of health and safety training
   • Published accident rates
   • Assigning responsibility for health and safety to a senior
     manager

(v)   Providing evidence of training and employee development systems
       including one or more of:

   • Annual training reviews for staff (more than 25 per cent of those
     staff where figures are available)
   • Providing significant data on time and money spent on training
   • Assigning responsibility for training and development to a
     senior manager

(vi)   Providing evidence of systems to maintain good employee
       relations including:

   • Union recognition agreements or other consultative arrange-
     ments (covering more than 25 per cent of staff where figures are
     available)
   • Assigning responsibility for pay and benefits issues to a senior
     manager

2.3 In practice/performance

(vii) Making charitable donations in excess of GBP50,000; operating
       payroll-giving schemes; providing gifts in kind or staff second-
       ments to community schemes or assigning responsibility for
       charitable donations or community relations to a senior manager.

(viii) Companies must not have breached the infant formula manu-
       facturing section of the International Code on Marketing of
       Breastmilk Substitutes according to the International Baby Food
       Action Network.

3 Human rights

In this area, *high impact* companies (that is, companies with the greatest
responsibility for the maintenance of human rights) have been identified
as those operating in businesses of strategic importance in countries with

the poorest human rights records. The FTSE4Good Advisory Committee will only assess high impact companies in this area. Companies that are not high impact will be deemed to have met the human rights selection criteria. The performance of these high impact companies will be assessed against the best practice framework in respect of having policies which meet any one of the three following conditions on a global basis:

- Have a policy statement specifically on human rights, which goes beyond employee rights
- Have a policy statement committing to at least two of the International Labour Organisation's Core Labour Standards for employees globally
- Have signed up to human rights initiatives such as the UN Global Compact, the Global Sullivan Principles, SA 8000, Ethical Trading Initiative, and Voluntary Principles on Security and Human Rights
- Are policies for managing risks to the company's value described?

Appendix 2

CSR schemes and criteria

CSR Scheme	Description	Key environmental criteria	Key social criteria	Key human rights criteria	Key labour criteria
Accountability 1000 (AA1000)	Issued by the Institute of Social and Ethical Accountability (ISEA) in 1999. The standard is used for internal and external audit procedures	• AA1000 is aligned and has close connections with the Global Reporting initiative (GRI) and ISO14001 in terms of environmental issues			• AA 1000 is aligned and has close connections with SA 8000 in terms of employment conditions
Caux Principles for Business	Issued in 1994 by the Caux Round Table of senior business leaders from Europe, Japan and North America	• A business should protect and, where possible, improve the environment; promote sustainable development; and prevent the wasteful use of natural resources	• A business should not trade in arms or other materials used for terrorist activities, drug traffic or other organized crime	• A business should contribute to human rights, education, welfare, and vitalization of the countries in which they operate	• A business should provide working conditions that respect each employee's health and dignity • A business should avoid discriminatory practices and guarantee equal treatment and opportunity in areas such as gender, age, race, and religion • A business should protect employees from avoidable injury and illness in the workplace

CSR Scheme	Description	Key environmental criteria	Key social criteria	Key human rights criteria	Key labour criteria
CERES Principles	Originally called the Valdez principles, the principles were developed by the Coalition for Environmentally Responsible Business (CERES) in the wake of the 1989 Exxon Valdez oil spill	• A business should work towards eliminating the release of any substance that may cause environmental damage • A business should make sustainable use of renewable natural resources • A business should reduce and where possible eliminate waste			• A business should strive to minimize the environmental, health and safety risks to their employees
Eco-Management & Audit Scheme (EMAS)	Launched by the European Commission in April 1995 and revised in 2001. Environmental management scheme, based on harmonized lines and principles throughout the European Union	• An organization should be compliant with all relevant environmental legislation • An organization should prevent pollution • An organization should aim to achieve continuous improvements in environmental performance			

CSR Scheme	Description	Key environmental criteria	Key social criteria	Key human rights criteria	Key labour criteria
Fair-Trade Labelling Organization International (FLO)	Founded in 1997 when national Fair Trade labelling initiatives united. FLO gives consumer labels to products that meet internationally recognized standards of fair trade		• Companies should pay a social premium for development purposes • Companies should offer a partial payment in advance to suppliers to avoid small producer organizations falling into debt • Companies should offer contracts that allow long-term production planning		Workers should have: • decent wages (at least the legal minimum) • good housing, where appropriate • minimum health and safety standards • the right to join trade unions • no child or forced labor
Forest Stewardship Council (FSC)	Founded in 1993, the FSC has developed procedures and standards that are used to accredit certification companies, that in turn evaluate forests aiming for certification according to FSC criteria	• Wood and paper products must come from a well-managed forest that abides by FSC criteria	• Companies should aim to improve the quality of life and relieve poverty for forest dependant people and workers		

CSR Scheme	Description	Key environmental criteria	Key social criteria	Key human rights criteria	Key labour criteria
Global Reporting Initiative	Established by the Coalition for Environmentally Responsible Economies (CERES) in 1997	• Companies should use environmental guidelines, such as the impact of processes, products and services on air, water, land, biodiversity and human health, in their reporting		• Companies should use human rights guidelines in their reports	• Companies should use labour guidelines, such as workplace health and safety, employee retention, labour rights, wages and working conditions in their company reports
Global Sullivan Principles	Introduced in 1999, the Global Sullivan principles expand upon the original Sullivan principles, which were developed by The Reverend Leon H. Sullivan in 1977 as a voluntary code of conduct for companies who were doing business in apartheid South Africa. The Global principles are aimed at multinational companies and their business partners	• Companies should protect the environment • Companies should promote sustainable development	• Companies should protect human health • Companies should promote fair competition • Companies should work with governments and communities in which they do business to improve the quality of life in those communities	• Companies should support universal human rights	• Companies should operate without unacceptable worker treatment • Companies should promote equal opportunity for all employees • Companies should respect employees' voluntary freedom of association • Companies should ensure all employees are paid at least enough to meet their basic needs • Companies should seek to provide opportunities for workers from disadvantaged backgrounds

CSR Scheme	Description	Key environmental criteria	Key social criteria	Key human rights criteria	Key labour criteria
GoodCorporation	Developed in association with the UK Institute of Business Ethics. Based on a charter committing signatory companies to incorporate social responsibility	• Companies should endeavour to protect and preserve the environment where they operate	• Companies should aim to make the communities in which they work and do business better places to live • Companies should aim to be sensitive to the local community's cultural, social and economic needs		• Companies should provide clear and fair terms of employment • Companies should provide healthy and safe working conditions • Companies should have a fair remuneration policy • Companies should encourage employees to develop skills • Companies should not tolerate any harassment or discrimination of its employees • Companies should seek to be honest and fair in their relationships with our suppliers and subcontractors

CSR Scheme	Description	Key environmental criteria	Key social criteria	Key human rights criteria	Key labour criteria
ICC Business Charter on Sustainable Development	Developed by the International Chamber of Commerce (ICC), launched in 1991	• Companies should conduct operations in an environmentally sound manner • Companies should contribute to the transfer of environmentally sound technology and management methods • Companies should measure environmental performance • Companies should endeavour to protect and preserve the environment where they operate			

CSR Scheme	Description	Key environmental criteria	Key social criteria	Key human rights criteria	Key labour criteria
ISO 14000	A family of environmental management and reporting standards developed by the International Standards Organization (ISO), launched in 1996. By 1999, more than 8000 organizations in 72 countries had formal certification under ISO 14001	• Companies should monitor and measure the environmental performance of their activities, products and services in order to continually improve their performance • Companies should consider the environmental impacts of their products and services			

CSR Scheme	Description	Key environmental criteria	Key social criteria	Key human rights criteria	Key labour criteria
Keidanren Charter for Good Corporate Behaviour	The charter is from Keidanren, the Japanese Federation of Economic Organizations, a nationwide business association whose membership includes more than 1,000 Japanese corporations and more than 100 industry groups	• Companies should recognize that coping with environmental problems is essential to corporate existence and their activities should reflect this	• Companies should develop and provide socially useful goods and services, giving full consideration to safety • Companies should communicate with society as a whole, actively and fairly disclosing corporate information • Companies should actively undertake philanthropic activities • In overseas operations, companies should respect the cultures and customs of the hosting society		• Corporations should strive to make it possible for employees to lead relaxed and enriched lives, guaranteeing a safe and comfortable work environment and respecting employees' dignity and individuality

CSR Scheme	Description	Key environmental criteria	Key social criteria	Key human rights criteria	Key labour criteria
Marine Stewardship Council (MSC)	MSC was developed by the World Wide Fund for Nature (WWF) and Unilever, and launched in 1996. It has developed a set of principles and criteria that are used to certify sustainable fisheries	• Companies should maintain and attempt to re-establish populations of targeted species • Companies should develop and maintain effective fishery management systems			
Natural Step	Launched in 1989 by the Swedish Natural Step Foundation. There are four 'system conditions': three environmental and one social	• Businesses should not produce substances faster than they can be broken down by natural processes • Businesses should not extract resources at a faster rate than they are replenished	• Businesses should help human needs to be met worldwide		

CSR Scheme	Description	Key environmental criteria	Key social criteria	Key human rights criteria	Key labour criteria
OECD Guidelines for Multinational Enterprises	Revised by the Organization for Economic Co-operation and Development (OECD) and relaunched in 2000.	• Companies should contribute to environmental progress • Companies should refrain from seeking or accepting exemptions in the statutory environmental regulatory framework	• Companies should contribute to social progress • Companies should refrain from seeking or accepting exemptions in the statutory health regulatory framework • Companies should abstain from any improper involvement in local political activities	• Companies should respect the human rights of those affected by their activities	• Companies should encourage human capital formation • Companies should refrain from seeking or accepting exemptions in the statutory labour regulatory frameworks • Companies should refrain from discriminatory action against employees
Principles for Global Corporate Responsibility	Revised and relaunched in 1998 by the US Interfaith Center for Corporate Responsibility (ICCR), Canada's Taskforce on the Churches and Corporate Responsibility (TCCR), and the UK Ecumenical Council for Corporate Responsibility (ECCR)	• Companies should protect the environment	• Companies should commit to sustainable economic development that increases the economic empowerment of communities	• Companies should respect the dignity of every person	• Companies should respect collective and individual employees' rights

CSR Scheme	Description	Key environmental criteria	Key social criteria	Key human rights criteria	Key labour criteria
Project SIGMA	SIGMA stands for 'Sustainability: Integrated Guidelines for Management'. SIGMA was launched in 1999 by the British Standards Institution (BSI), Forum for the Future, and the Institute for Social and Ethical Accountability, with backing from two UK government departments	• Environmental principles are based on the three 'system conditions' of The Natural Step	• Businesses should think positively about the social impact they can make to society		

CSR Scheme	Description	Key environmental criteria	Key social criteria	Key human rights criteria	Key labour criteria
Social Accountability 8000 (SA8000)	SA8000 was developed by Social Accountability International. It is a voluntary, factory-based monitoring and certification standard for assessing labour conditions in global manufacturing operations			• Companies must respect human rights • Companies must not engage in or support the use of corporal punishment, mental or physical coercion, verbal abuse	• Companies must not engage in, or support the use of child labour • Companies must not engage in or support the use of forced labour • Companies must provide a safe and healthy working environment • Companies must respect the right of all personnel to form and join trade unions of their choice and to bargain collectively • Companies must not engage in or support discrimination • Companies must ensure that wages paid for a standard working week shall always meet at least legal or industry minimum standards

CSR Scheme	Description	Key environmental criteria	Key social criteria	Key human rights criteria	Key labour criteria
Sunshine Standards for Corporate Reporting to Stakeholders	Proposed in 1996 by the US-based Stakeholder Alliance	• Information shall be disclosed necessary for customers to make informed decisions for purchase and use of products and services, and to satisfy concerns regarding environmental impact, commitment to sustainability, and other areas of CSR			• Information shall be provided that will enable present and potential employees to make fully informed employment decisions, and to protect themselves in the workplace and in other relations with the company • Information shall be provided that will enable consumers, government agencies, and other stakeholders to fairly assess the company's workplace conditions on issues such as fair pay, child labour, sweatshop conditions, and the right to organize

CSR Scheme	Description	Key environmental criteria	Key social criteria	Key human rights criteria	Key labour criteria
Universal Declaration of Human Rights	Adopted by the General Assembly of the United Nations in 1948. Sets a common standard of achievement for all peoples and all nations. A foundation stone for the UN Global Compact			• Organizations must recognize the inherent dignity and equal and inalienable rights of all humans • No one shall be held in slavery or servitude • No one shall be subjected to torture or to cruel, inhuman or degrading treatment or punishment	
UN Global Compact	Developed by the United Nations and announced by Secretary-General Kofi Annan at the World Economic Forum in 1999. Businesses are encouraged to embrace a set of nine principles in their own operations and support complementary public policy initiatives.	• Businesses must support a precautionary approach to environmental challenges • Businesses must undertake initiatives to promote greater environmental responsibility • Businesses must encourage the development and the diffusion of environmentally friendly technologies		• Businesses must support and respect the protection of international human rights • Businesses must make sure their own corporations are not complicit in human rights abuses	• Businesses must uphold the right to freedom of association and collective bargaining • Businesses must eliminate all forms of forced and compulsory labour • Businesses must abolish child labour • Businesses must end discrimination in respect of employment and occupation

Resource list

Websites

Accountability 1000	www.accountability.org.uk
Bank Sarasin	www.sarasin.com
Business for Social Responsibility	www.bsr.org
Business in the Community	www.bitc.org.uk
Caux Principles for Business	www.cauxroundtable.org
Coalition for Environmentally Responsible Economies (CERES) Principles	www.ceres.org
Dow Jones Sustainability Group index	www.sustainability-index.com
Eco-Management and Audit Scheme (EMAS)	europa.eu.int/comm/ environment/emas
Environics	www.environics.net
Ethical Corporation magazine	www.ethicalcorp.com
European Sustainability and Responsible Investment Forum (Eurosif)	www.eurosif.info
Fairtrade Labelling Organization International (FLO)	www.fairtrade.net
Forest Stewardship Council (FSC)	www.fscoax.org
FTSE4Good index	www.ftse4good.com
Global Reporting Initiative	www.globalreporting.org
Global Sullivan Principles	www.globalsullivanprinciples.org
GoodCorporation	www.goodcorporation.com
Institute of Business Ethics	www.ibe.org.uk
International Chamber of Commerce (ICC) Business Charter on Sustainable Development	www.iccwbo.org/home/ environment
ISO 14000	www.iso14000.com
Keidanren Charter for Good Corporate Behaviour	www.keidanren.or.jp/english/policy
Marine Stewardship Council (MSC)	www.msc.org
OECD Guidelines for	www.oecd.org/daf/

Multinational Enterprises	investment/guidelines
Prince of Wales Business Leaders Forum	www.pwblf.org
Project SIGMA	www.projectsigma.com
Social Accountability 8000 (SA8000)	www.sa-intl.org
Social Investment Forum	www.socialinvest.org
Sunshine Standards for Corporate Reporting to Stakeholders	www.stakeholderalliance.org/ sunstds.html
The Natural Step	www.naturalstep.org
Tomorrow's Company	www.tomorrowscompany.com
UN Environmental Programme (UNEP)	www.un.orrg
UN Global Compact	www.unglobalcompact.org
Universal Declaration of Human Rights	www.un.org/Overview/rights.html
World Business Council for Sustainable Development	www.wbcsd.ch
Worldwatch Institute	www.worldwatch.org

Articles and reports

Association of British Insurers, *Investing in Social Responsibility: Risks and Opportunities*, 2001

Buried Treasure: Uncovering the Business Case for Corporate Sustainability, SustainAbility, 2001

Environics International, *GlobeScan Survey of Sustainability Experts*, 2001

Environics International, The Conference Board and the Prince of Wales Business leaders' Forum, 'The Millenium Poll on Corporate Social Responsibility', 1999

Little, Arthur D., *Realising the Business Value of Sustainable Development*, Arthur D. Little Inc., Cambridge, MA, 1999

Modern Company Law: Developing the Framework, Company Law Review Steering Group, HMSO, November 2000

O'Connor, N., 'UK Corporate Reputation Management: The Role of Public Relations Planning, Research and Evaluation in a New Framework of Company Reporting', *Journal of Communication Management*, 6 (1), 2001

OECD Trade Directorate, *Codes of Corporate Conduct: An Inventory*, OECD, Paris, 1999

Rucci, A.J., Kim, S.P. and Quinn, R.T., *The Employee-Customer-Profit Chain at Sears*, Harvard Business Review, 76 (1), Jan–Feb 1998

Social Investment Forum, *Report on Socially Responsible Investing Trends in the United States*, 2001

The Novo Group, *Environmental and Social Report*, 2001

Weiser, J., Zadek, S., *Conversations with Disbelievers*, The Ford Foundation, 2000

Zadek, S., Hojensgard, N. and Raynard, P., *The New Economy of Corporate Citizenship*, The Copenhagen Center, Copenhagen, 2000

Books

Centre for Tomorrow's Company and GPL, *Leading and Managing in the New Economy*, Centre for Tomorrow's Company, 2001

Elkington, J., *The Chrysalis Economy: How Citizen CEOs and Corporations Can Fuse Values and Value Creation*, Capstone, Oxford, 2001

Goyder, Mark, *Living Tomorrow's Company*, Gower, 1998

Sadler, Phillip, *Leadership in Tomorrow's Company*, Centre for Tomorrow's Company, 1999

Zadek, S., *The Civil Corporation: The New Economy of Corporate Citizenship*, Earthscan, London, 2001

Conclusion

Since I started to write this book, unprecedented upheaval in the performance of corporate America has illustrated the deficit in confidence and trust that poor governance (let alone outright dishonesty) delivers and its direct impact on reputation as well as financial performance. When I started on the first chapter, the US stock market was worth around $24 trillion. By the summer of 2002 it had plummeted to $11 trillion. The failure of Enron and associated demise of Arthur Andersen; the fall of WorldCom, tax evasion charges against the CEO of Tyco; charges of corporate looting against the founder and family members of cable operator Adelphia; scandals associated with covering up manufacturing errors at Johnson & Johnson, and of exploiting a monopoly position at Bristol-Myers Squibb; claims of dubious accounting practices at Xerox, Global Crossing, Qwest, Merck, AOL Time Warner and even the mighty GE, have all combined to create a collapse in investor confidence and stockmarket free-fall. At the centre of these woes is the question of governance – are corporations being economical with the truth by bending the rules of accounting and reporting in order to project a far rosier picture of performance? And if so, who is responsible, not least for the carnage among the stock-based savings that underpin the retirement plans of older Americans?

In the US the CEO is king; chief executives are the people who heroically run the world virtually unquestioned and with little regard for the board as a significant balance of power in the organization. However, a pervading sense of corporate greed and paucity of transparent governance is eroding investor confidence and, crucially, wider public trust. It is also giving a new lease of life to law firms that sue companies on behalf of their shareholders. According to Stanford Law School, shareholders filed 327 federal class action lawsuits against US companies last year – a rise of 60 per cent over the previous year. The resurgence of such action is viewed by corporate executives as little better than an extortion racket designed to enrich unscrupulous lawyers, while others see the threat of costly litigation as one way of encouraging US corporations to treat their investors better. What is in no doubt is that the 'Enron *et al.*' landslide has highlighted a significant deterioration in US corporate governance.

In testimony to Congress in July 2002, the Federal Reserve Chairman, Alan Greenspan, described the CEO as "the fulcrum of governance" and reflected a mood swing towards pressure for CEOs to certify accounts and keep a closer eye on the running of the company, greater accountability in the boardroom, and more external, independent representation on the board. Debate over the merits of splitting the role of CEO and Chairman, a development that has been actively pursued in the UK in response to recommendations on improving governance guidelines, may yet be a bridge too far for US executives. However, Coca-Cola's decision to break with the widespread tradition of not charging stock option costs against profits was seen to be a well-timed response to growing political, regulatory and activist pressure for change.

Trust and belief underpin reputation and yet trust is easily squandered with little recognition that it is a non-renewable asset. And there is now growing evidence that the primary damage distrust inflicts *is* on economic performance, in addition to emotional well-being and social cohesion.

A key threat to reputation is risk perception, compounded by irresponsible media reporting, scaremongering pressure groups and lack of transparent government. Sensationalism around environmental health scares has flourished because politicians have not been straight with the public. European consumers panicked over BSE because authorities ignored or concealed, for far too long, evidence that the disease could spread to humans. Stonewalling about the potential health risks of depleted uranium in the US and the UK has amplified suspicion and undermined the legitimacy of government, resulting in policies being dictated by populism not principle. Instead of basing decisions on proper risk assessment, frightened and opportunistic politicians have surrendered to emotive and ill-judged claims by activists.

I have argued the case for treating reputation as a valuable but vulnerable asset, which must be actively managed from the top of the organization. Risk is a constant theme in managing reputation which is why it must be owned in the boardroom. The ability to recognize the threats and opportunities around current and emerging reputation risks should be treated no differently from the way in which any operational risk is identified, assessed and mitigated against. Establishing and maintaining a finely tuned radar that enables you to look and listen will help you to understand your responsibilities to your different stakeholders and deliver against your own code of good behaviour. Treat them intelligently and the goodwill payback will be worth its weight in gold.

And remember that today's business environment is like a goldfish bowl – there is no hiding place, so work as though everything you say and do is public.

In an uncertain world, there are few certainties other than death – and taxes! In the absence of certainty, then, openness and accountability, underpinned by an organization's ability to anticipate the potential for change and align its relationships with stakeholders, are the only important beacons on the course to successful strategic reputation risk management. By following these principles, the power of business to help build healthy and prosperous societies will be harnessed.

Index